SWIFT, SILENT AND SURROUNDED

MSgt A. A. Bufalo USMC (Ret)

ISBN 978-0-9745793-0-6

First Printing – April 2003
Printed in the United States of America

www.AllAmericanBooks.com

Swift, Silent and Surrounded

DEDICATION

This book is dedicated to the following warriors who died in the service of our country. Each perished in the line of duty while working to perfect their formidable skills as Reconnaissance Marines. It was a privilege serving with such fine Americans.

Staff Sergeant Vincent Sabasteanski .... 1st Force Recon Co - 1999

Staff Sergeant Jeffrey R. Starling .... 1st Force Recon Co - 1999

Staff Sergeant David Galloway .... 1st Force Recon Co – 1999

Hospital Corpsman 1st Class Jay J. Asis........... 1st Force Recon Co - 1999

Sergeant James L. Burns................................ 1st Force Recon Co - 1997

Sergeant Robert Reyes.................................. 2nd Force Recon Co -1988

Sergeant James J. Pechiney........................... Co A, 2nd Recon Bn - 1978

Corporal Mark M. Baca Jr. .... 1st Force Recon Co - 1999

PREFACE

Back in the early 1980s I was standing at the bar in the 1st Marine Corps District all-ranks club in Garden City New York when a Lieutenant Colonel named Abele asked if I had read the book *Brown Side Out* by a retired Major named Gene Duncan. I hadn't, but on his recommendation went out and got myself a copy. I have never regretted it.

The inspired wisdom in each of Major Duncan's books provided me with food for thought as I developed my own leadership style, and I put many of the lessons learned from his writings to use as I progressed in my career. This book is something of a tribute to him, although it could very easily have been titled "Chicken Soup for the Jarhead's Soul."

I soon realized I had some stories of my own to tell, and thought perhaps someone might benefit from my experiences and learn from my mistakes - as well as those made by a few others - and hopefully enjoy a few chuckles in the process. I know I had a great time putting it together.

The title *Swift, Silent and Surrounded* is derived from the motto of Marine Reconnaissance Battalions, which is Swift, Silent and Deadly – or in the case of 3rd Recon, "Celer, Silens et Mortalis." I always felt "surrounded" was more accurate because we operated in small teams in the middle of Indian Country, and survived by stealth and guile rather than firepower. It also illustrates that our Corps is one of the last bastions of warrior culture in these kinder and gentler times, and that we are surrounded by special interest groups whose self-serving "causes" are chipping away at our ability to fight and win future wars.

This book is divided into sections which reflect the fourteen Leadership Traits, since they are the building blocks of all great leaders. Too many young Marines memorize the traits themselves, without really learning what they are all about. Each story in some way relates to the trait under which it is found, although many could be applied to others as well –and it is up to the reader to figure out the message.

I owe a great deal to the Marine Corps, and hope this volume helps repay that debt in some small measure. I am certain of one thing - anyone who has not been a Marine has been cheated by life. Most people simply have to be content with *knowing* those who wear the Eagle, Globe and Anchor, although they will never really understand the intangibles which make us "the Few and the Proud."

Many of the stories contained in this volume are inspirational in nature, and will hopefully give the uninitiated some small understanding of what it is to be a Marine. As for those of us who have worn the uniform, it is difficult to read about the exploits of our brothers-in-arms without swelling with pride or, in some cases, shedding a tear.

There are also quite a few stories about "nimrods" in this book, but there is a reason for that. Nimrods make for great stories! Fortunately they are a minority in the Corps, but the comic relief they provide is always a welcome diversion. I have of course changed their names where appropriate in order to avoid publicly embarrassing anyone. After all, even nimrods deserve a modicum of dignity!

Not surprisingly many of my stories involve Recon or the MSG program, since those were the units I served the most time with. A glossary of terms has been included to help the reader through any passages containing unfamiliar acronyms, but for the most part I have embraced the KISS principle – Keep It Simple, Stupid!

I must warn you that many of my opinions are not "politically correct," and I am not afraid to express them. Too many people are afraid to tell it like it is, and as far as I'm concerned that amounts to moral cowardice. You may not always agree with *how* I feel, but you will always know *why* I feel that way.

Readers who have served in other branches of the armed forces may not share some of my views of their service, but that is okay too. This book was written *by* a Marine, *about* Marines, and *for* Marines. I have respect for <u>anyone</u> who has served our country and gone in harm's way - hell, my own Dad was in the Army and landed at Normandy! But that doesn't mean I'm going to sugar-coat things.

Interspersed throughout my ramblings are the writings of many others to whom I am grateful. Their insights offer unique perspectives on a number of topics, and also serve to give the reader a break from listening to yours truly. I would like to take this opportunity to thank the many contributors and sources of information who have made this project possible. They are all fine Americans.

Semper Fi!

Swift, Silent and Surrounded

TABLE OF CONTENTS

Swift, Silent and Surrounded

BROTHER TO BROTHER

"We sometimes forget, but freedom isn't free."
- Johnny Spann, father of CIA officer & Former Marine Mike Spann, who was the first U.S. casualty in the war on terrorism

John Tanney enlisted in 1967 as he always felt it was his duty to serve his country. He was a true patriot in every sense of the word. While at Khe Sahn at the age of eighteen John wrote a letter to his baby brother Bob, who was only seven months old at the time. It was written just before the 26th Marines launched their assault on Hill 881 North, and was only to be opened in the event of John's death. John was wounded by mortar fire at the siege of Khe Sahn in April of 1968, where he received his first Purple Heart.

After his death, the letter was opened by his parents. Congressman Alexander Pirnie also read it and asked permission to read it in a Congressional session, where it is now a permanent part of the Congressional record. Here is the text of that letter exactly as he wrote it:

Dear Brother Bob,

I know that you won't be able to read this for awhile, but I just felt a compulsion to write to you anyway. I'm waiting to be picked up by helicopter with the rest of my buddies to push on to Hills 861, 881, 881 North, and 689. My platoon is spearheading the assault up Hill 881 North. The enemy has many soldiers up top and they are dug in as well as we are at Khe Sahn (a Viet Cong siege of U.S.Marines). It will be a hard and bitter struggle, but as always we Marines will take the objective.

You are little now and haven't the slightest idea of what is going on in the world, but what we are doing here concerns all. It is important for you to remember that we are fighting for freedom for Viet Nam. The Bible says "I am my brother's keeper." This is also true for our Vietnamese brothers.

Someday, when you come of age, you too will render your services to your country. You do not have to join the Marine Corps because I did. Just fulfill your duty - your privilege. Yes, it is a privilege to fight for a noble cause. War is far, far worse than hell.

Men are torn apart like a worn-out rag doll. War has a smell to it. It is the smell of charred flesh. War has sounds. They are the sounds of men dying. Bob - I hope that you will never have to go to war. I hope that we can stop this thing from spreading. I hope that the men of peace will sit down and discuss living in peace - but, alas, I hope in vain.

I am nearly going crazy thinking about assaulting that hill. But, I am a Marine and I shall not falter. I will be confident in the Lord and in my training as a Marine. Bob - if anything should happen, remember this: I am fighting for what I believe in - you, Mom, Dad, Tom and Cindy. I am fighting for the right to choose my own religion, make my own decisions, and to be my own man. And yes, I am fighting for my flag. My country means a lot to me and I am proud to fight for it. I know that you will be too.

You know, I am over eighteen years older than you and I have spent so little time with you. But, you are near to me not so much in my mind as in my heart. I hope that your generation of people will respect what we are doing here. I hope that they will understand that we, too, love life. We have lost many friends, and now it is time for the enemy to lose some.

We are United States Marines. We are the best troops in the world. We fight odds that are heavily against us - and win! Our spirit is indomitable, our courage unexcelled, and our loyalty is unquestionable.

I felt like writing to you. Perhaps it sounds foolish. Perhaps it is. But you can never imagine what it is like - not knowing if I'm coming back down that hill. I wanted you to have something from me to you. I love you, Bob, but you are too young to know it.

Someday you will know. I will leave now - time is short.

Love to you,

Brother John

THE LITTLEST MARINE

By Jay Stuller

"Some people spend an entire lifetime wondering if they made a difference in the world. But, the Marines don't have that problem."
- Ronald Reagan, President of the United States; 1985

On a spring day in 1983, Marine Staff Sergeant Robert Menke was waiting for a hot enlistment prospect he had talked to on the phone. Hunched over paperwork in the Corps' Huntington Beach California recruiting station, Menke heard the front door open and looked up. In came a boy in a motorized wheelchair, followed by his father. Menke noted the boy's frail body and thin arms. "Can I help you?" he asked.

"Yes," the boy answered firmly. "My name is John Zimmerman."

It took the startled Marine a moment to realize that this was indeed his prospect. "I'm Staff Sergeant Menke," he said, shaking his visitor's small hand. "Come on in."

Menke, a shy man uncomfortable with recruiting, quickly found himself captured by the articulate thirteen-year-old youth with an easy, gap-toothed grin. For more than an hour they spoke – of training and overseas assignments and facing danger. The kid loved the Marine Corps. Not a word was exchanged about the younger Zimmerman's condition or the wheelchair.

There was one basic reason behind the visit to the Marine Corps recruiting office that day. From the moment Richard and Sandra Zimmerman learned their fourteen month old son had Werdnig-Hoffman syndrome, a rare neurological disease, they vowed to treat him like a normal child. Told

4

that John probably would not live past age two, they refused to believe he would die. Despite tremendous weakness in his legs and back and susceptibility to colds, John simply *looked* well. They had him fitted with a rigid body jacket to help him sit upright, and took him on vacation trips all over the country. They didn't get a wheelchair for him until he was three. Even then, Richard Zimmerman often carried his son, who weighed around thirty pounds, lugging him through amusement parks, into restaurants and to movies.

Werdnig-Hoffman syndrome victims have difficulty fighting off upper respiratory problems. Before the age of five John was hospitalized three times with pneumonia, with each bout putting him on the edge of death. Richard Zimmerman believed Chicago's cold winter climate was partly to blame, and in 1975 he arranged a job transfer so the family could move to Southern California. There, the boy suffered fewer bouts with respiratory illness.

John, then six, was enrolled in classes for orthopedically handicapped children at the Plavan School in Fountain Valley. About this time he became aware of the Marine Corps at a week-long summer camp for disabled children. Many of his counselors at the camp in Cuyamaca Rancho State Park near San Diego were Marine volunteers. Each summer John would get to know another Marine through the camp's one-to-one counseling program. This sparked an interest that evolved into a passion.

While other children worshipped athletic heroes and rock stars, John gathered every bit of material about the Marines he could find. He plastered his room with Corps recruiting posters, his wheelchair with Marine stickers. His hero was John Wayne. He even dressed like a Marine and, much to his mother's consternation, got a Corps "burr" haircut.

After his initial visit to the Huntington Beach recruiting center, John kept in contact with Menke and Menke's boss, Gunnery Sergeant John Gorsuch. Occasionally he dropped by with his father; more often, he phoned to ask questions or just to talk. He frequently devoted his school reports to Marine tactics, campaigns or equipment. When new recruiting posters arrived, Menke or Gorsuch would mail or personally deliver one to John. In turn John built model airplanes, trucks and tanks for his Marine buddies. Though delicate and intricate chores were difficult – and even painful – for him, John would work night after night on the models.

While Marines inspired John, he gave back as much as he got. One afternoon Gorsuch had scheduled seven appointments for potential recruits. Five hadn't shown up, and the other two had to be disqualified. John called to ask questions for a school report. "What's wrong, Gunny," John asked. "You don't sound right." Gorsuch explained. "Ah, come on Gunny," John said. "Look, you're a smooth operator, and for every one you lose you'll get two more." Gorsuch began to laugh. "You're right Johnny," he said. "You know… you're right."

An attempt to move John into a standard fourth-grade class at Plavan failed; because he could not write quickly, he could not keep up. But he made it in the sixth grade after his teachers allowed him to dictate some of his work.

John's family also benefited from his forceful personality. When told something couldn't be done, he would respond, "But, did you ask?" Although he realized he probably never could hold a regular job he had no fear of talking with strangers, and figured one day he could help his father, a commercial real estate broker, by making the "cold" call the elder Zimmerman dreaded. As close as he was to his Marine friends, he was even closer to his father. Richard

Swift, Silent and Surrounded

Zimmerman helped his son dress in the morning, helped him with baths and put him to bed each evening.

John rarely talked about the consequences of his disease, but he understood. On a trip to Hawaii in 1982, as the family visited the National Memorial Cemetery of the Pacific, the famed "Punchbowl," John whispered to his father, "I want to be buried here when I die. Can we do it?" Richard Zimmerman was taken aback. "I don't know if it's possible. But sure, John. Sure."

In the spring of 1984, not long before John was to graduate from the eighth grade, his condition began to worsen. His twisted spine was pressing into his internal organs, pinching nerves that sent searing pain through his back and legs. He had difficulty digesting food, and he began to lose weight. But he was determined to attend graduation.

On the night of the ceremony John was weak and nauseated, but to his surprise a Marine sergeant was there to escort him. He and the sergeant led the procession of students into the auditorium. John, thin and twisted, had to use the armrest of his wheelchair to prop himself up. His head, normal size, looked much too large for a body that was deserting an able mind. But to a rousing ovation, he flashed his biggest smile. Then another surprise: it was announced that John was a co-recipient of Plavan's Sergio Duran award, given annually to the handicapped graduate who best overcomes his limitations.

That summer John's condition improved slightly, and he entered Fountain Valley High School in the fall of 1984. During the first semester, however, his condition began to decline again, and his weight dropped to less than forty pounds. While he would have preferred to stay home and sleep, he attended school, confiding to his sister that he went "Mainly because it makes Mom and Dad happy."

7

On New Year's Eve John went into respiratory failure and was rushed to the hospital. Gorsuch and Menke visited daily. Realizing their fifteen year old friend's remaining days would be few, they set out to make him a Marine. Menke secured permission to name John an honorary member of the Corps. Then one of Menke's friends penned a one-of-a-kind proclamation. On January 15, in a hospital room crowded with family and Marines, Major Robert Robichaud, area recruiting director, read the document. "By reposing special trust and confidence in the fidelity and abilities of John Zimmerman, I do hereby appoint him an Honorary Marine..."

Two days later John looked at Sandra and said, "I'm a fighter, Mom. A helluva fighter." That night, he spoke to his nurses about dying, saying that his only fear was how his parents and sister would fare without him. In the early hours of January 18, John Zimmerman, U.S. Marine, passed on.

In a eulogy at John's memorial service Gorsuch, his voice cracking, said, "Marines learn never to give up, and John definitely had that quality. We have a motto in the Marines, the Latin words for always faithful. This is for Johnny Zimmerman," he concluded. "*Semper Fi.*" After the service the two Marines approached John's casket. Slowly, Menke and Gorsuch unpinned the Marine emblems from their coat collars and gently placed these symbols of fidelity into the casket with their friend.

During the final week of his life, no longer able to talk, John had scrawled a note to his father, reminding him of a promise made nearly three years before. "Punchbowl – will you visit me?" His father nodded. "If that's what you want, we'll do it," he said. In reality, Richard had no idea if it would even be possible. Yet his son's favorite phrase kept coming back to him: "But Dad, did you ask?" Richard looked into the matter and discovered that such cemeteries are reserved for military personnel and their families. Even though Menke had volunteered to give up his cemetery plot, the Veterans Administration would not permit it, or grant John's wish. Richard decided to try again. This time he wrote to California Senator Pete Wilson and learned that to circumvent the rules he would need authorization from the President. The Senator, a former Marine, was willing to help.

"He never had the opportunity to serve his country in the Marine Corps as he so wished he could have," Wilson wrote to President Reagan. "However, his dedication and courage no doubt had very positive effects on many young Marines and civilians..." The President granted the request, and the Marine Corps went into action. At Camp Smith on Oahu, about thirty Marines volunteered for the funeral detail. And on a windy day in the Punchbowl, with the cemetery's flag at half-staff, John Zimmerman was put to rest with full military honors.

Prior to a 21-gun salute, U.S. Navy Chaplain Jack Graham spoke. "Courage isn't limited to battlefields," he said. "The Marines have a saying: 'The Marines need a few good men.' They found one in John Zimmerman.

THE REAL HEROES

"Come on, you sons of bitches! Do you want to live forever?"
- GySgt Daniel J. "Dan" Daly as he led the 5th Marines' attack into Belleau Wood, 6 June 1918

When Army PFC Jessica Lynch was rescued after being captured by the Iraqis it was a joyous occasion to be sure. No one was happier than I when she was rescued, since I have two daughters of my own and could imagine how her family must have felt. But the press, as they are in the habit of doing, took a positive thing and turned it into a circus by running stories *ad nauseum* about such things as her kindergarten teacher and her meal requests at Landstuhl hospital. My compassion and interest extended only so far, and the fact that she asked for "roast turkey, apple sauce, and steamed carrots" was a bit more than anyone wanted or needed to know.

It is sad that the saga of a well-meaning young lady who joined the armed forces solely for the purpose of obtaining a college education, and who was captured as the result of making a wrong turn, overshadowed the professionals who risked their lives to rescue her. A TV news station even went so far as to call her the best known *hero* of the war with Iraq. The word hero gets used much too freely these days. The Marines, Rangers and SEALs who put together and executed a successful *in-extremis* mission were the ones who should have been getting the press. But I can't say I was surprised.

Needless to say the indiscriminate use of the word hero became something of a pet peeve, and I wasn't the only one who felt that way. When I retired from the Corps I moved to a town near the city of Tampa, Florida and began to acquaint myself with the local scene, and one of the most prominent television personalities in the area was a news anchor named Bob Hite - who enjoyed a reputation among the locals as a straight shooter. I immediately liked his style, and it wasn't long before I learned a bit more about his background.

As many of you will remember an Air Force Captain named Scott O'Grady was shot down over Bosnia a few years back and was forced to evade capture for several days. It so happened O'Grady was in Tampa for a speaking engagement, and the correspondent assigned to cover the story made it a point to call him a "hero" on several occasions. No mention was made of the Marines who had conducted a "TRAP" mission to rescue him.

When the camera cut back to Mr. Hite he was visibly agitated. "How," he asked, "does getting a twenty million dollar plane shot out from under him make O'Grady a hero? The real heroes were the Marines who went in and rescued him!"

Hite's female co-anchor seemed surprised by his outburst for a moment, but then she smiled and exclaimed, "Oh that's right Bob, I forgot… you were in the Marines."

Hite puffed out his chest and proudly replied, "You're darn right I was!"

THE PRICE OF SILENCE

"All that is necessary for evil to succeed is that good men do nothing." – Edmund Burke

Calamity seems to follow me wherever I go. When I sailed to the Mediterranean, Beirut had to be evacuated. I went to the Philippines and Marcos was overthrown. I deployed to Panama and all hell broke loose. A visit to Korea was followed by major rioting. An assignment in the Congo led to civil war. If anyone ever gets wind of this I may become *persona non grata* everywhere on the planet.

With all that history it should not come as much of a surprise to learn I moved to the State of Florida in the year 2000. I became a resident and changed my voter registration to that state prior to the Presidential election, and shortly thereafter the term "hanging chad" became part of every American's vocabulary. To say what transpired during the so-called "recount" was a travesty would be a gross understatement, but through all of the litigation and political maneuvering one tactic struck me as particularly heinous. The attempt to exclude absentee ballots submitted by members of the armed forces was absolutely unconscionable. The Americans whose very service guarantees the right of each and every citizen to vote were being denied that same opportunity.

If you were to ask a dozen Marines the reason they joined the Corps you might be surprised by how many different responses you would get. The need for discipline, steady pay, technical training, family tradition, the GI Bill, dress blues – the list goes on. Not too many years ago "the judge said I had a choice between the Marine Corps and jail" made the list with some regularity as well, but fortunately that one has fallen out of favor in recent years.

The common thread is a Marine's love of country, desire to protect our democracy, and belief in liberating the oppressed. Most of us join this gun club, at least in part, because we believe in what our country stands for. Every one of us is an instrument of democracy and weapon for freedom – yet the sad irony is most members of the armed forces fail to employ the most potent weapon in their arsenal.

Nuclear submarines and stealth bombers are formidable weapons systems to be sure, but they are impotent without a coherent foreign and national policy. Sit around any barracks lounge during the six o'clock news and more than likely some report about a government policy affecting the military will touch a nerve and trigger an impromptu "gripe" session. Pay raises, homosexual policies, and deployment of forces to places such as Bosnia are not abstract news items to military members – they impact them directly. Yet out of that same group of gripers, how many actually voted in the last general election? They are the cream of America's youth, the enforcers of foreign policy and the *guardians of democracy* – yet the vast majority don't bother to vote.

Why is this so? As far as I can tell there are three primary reasons: apathy, ignorance, and inconvenience. I am not going to address apathy at length because although it is a regrettable trait, the sad fact is it permeates not only the armed forces, buy society at large. I will simply say this – shame on you! (and you know who you are).

Ignorance and inconvenience, on the other hand, are easily eliminated. The Marine Corps appoints voting officers and publishes voting policy, and I'm sure the other services do as well. The problem is many voting officers view this collateral duty as a burden and do not aggressively pursue the duties associated with it. Most troops don't even know who their voting officer is, much less how to obtain and fill out an absentee ballot. Commanders need to start asking PFCs to identify the voting officer in addition to memorizing the chain of command, and should require NCOs to know how to submit a Federal Post Card application in addition to being able to conduct close order drill. We conduct classes on everything from digging a straddle latrine to sexual harassment, yet most units can't seem to find room on the training schedule for a simple voting orientation during an election year.

The simple measure of requiring voting officers take their job seriously and conduct a voting class will go a long way toward eliminating ignorance as an excuse, so that leaves inconvenience as the remaining roadblock. Deployments, operational tempo, and special duty are all serious impediments to the implementation of a Marine Corps-wide voting effort, yet those very same problems always seem to be overcome during the Combined Federal Campaign and Navy/Marine Corps Relief fund drives. Thermometers measuring participation suddenly appear at every base, and there is a requirement for all personnel to be contacted – even while at sea. I am certainly not questioning the importance of those worthy charities, but instead am at a loss to understand why our most sacred right - the vote - is not given the same attention. It's time for leaders to start educating Marines about the importance of voting, and for our voting assistance officers to start assisting by providing the means and guidance necessary.

I am not trying to tell anyone *how* to vote, but am simply trying to encourage Marines, and all members of the armed forces, to take the time to *do* it. It's in our own best interest to take an active part in choosing those who lead the nation and shape the policies our troops must live, and perhaps die, by. Many people rationalize that one more vote one way or the other will have no effect on the outcome of an election, but the truth is a single ballot can be just as effective as the single, well-aimed round fired by a Marine sniper. You need look no further than the 2000 Presidential election for an object lesson in the value of a single vote.

Bottom line: If you can get by with a smaller pay raise, if you don't mind bunking with a homosexual, and if you are happy to deploy to Bosnia or some other far off land at the behest of a President who dodged the draft, well, that's certainly your right. I just don't want to hear you complaining during the six o'clock news, because as far as I'm concerned you gave up *that* right when you chose not to vote. Such is the price of silence.

A SPECIAL VISIT
To the Iwo Jima Memorial

Author Unknown

"The raising of that flag on Suribachi means a Marine Corps for the next five hundred years." - Secretary of the Navy James Forrestal

Each year I am hired to go to Washington, D.C. with the eighth grade class from Clinton, Wisconsin to videotape their trip. I greatly enjoy visiting our nation's capitol, and each year I take some special memories back with me.

This fall's trip was especially memorable. On the last night of our trip we stopped at the Iwo Jima memorial. This memorial is the largest bronze statue in the world and depicts one of the most famous photographs in history - that of the six brave soldiers raising the American Flag at the top of a rocky hill on the Island of Iwo Jima, Japan during WW II.

Over one hundred students and chaperones piled off the buses and headed towards the memorial. I noticed a solitary figure at the base of the statue, and as I got closer he asked, "Where are you guys from?" I told him that we were from Wisconsin. "Hey, I'm a Cheesehead too! Come gather around Cheeseheads, and I will tell you a story."

James Bradley just happened to be in Washington D.C. to speak at the memorial the following day. He was there that night to say good night to his dad, who has since passed away. He was just about to leave when he saw the buses pull up. I videotaped him as he spoke to us, and received his permission to share what he said from my videotape. It is one thing to tour the incredible monuments filled with history in Washington DC, but it is quite another to get the

16

kind of insight we received that night. When all had gathered around he reverently began to speak.

"My name is James Bradley and I'm from Antigo, Wisconsin. My dad is on that statue, and I just wrote a book called *Flags of Our Fathers* which is number five on the New York Times Best Seller list right now. It is the story of the six boys you see behind me. Six boys raised the flag.

The first guy putting the pole in the ground is Harlon Block. Harlon was an all-state football player. He enlisted in the Marine Corps with all the senior members of his football team. They were off to play another type of game - a game called 'War.' But it didn't turn out to be a game. Harlon, at the age of twenty-one, died with his intestines in his hands. I don't say that to gross you out, I say that because there are generals who stand in front of this statue and talk about the glory of war. You need to know that most of the boys in Iwo Jima were seventeen, eighteen, and nineteen years old.

He pointed to the statue. You see this next guy? That's Rene Gagnon from New Hampshire. If you took Rene's helmet off at the moment this photo was taken, and looked in the webbing of that helmet, you would find a photograph. A photograph of his girlfriend. Rene put that in there for protection, because he was scared. He was eighteen years old. Boys won the battle of Iwo Jima. Boys, not old men.

The next guy here, the third guy in this tableau, was Sergeant Mike Strank. Mike is my hero. He was the hero of all these guys. They called him the 'old man' because he was so old. He was already twenty-four. When Mike would motivate his boys in training camp, he didn't say, 'Let's go kill some Japanese' or 'Let's die for our country.' He knew he was talking to little boys. Instead he would say, 'You do what I say, and I'll get you home to your mothers.'

The last guy on this side of the statue is Ira Hayes, a Pima Indian from Arizona. Ira Hayes walked off Iwo Jima. He went to the White House with my dad. President Truman told him, 'You're a hero.' He told reporters, 'How can I feel like a hero when two hundred and fifty of my buddies hit the island with me and only twenty-seven of us walked off alive?' So you take your class at school. Two hundred fifty of you spending a year together having fun, doing everything together. Then all of you hit the beach, but only twenty-seven of your classmates walk off alive. That was Ira Hayes. He had images of horror in his mind. Ira Hayes died dead drunk, face down, at the age of thirty-two. Ten years after this picture was taken.

The next guy, going around the statue, is Franklin Sousley from Hilltop Kentucky. A fun-lovin' hillbilly boy. His best friend, who is now seventy told me, 'We pushed two cows up on the porch of the Hilltop General Store. Then we strung wire across the stairs so the cows couldn't get down. Then we fed them Epson salts. You know what happened.' Yes, he was a fun-lovin' hillbilly boy. Franklin died on Iwo Jima at the age of nineteen. When the telegram came to tell his mother that he was dead, it went to the Hilltop General Store. A barefoot boy ran that telegram up to his mother's farm. The neighbors could hear her scream all night and into the morning. The neighbors lived a quarter of a mile away.

The next guy, as we continue to go around the statue, is my dad, John Bradley from Antigo, Wisconsin, where I was raised. My dad lived until 1994, but he would never give interviews. When Walter Cronkite's producers, or the *New York Times* would call, we were trained as little kids to say, 'No, I'm sorry sir, my dad's not here. He is in Canada fishing. No, there is no phone there sir. No, we don't know when he is coming back.' My dad never fished or even went to Canada. Usually he was sitting there right at the table eating his Campbell's soup. But we had to tell the press that he was out fishing. He didn't want to talk to the press.

You see, my dad didn't see himself as a hero. Everyone thinks these guys are heroes, because they are in a photo and a monument. My dad knew better. He was a medic. John Bradley from Wisconsin was a caregiver. On Iwo Jima he probably held over two hundred boys as they died. And when boys died on Iwo Jima, they writhed and screamed in pain.

When I was a little boy my third grade teacher told me that my dad was a hero. When I went home and told my dad that, he looked at me and said, 'I want you always to remember that the heroes of Iwo Jima are the guys who did not come back. Did *not* come back.'

So that's the story about six nice young boys. Three died on Iwo Jima, and three came back as national heroes. Overall seven thousand boys died on Iwo Jima in the worst battle in the history of the Marine Corps. My voice is giving out, so I will end here. Thank you for your time."

Suddenly the monument wasn't just a big old piece of metal with a flag sticking out of the top. It came to life before our eyes with the heartfelt words of a son who did indeed have a father who was a hero. Maybe not a hero for the reasons most people would believe, but a hero nonetheless.

AT DAWN THEY SLEPT

"We signed up knowing the risk. Those innocent people in New York didn't go to work thinking there was any kind of risk." - Pvt. Mike Armendariz-Clark, USMC; Afghanistan, September 20, 2001

The events of 9/11 made a lot of us think back to the Beirut bombing. I suppose it's natural to compare the two disasters. In each case a large explosion brought down a building and killed a bunch of Americans, but when you think about it the similarity stops there. The two incidents occurred in far different environments, and it's important to remember that.

One of the things which differentiates an act of terror from an act of war is the target chosen. When the IRA attacks people in a pub, a bomb goes off on a bus in Israel, or an airliner crashes into the World Trade Center it is *terrorism*, cut and dried. The killing of unsuspecting noncombatants is inexcusable, and those who do it are cowards.

The sneak attack on Pearl Harbor is in something of a gray area. Although the target was certainly military in nature, no state of war existed between the United States and Japan at the time. It can be argued that the Japanese used surprise as a legitimate strategy against a superior foe, but the issue of morality is something else entirely.

The Beirut bombing was launched against a military target during an armed conflict, and it is OUR fault the defenses around the Marine barracks were penetrated. If they had dropped a bomb from an airplane or launched a missile, people would have viewed the attack as an act of war. But the perpetrators simply didn't have the resources to do that. Keep in mind the Japanese employed kamikazes as an act of

20

desperation during World War II, and those acts were never considered terrorist in nature.

The people who carried out the Beirut bombing knew they couldn't whip Marines in a fair fight, so they used guerrilla tactics similar to the ones our minutemen employed in the early days of the American Revolution. It was a grisly episode in our history, but we must learn a lesson from it. Otherwise two hundred and forty-one Americans will have died for nothing.

In October of 1983 I was visiting with my friend Eddie Fleck at his home in New York when he received a phone call. He was told that "Mr. Smith from Connecticut" was on the line, and he answered the phone expecting it to be his friend Tom. Staff Sergeant Tom Smith was a platoon sergeant with 2nd Recon Battalion, and had served with Eddie when he was still on active duty. The caller turned out to be Tom's Dad, and he was calling to tell Eddie of his son's death in Beirut. It was tragic.

The Marine Corps is a small family, and I discovered *how* small a couple of years later. I read a book about Beirut entitled *The Root* by Eric Hammel, and he gave a detailed account of what happened to a number of Marines who were there. I returned to active duty the month after the attack, and after a stint in Okinawa found myself in the same company with Sergeant Pablo Arroyo, one of those who had been profiled. A couple of years later I became friends with yet another, a Marine named Burnie Matthews. Tom Smith had been platoon sergeant for both.

Politicians cannot tie the hands of the military with unrealistic rules of engagement ever again. Marines with empty weapons in an environment like Beirut was in 1983 are sitting ducks. We all knew the risks when we joined the

Corps, but when our time comes we want to die with our boots on.

There is a memorial to those who lost their lives in Beirut outside the gates of Camp Johnson, which is adjacent to Camp Lejeune. Every October 23rd a ceremony is held there to honor those who died that day. If you are ever there during that time of year stop by and remember those who fell.

YES SIR, NO SIR...
Three Bags Full!

"Knowing the right thing to do is usually easy, but consistently doing the right thing in the face of adversity is something else. That is the true test of character." – Judith K. Molloy

Integrity is invariably cited as the most important of the fourteen Leadership Traits, but in my humble opinion it is the one most often violated in today's military. How many of us, from the Commandant down to the last Private in the rearmost rank, have lied when asked our opinion about a controversial subject? After all, it's much simpler to tell our constituency or chain-of-command what we think they *want* to hear, rather than take a chance on being "politically incorrect."

I believe courage surpasses integrity as the most indispensable leadership quality in this age of "don't ask, don't tell" politics. I'm not talking about the sort of physical courage normally associated with heroism, but moral courage. As Marines we revere those who perform courageous acts in combat, yet when someone dares to demonstrate moral courage they are often admonished for committing professional suicide. How many fitness reports contain the reporting senior's *honest* assessment of someone's deficiencies? The new performance evaluation system has done much to eliminate the walk-on-water syndrome that was so prevalent - but it has not disappeared altogether. The opportunity to dive on a live grenade is rare, but chances to express honest opinions, and perhaps make a difference, are everywhere.

23

I always made it my policy to be brutally candid with my seniors, and made it clear to my juniors I expected them to afford me the same courtesy. I am not in any way suggesting tact should be dispensed with. On the contrary, I encouraged Marines to tell me what they really thought within the framework of military courtesy. The alternative is to cultivate a Marine Corps filled with camouflage clad Madison Avenue yes-man types who live by the credo "don't rock the boat."

Throughout my career I always admired leaders who were not afraid to do or say what they thought was right even when it went against the party line. A good example occurred during General Mundy's tenure as Commandant. Many Marines, myself among them, mourned the departure of General Gray when he retired. We felt that a seemingly aristocratic politician such as Mundy had no hope of filling the boots of "Warrior Al." At least that was the case until he released the now infamous, and short-lived, ALMAR on married enlistees. My respect for the Commandant skyrocketed because he had the courage to put forth a politically unpopular policy that happened to make sense both financially and operationally.

I developed a bit of a reputation as a boat rocker myself, and there is no doubt it occasionally had a negative impact on my career. But I was willing to suffer the slings and arrows of the unenlightened in order to be heard, because every now and then someone was actually listening. Do you remember what Gunny Highway said to the MEU Commander in the movie *Heartbreak Ridge* when asked his opinion of a readiness exercise? "It's a clusterfuck, Sir" was his unvarnished appraisal, in contrast to the unabashed brown-nosing of Major Powers. Which one deserves our respect, and which is displaying both courage and integrity?

It must be noted that disagreement for disagreement's sake serves no constructive purpose. Just because the CO says "tastes great" does not mean you have to automatically respond with "less filling." On the other hand, if you possess information not available to the rest of the beer quaffing public by all means make the boss aware of it. Anyone who does less in order to stay off the skyline not only lacks courage, but is derelict in his duty as well.

Marine leaders must have the *courage* to exercise good *judgment* by having the *integrity* to *tactfully* point out something is not the way it ought to be, no matter how unpopular their position. Notice any leadership traits in that last sentence? We need Marines who are blissfully ignorant of the term "politically incorrect." Just carry out your duties in a quiet but professional manner until someone asks what you think about women in combat (or *whatever*). Then tell them what you *really* think. After all, if they didn't want your opinion they shouldn't have asked!

HEROES
Of the Vietnam Generation

By James Webb

"A country is not just an area of land. It's a principle, and patriotism is loyalty to that principle."

The rapidly disappearing cohort of Americans who endured the Great Depression and then fought World War II is receiving quite a send-off from the leading lights of the so-called "60's generation." Tom Brokaw has published two oral histories of "The Greatest Generation" that feature ordinary people doing their duty which suggest that such conduct was historically unique.

Chris Matthews of "Hardball" is fond of writing columns praising the Navy service of his father while castigating his own baby boomer generation for its alleged softness and lack of struggle, William Bennett gave a condescending speech at the Naval Academy a few years ago comparing the heroism of the "D-Day Generation" to the drugs-and-sex nihilism of the "Woodstock Generation," and Steven Spielberg, in promoting his film *Saving Private Ryan*, was careful to justify his portrayals of soldiers in action based on the supposedly unique nature of World War II.

An irony is at work here. Lest we forget, the World War II generation now being lionized also brought us the Vietnam War, a conflict which today's most conspicuous voices by and large opposed, and in which few of them served. The "best and brightest" of the Vietnam age group once made headlines by castigating their parents for bringing about the war in which they would not fight, which has become the war they refuse to remember.

Pundits back then invented a term for this animus: the "generation gap." Long, plaintive articles and even books were written examining its manifestations. Campus leaders, who claimed precocious wisdom through the magical process of reading a few controversial books, urged fellow baby boomers not to trust anyone over thirty. Their elders, who had survived the Depression and fought the largest war in history, were looked down upon as shallow, materialistic, and out of touch.

Those of us who grew up on the other side of the picket line from that era's counter-culture can't help but feel a little leery of this sudden gush of appreciation for our elders from the leading lights of the old counter-culture. Then and now, the national conversation has proceeded from the dubious assumption that those who came of age during Vietnam are a unified generation in the same sense as their parents were, and thus are capable of being spoken for through these fickle elites.

In truth, the "Vietnam generation" is a misnomer. Those who came of age during that war are permanently divided by different reactions to a whole range of counter-cultural agendas, and nothing divides them more deeply than the personal ramifications of the war itself. The sizable portion of the Vietnam age group who declined to support the counter-cultural agenda, and especially the men and women who opted to serve in the military during the Vietnam War, are quite different from their peers who for decades have claimed to speak for them.

In fact, they are much like the World War II generation itself. For them Woodstock was a side show, college protestors were spoiled brats who would have benefited from having to work a few jobs in order to pay their tuition, and Vietnam represented not an intellectual exercise in draft avoidance, or protest marches, but a battlefield that was just as brutal as those their fathers faced in World War II and Korea.

Few who served during Vietnam ever complained of a generation gap. The men who fought World War II were their heroes and role models. They honored their father's service by emulating it, and largely agreed with their father's wisdom in attempting to stop Communism's reach in Southeast Asia.

The most accurate poll of their attitudes (Harris, 1980) showed that ninety-one percent were glad they'd served their country, seventy-four percent enjoyed their time in the service, and eighty-nine percent agreed with the statement that "our troops were asked to fight in a war which our political leaders in Washington would not let them win." And most importantly, the castigation they received upon returning home was not from the World War II generation, but from the very elites in their age group who supposedly spoke for them.

Nine million men served in the military during Vietnam War, three million of whom went to the Vietnam Theater. Contrary to popular mythology, two-thirds of these were volunteers, and seventy-three percent of those who died were volunteers. While some attention has been paid recently to the plight of our prisoners of war, most of whom were pilots, there has been little recognition of how brutal the war was for those who fought it on the ground.

Dropped onto the enemy's terrain 12,000 miles away from home, America's citizen-soldiers performed with a tenacity and quality that may never be truly understood. Those who believe the war was fought incompletely on a tactical level should consider Hanoi's recent admission that 1.4 million of its soldiers died on the battlefield, compared to 58,000 total U.S. dead.

Those who believe that it was a "dirty little war" where the bombs did all the work might contemplate that is was the most costly war the U.S. Marine Corps has ever fought - five times as many dead as World War I, three times as many dead as in Korea, and more total killed and wounded than in all of World War II.

Significantly, these sacrifices were being made at a time the United States was deeply divided over our effort in Vietnam. The baby-boom generation had cracked apart along class lines as America's young men were making difficult, life-or-death choices about serving. The better academic institutions became focal points for vitriolic protest against the war, with few of their graduates going into the military. Harvard College, which had lost 691 alumni in World War II, lost a total of twelve men in Vietnam from the classes of 1962 through 1972 combined. Those classes at Princeton lost six, at MIT two. The media turned ever more hostile. And frequently the reward for a young man's having gone through the trauma of combat was to be greeted by his peers with studied indifference or outright hostility.

What is a hero? My heroes are the young men who faced the issues of war and possible death, and then weighed those concerns against obligations to their country. Citizen-soldiers who interrupted their personal and professional lives at their most formative stage, in the timeless phrase of the Confederate Memorial in Arlington National Cemetery, "not for fame of reward, not for place of rank, but in simple obedience to duty, as they understood it." Who suffered loneliness, disease, and wounds with an often-contagious élan. And who deserve a far better place in history than that now offered them by the so-called spokesman of our so-called generation.

Mr. Brokaw, Mr. Matthews, Mr. Bennett, and Mr. Spielberg - meet my Marines. 1969 was an odd year to be in Vietnam. Second only to 1968 in terms of American casualties, it was the year made famous by Hamburger Hill, as well as the gut-wrenching *Life* cover story showing pictures of 242 Americans who had been killed in one average week of fighting. Back home, it was the year of Woodstock, and of numerous anti-war rallies that culminated in the Moratorium march on Washington. The My Lai massacre hit the papers, and was seized upon by the anti-war movement as the emblematic moment of the war. Lyndon Johnson left Washington in utter humiliation.

Richard Nixon entered the scene, destined for an even worse fate. In the An Hoa Basin southwest of Danang, the Fifth Marine Regiment was in its third year of continuous combat operations. Combat is an unpredictable and inexact environment, but we were well led. As a rifle platoon and company commander, I served under a succession of three regimental commanders who had cut their teeth in World War II, and four different battalion commanders, three of whom had seen combat in Korea. The company commanders were typically captains on their second combat tour in Vietnam, or young first lieutenants like myself who were given companies after many months of "bush time" as platoon commanders in the Basin's tough and unforgiving environs.

The Basin was one of the most heavily contested areas in Vietnam, its torn, cratered earth offering every sort of wartime possibility. In the mountains just to the west, not far from the Ho Chi Minh Trail, the North Vietnamese Army operated an infantry division from an area called Base Area

112. In the valleys of the Basin, main-force Viet Cong battalions whose ranks were eighty percent North Vietnamese Army regulars moved against the Americans every day. Local Viet Cong units sniped and harassed. Ridgelines and paddy dikes were laced with sophisticated bobby traps of every size, from a hand grenade to a 250-pound bomb. The villages sat in the rice paddies and tree lines like individual fortresses, crisscrossed with the trenches and spider holes, their homes sporting bunkers capable of surviving direct hits from large-caliber artillery shells. The Viet Cong infrastructure was intricate and permeating. Except for the old and the very young, villagers who did not side with the Communists had either been killed or driven out to the government controlled enclaves near DaNang.

In the rifle companies, we spent the endless months patrolling ridgelines and villages and mountains, far away from any notion of tents, barbed wire, hot food, or electricity. Luxuries were limited to what would fit inside one's pack, which after a few "humps" usually boiled down to letter-writing material, towel, soap, toothbrush, poncho liner, and a small transistor radio.

We moved through the boiling heat with sixty pounds of weapons and gear, causing a typical Marine to drop twenty percent of his body weight while in the bush. When we stopped we dug chest-deep fighting holes, and slit trenches for toilets. We slept on the ground under makeshift poncho hootches, and when it rained we usually took our hootches down because wet ponchos shined under illumination flares, making great targets. Sleep itself was fitful, never more than an hour or two at a stretch for months at a time as we mixed daytime patrolling with night-time ambushes, listening posts, foxhole duty, and radio watches. Ringworm, hookworm, malaria, and dysentery were common, as was trench foot

31

when the monsoons came. Respite was rotating back to the mud-filled regimental combat base at An Hoa for four or five days, where rocket and mortar attacks were frequent and our troops manned defensive bunkers at night. Which makes it kind of hard to get excited about tales of Woodstock, or camping at the Vineyard during summer break.

We had been told while training that Marine officers in the rifle companies had an eighty-five percent probability of being killed or wounded, and the experience of "Dying Delta," as our company was known, bore that out. Of the officers in the bush when I arrived, our company commander was wounded, the weapons platoon commander wounded, the first platoon commander was killed, the second platoon commander was wounded twice, and I, commanding the third platoon, fared no better. Two of my original three-squad leaders were killed, and the third was shot in the stomach. My platoon sergeant was severely wounded, as was my right guide. By the time I left my platoon had gone through six radio operators, five of them casualties.

These figures were hardly unique; in fact, they were typical. Many other units, for instance those who fought the hill battles around Khe Sanh, or were with the famed Walking Dead of the Ninth Marine Regiment, or were in the battle of Hue City or at Dai Do, had it far worse.

When I remember those days and the very young men who spent them with me I am continually amazed, for these were mostly recent civilians barely out of high school, called up from the cities and the farms to do their year in hell and then return. Visions haunt me every day, not of the nightmares of war but of the steady consistency with which my Marines faced their responsibilities, and of how uncomplaining most of them were in the face of constant danger. The salty, battle-hardened twenty-year-olds teaching green nineteen-year-olds the intricate lessons of the hostile battlefield. The unerring skill of the young squad leaders as we moved through unfamiliar villages and weed-choked trails in the black of night. The quick certainty when a fellow Marine was wounded and needed help. Their willingness to risk their lives to save other Marines in peril. To this day it stuns me that their own countrymen have so completely missed the story of their service, lost in the bitter confusion of the war itself.

Like every military unit throughout history we had occasional laggards, cowards, and complainers. But in the aggregate, these Marines were the finest people I have ever been around. It has been my privilege to keep up with many of them over the years since we all came home. One finds in them very little bitterness about the war in which they fought. The most common regret, almost to a man, is that they were not able to do more for each other and for the people they came to help.

It would be redundant to say that I would trust my life to these men because I already have, in more ways than I can ever recount. I am alive today because of their quiet, unaffected heroism. Such valor epitomizes the conduct of Americans at war from the first days of our existence. That the boomer elites can canonize this sort of conduct in our fathers generation, and not in ours, constitutes a continuing travesty.

Senator and Former Secretary of the Navy James Webb was awarded the Navy Cross, Silver Star, and Bronze Star medals for heroism as a Marine in Vietnam.

NOT FOR SELF
But For Country

"He who lives only for himself does not have very much to live for."

The following is an excerpt from a speech delivered to the graduates of the Hebert School of Medicine, the Graduate School of Nursing, and the Graduate School of Medicine by General Charles Krulak, Commandant of the Marine Corps, telling of one selfless act of bravery:

"Last month, I had the opportunity to visit the island of Iwo Jima. Known to the Japanese as Sulfur Island, it is a hot, bubbling, volcanic atoll that to this day still has active sulfur vents. During February and March 1945 it was the scene of one of the most horrific battles of World War II.

During the thirty-six day campaign to take that island, a Marine fell to Japanese fire every two minutes - every two minutes for thirty-six days a Marine was killed or wounded. It was the only battle in the history of our Corps where Marines suffered more casualties than the enemy. Today, the island still bears the scars of that titanic struggle. It is a place heavy with history and long on memories. The winds that constantly blow across the black sands of the Iwo Jima beaches seem, at times, to carry the voices of the warriors who fought there so long ago.

It is a mournful and reverent place. Joining me on that tortured ground was the family of the late John Bradley. They had never been there before, and wanted to see where their husband and their father had fought. John Bradley, who survived the battle, rarely spoke to his family about his experiences on Iwo Jima. When pressed, he would gloss over and downplay how he had won the Nation's second highest award for bravery... the Navy Cross. He earned that decoration by rushing to the aid of two wounded Marines, and then shielding them with his body while he tended to their wounds. When Bradley hurried to their aid, he didn't exactly rush. He crawled! Crawled, because he himself had been shot through both legs just a few minutes before.

Another reason the Bradley family wanted to visit Iwo Jima was because they wanted to see the site of the most famous battle photograph ever taken; the raising of the American flag on Mount Suribachi. That memorable event, captured in a bronze and granite sculpture, is known today as the Marine Corps War Memorial. Five Marines and one Navy Corpsman took part in that flag raising. Three did not survive the battle. The Navy Corpsman did... and as you have probably guessed, his name was Pharmacist Mate Second Class John Bradley.

Let me encourage you to visit the War Memorial one day. Run your hands across the cool granite. Step back and read the engraved words: 'Where Uncommon Valor Was a Common Virtue,' and then let your eyes travel up to the sculptured figures, young men forever captured in bronze. Look for Corpsmen John Bradley - you'll recognize him - he's the one with the empty canteen pouch.

You see, prior to climbing Mount Suribachi, he gave the last of his water to a dying Marine. On that hot bubbling Sulfur Island John Bradley would go the next twenty-four hours without water.

What I want to talk to you about today goes beyond bravery; goes beyond sacrifice. I want to talk to you about selflessness. John Bradley was a brave man and he sacrificed greatly. But most of all he was selfless. His brave acts were not done for any reward. Nor were they intended to be captured by NewsCam 4 or CNN. There was no public glory in what he did. In fact men under fire rarely speak of glory. Instead, they speak of, 'who can be counted upon and who cannot.' Above all, they speak about and remember the small individual acts of selflessness.

When Felix de Weldon, the sculptor of the Marine Corps War Memorial, asked John Bradley what had happened to his canteen, John couldn't even remember. In the heat of battle he had completely forgotten. But the surviving Marines of Bradley's unit knew, and they remembered, and they told de Weldon the story of his sharing his water.

Selflessness is unforgettable. Even the smallest acts of selflessness are unforgettable. Today, when you leave here, you will find yourselves placed into positions of great responsibility. You will be men and women of letters and possess a special and unique educational experience. That alone will cause the mantle of responsibility to be thrust upon you. And because of who and what you are you must don that mantle of responsibility. With responsibility comes many challenges. These challenges normally are translated into choices. A choice to operate. A choice for therapy. A choice to do nothing. But of all the choices you will face, there is none greater than the choice between self or selflessness. Is the benefit for you? Or is it for your team, or your patient, or your clinic, or your family?

Over the chapel doors at the United States Naval Academy is a simple Latin inscription: 'Non Sibi Sed Patriae' ('Not for self, but for country'). Simple, but powerful. Selflessness takes time to develop. Rarely does a man or woman suddenly grow a brain and a spine in the middle of an operating room or on a battlefield. Likewise, rarely does a person develop a sense of selflessness in one single moment in time. Spontaneous selfless acts rarely happen. Instead, they are built on a strong moral foundation and then carefully layered by doing the right thing time and time again.

All of you possess a strong character, strong morals, and a strong sense of duty. Let me encourage you to add to those strengths a spirit of selflessness. That spirit is within you now. Draw from it, use it and encourage it from others. Use it to lead, to build your team and to serve those you know and those you know not.

John Bradley gave the last of his water to a wounded Marine on 23 February 1945. That afternoon, he was struggling to climb the fire swept heights of Mount Suribachi. The next day he braved enemy fire to aid two wounded Marines and just a few days later, though wounded himself, he again braved enemy fire to aid two *more* Marines. It was not for sense of self that he performed those brave deeds. It was for others, for those he knew and for those he knew not. Deep within his soul John Bradley instinctively understood that 'Non Sibi Sed Patriae' is contagious.

After aiding those final two wounded Marines Corpsman John Bradley, badly wounded, lost consciousness. He awoke thirty-six hours later aboard the hospital ship *USS Solace*. How he arrived there is unknown. The names of those Marines and Sailors who carried him off the fire swept field of battle, who placed him on the small boat, and who carried him to the ship have been lost to history. Only their selfless deed remains. Even small acts of selflessness are unforgettable."

Semper Fi!

WHERE DO WE FIND THEM?

"The person who has nothing for which he is willing to fight, nothing which is more important than his own personal safety, is a miserable creature and has no chance of being free unless made and kept so by the exertions of better men than himself." – John Stewart Mill

A story from Operation Iraqi Freedom that appeared on April 5, 2003:

Martin Savidge of CNN, embedded with the 1st Marine Division, was talking with four young Marines near his foxhole ones morning live on CNN. He had been telling the story of how well the Marines had been looking out for and taking care of him since the war started. He went on to tell about the many hardships the Marines had endured since the war began, and how they all looked after one another.

He turned to the four and said he had cleared it with their commanders for them to use his video phone to call home. The nineteen-year-old Marine next to him asked Martin if he would allow his platoon sergeant to use his turn to call his pregnant wife back home, whom he had not been able to talk to in three months. A stunned Savidge, who was visibly moved by the request, shook his head and the young Marine ran off to get the sergeant.

Savidge recovered after a few seconds and turned back to the three young Marines still sitting with him and asked which one of them would like to call home first. The Marine closest to him responded without a moment's hesitation, "Sir, if it's all the same to you we would like to call the parents of a buddy of ours, Lance Corporal Brian Buesing of Cedar Key, Florida who was killed on March 23rd near Nasiriya, to see how they are doing."

At that Martin Savidge totally broke down and was unable to speak. All he could get out before signing off was "Where do they get young men like this?"

THE VISIT

By Tre' M. Barron

"We few, we happy few, we band of brothers..." - William Shakespeare

My Dad, Angelo, was in the hospital in Tacoma, Washington. A former Marine and veteran of the Korean War, he was having his third knee-replacement surgery.

A long and very painful operation was going to be made even worse because Dad was going through it alone. There was no one to hold his hand, no familiar soft voices to reassure him. His wife was ill and unable to accompany him or even visit during his weeklong stay. My sisters and brother lived in California, and I lived even farther away in Indiana. There wasn't even anyone to drive him to the hospital, so he had arrived that morning by cab. The thought of my Dad lying there alone was more than I could stand. But what could I do from here?

I picked up the phone and called information for the Puyallup, Washington Marine Corps recruiting station, where I had joined the Marines ten years before. I thought that if I could talk to a Marine and explain the situation, maybe one of them would visit my Dad.

I called the number. A man answered the phone and in a very confident voice said, "United States Marines, Staff Sergeant Van-es. May I help you?"

Feeling just as certain, I replied, "Sergeant Van-es, you may find this request a little strange, but this is why I am calling..." I proceeded to tell him who I was and that my father was also a former Marine and one hundred percent disabled from the Korean War. I explained that he was in the hospital alone, without anyone to visit, and asked if Sergeant Van-es would please go and see him.

Without hesitation, he answered, "Absolutely."

Then I asked, "If I send flowers to the recruiting station, would you deliver them to my Dad when you go to the hospital?"

"Ma'am, I will be happy to take the flowers to your Dad. I'll give you my address. You send them, and I will make sure that he receives them," he replied.

The next morning I sent the flowers to Sergeant Van-es' office just as we had planned. I went to work, and that evening I returned home and phoned my Dad to inquire about his surprise visitor.

If you have ever talked with a small child after that child has just seen Santa Claus, you will understand the glee I heard in my Dad's voice. "I was just waking up when I thought I saw two Marines in their dress blue uniforms standing at the foot of my bed," he told me excitedly. "I thought I had died and gone to heaven. But they were really there!"

I began to laugh, partly at the excitement, but also because he didn't even mention his operation. He felt so honored: Two Marines he had never met took time out to visit an old Marine like him. He told me again and again how sharp they looked and how all the nurses thought he was so important. "But how did you ever get them to do that?" he asked me.

"It was easy. We are all Marines, Dad, past and present. It's the bond.

After hanging up with my Dad I called Sergeant Van-es to thank him for visiting my Dad. And to thank him for the extra things he did to make it special: wearing his dress blue uniform, bringing another Marine along – he even took a digital camera with him. He had pictures taken of the two

Marines with my Dad right beside his bed. That evening he e-mailed them to me so I could see for myself that my Dad was not alone and that he was going to be okay.

As for the flowers, they hardly mattered, but I was glad for the opportunity to express my feelings. The card read: "Daddy, I didn't want just anyone bringing you flowers... so I sent the World's Finest. Semper Fi."

This story originally appeared in "Chicken Soup for the Veteran's Soul."

TOYS FOR TOTS

"Bring the joy of Christmas to America's needy children."

Toys for Tots began in 1947 when Major Bill Hendricks, USMCR and a group of Marine Reservists in Los Angeles collected and distributed 5,000 toys to needy children. The idea came from Bill's wife, Diane. In the fall of 1947 Diane handcrafted a Raggedy Ann doll and asked Bill to deliver it to an organization which gave toys to needy children at Christmas. When Bill determined that no such agency existed, Diane told him that he should start one. He did. The 1947 campaign was so successful that the Marine Corps adopted Toys for Tots in 1948 and expanded it into a nationwide campaign. That year Marine Corps Reserve units across the nation conducted Toys for Tots campaigns in each community in which a Reserve Center was located, and Marines have conducted successful nationwide campaigns at Christmas each year since then.

Bill Hendricks, a Marine Reservist on weekends, was in civilian life the Director of Public Relations for Warner Brothers Studio. This enabled him to convince a vast array of celebrities to provide their support. In 1948 Walt Disney designed the Toys for Tots logo, which is still used today. Disney also designed the first Toys for Tots poster used to promote the nationwide program. Nat "King" Cole, Peggy Lee, and Vic Damone recorded the Toys for Tots theme in 1956, and Bob Hope, John Wayne, Doris Day, Tim Allen and Kenny Rogers are but a few of the long list of celebrities who have given their time and talent to promote this worthy charity. First Lady Barbara Bush served as the national spokesperson in 1992, and in her autobiography named Toys for Tots as one of her favorite charities.

My own affiliation with the Toys for Tots program began during my days with 2nd Battalion, 25th Marines in Garden City, New York. Collection points were set up at Shea Stadium prior to a Jets football game one Christmas season, and volunteers were needed to man them. I admit my motive wasn't completely noble that day – participants were allowed into the stadium to watch the second half for free. But the experience did teach me a lot about the spirit of giving.

Once I returned to active duty, deployments and operational tempo often limited my participation in the program - but I still donated toys whenever possible. When I reported for duty in the Congo during the later part of 1992 one of the first things that struck me was the overwhelming poverty of the Congolese people. I wanted to help in some small way, so my Marines placed a large box under the Embassy Christmas Tree and sent a memo to every office soliciting the donation of toys. Everyone was very generous, and what we collected was distributed to local children by missionaries working in the area.

My next assignment was in Australia. While there was nothing like the poverty I saw in the Congo, there were still a lot of needy kids all the same. Once again a collection point was set up under the Embassy Christmas Tree, and once again we were overwhelmed by the generosity of everyone who worked there. Since there was no official Toys for Tots distribution system there we turned the toys over to the Australian Salvation Army, and they in turn brought them to children's hospitals where the neediest children received an unexpected visit from Santa Claus.

No story about Toys for Tots would be complete without mentioning the late Sam Dipoto, who ran the program for the

Marine Corps League in the Tampa/St. Petersburg area of Florida for nearly twenty years. Sam loved to tell the story of a woman who donated a dozen brand new bicycles one Christmas. When he tried to thank her she said it was just *her* way of thanking Toys for Tots. It turned out a couple of years earlier the woman had been out of work and destitute, but the Marines had come through with a bicycle for her young son.

I have no doubt that there are many like Sam all across the country, and hopefully there will be many more to follow in their footsteps. The kids are counting on it.

If you would like to donate a toy, make a cash contribution or donate your time contact the Marine Toys For Tots Foundation, PO Box 1947 Quantico, VA 22134. They can also be reached at (703) 640-9433 or via the worldwide web by visiting www.toysfortots.org.

RESOLUTE RESPONSE

"They told (us) to open up the Embassy, or 'we'll blow you away.' And then they looked up and saw the Marines on the roof with these really big guns, and they said in Somali, 'Igaralli ahow,' which means 'Excuse me, I didn't mean it, my mistake.'" - Karen Aquilar, U.S. Embassy Mogadishu, Somalia, 1991

The Moscow Station scandal brought a lot of bad publicity to the Marine Security Guard program, but it was not an true indication of the type of Marines we had out there guarding our Embassies and Consulates. When the following incident occurred I took a bit of a personal interest since our Embassy in Nairobi was headquarters for Company F and I had visited there on several occasions. These Marines are far more representative of the MSG program than the likes of Clayton Lonetree:

On the morning of August 7, 1998 Corporal Samuel Gonite was standing duty at Post One of the American Embassy in Nairobi. Another MSG who was off duty at the time, Sergeant Jesse Aliganga, stopped by to chat with Gonite for a few minutes on his way to cash some checks for a Marine social function scheduled for that evening. When their conversation concluded Aliganga left Post One and got on the elevator. It was at that moment that a bomb was detonated by terrorists in the Embassy parking garage.

Gonite heard the explosion and checked the closed circuit television monitors to see if there had been a car accident on the street in front of the Embassy. A split second later he was knocked to the ground by a second explosion. When he opened his eyes he couldn't see anything due to the dust, and a few moments later he heard someone pounding on the door to his post. He opened it and discovered it was his Detachment Commander, Gunnery Sergeant Gary Cross. Cross had been thrown to the bottom of a stairwell as he responded to the first explosion, and he directed Gonite to secure classified material and aid people as they evacuated the building.

At the time of the explosion two other Marines, Sergeants Aaron Russell and Daniel Briehl, were waiting for Alingala by their car in front of the Embassy. They decided to go inside to wait, and had just started moving toward the entrance when the bomb exploded. Briehl dove for cover by their car as debris began to fall on him, and Russell sprinted to Post One to check on Gonite. A few moments later Russell heard a muffled yell and realized that Briehl, who had followed him into the Embassy by that time, had fallen down the elevator shaft while trying to feel his way through the smoke to Post One. Debris was falling down the shaft on top of Briehl, who had sustained three broken ribs in the fall. Despite his injuries he assisted a group of people who had been trapped below in climbing up and out to safety. When Cross found him a bit later he sent the Marine to the hospital for treatment.

Gunny Cross immediately set about the task of securing a perimeter around the Embassy. He, Russell and Gonite donned their react gear and surrounded the Embassy as best they could until Cross was able to enlist the aid of additional military personnel.

While all this was happening Sergeants Armando Jiminez and Raymond Outt heard what was happening over their radio at the Marine House. They ran outside, flagged down a passing diplomatic vehicle, and headed for the Embassy. When they couldn't get through the snarl of traffic the Marines jumped from the vehicle and ran to the Embassy.

Their Detachment Commander later commented that they "probably ran the fastest PFT of their lives." Upon arriving at the scene thirty minutes after the explosion the two reported to Cross and asked what they could do.

Another member of the detachment, Sergeant Harper, had been on leave in Mombasa where he had gone on safari. As he returned from the airport later that evening he heard about the bombing, and he headed straight for the Embassy to see what he could do.

Eventually seven search parties were organized, and Gunny Cross was asked if his Marines would be willing to help since they were intimately familiar with the layout of the Embassy. It was emphasized that since the building was unstable it was strictly a voluntary effort, and no one could be ordered to go back inside. Every single Marine volunteered without hesitation.

Cross and his detachment immediately reentered the shattered building in an effort to locate Aliganga and other Embassy personnel who had been killed or injured. Digging with their bare hands at first, they were determined to locate their brother Marine. Twenty-seven hours later they found him – dead.

The Marines draped their comrade in an Embassy flag that had been blown from its pole by the blast, and when Cross, Outt, Harper and Jiminez carried out the body onlookers grew silent.

At one point, as Cross helped carry a stretcher out of the Embassy, he noticed that Briehl was back from the hospital and standing guard. He was still wearing his hospital gown, over which he had donned his flak jacket and helmet. When Cross asked him what he was doing there, Briehl simply replied "I knew you needed me down here, so I checked myself out of the hospital." Cross ordered him to go back.

The six Marines had been on duty for roughly thirty-six hours by the time MSGs from other posts in the region arrived to relieve them. Search and recovery efforts continued for the next six days, and the Marines continued their mission. A senior State Department official commented that "the Marines did a tremendous job. While most people were running out of the building, they were running in, despite the obvious danger."

Many of the Embassy staff described the building as unrecognizable after the bombing, but through the smoke, flames, death and destruction one thing remained easy to recognize. Esprit de Corps.

A YOUNG MARINE
Restores My Faith

By Ann Baker

"It's not the size of the man in the fight, it's the size of the fight in the man"!

It was our normal Thursday morning business meeting at our real-estate office. No big deal. Before the meeting we hung around the bagel table, as usual, with our coffee. He stood aside, looking a little shy and awkward and very young, a new face in a room full of extroverted salespeople. An average looking guy, maybe five feet, eight inches. A clean-cut, sweet-faced kid. I went over to chat with him. Maybe he was a new salesman?

He said he was just back from Kabul, Afghanistan. A Marine. Our office (and a local school) had been supportive by sending letters to him and other troops, which he had posted on the American Embassy door in Kabul. He stood guard there for four months and was shot at daily. He had come to our office to thank us for our support, for all the letters during those scary times. I couldn't believe my ears. He wanted to thank *us*? We should be thanking him. But how? How could ever show him my appreciation?

At the end of the sales meeting he stepped quietly forward, no incredible hulk. As a matter of fact, he looked for all the world fifteen years old to me. (The older I get, the younger they look.) This young Marine, this clean-faced boy, had no qualms stepping up to the plate and dodging bullets so that I might enjoy the freedom to live my peaceful life in the land of the free - no matter the risk. Suddenly the most stressful

50

concerns of my life seemed as nothing, my complacency flew right out the window with his every word. Somewhere, somehow, he had taken the words honor, courage and commitment into his very soul and laid his life on the line daily for me and us. A man of principle. He wants to do it. Relishes it. And he came to thank *us*? For a few letters? I fought back the tears as he spoke so briefly and softly.

He walked forward to our manager and placed a properly folded American flag in his hands. It had flown over the Embassy. He said thanks again. You could hear a pin drop. As I looked around I saw red faces everywhere fighting back the tears.

In a heartbeat, my disillusionment with young people today quickly vanished. In ordinary homes, in ordinary towns, kids like him are growing up proud to be an American and willing to die for it. Wow. We'll frame the flag and put it in the lobby. He only came to my office once, for just a few minutes. But I realized I had rubbed shoulders with greatness in the flesh, and in the twinkling of an eye my life was forever changed. His name is Michael Mendez, a corporal in the USMC. We are a great nation. We know, because the makings of it walked into my office that day.

This letter was authored by Ann Baker of Huntington Beach, California and originally appeared in the Orange County Register on June 30, 2002.

VIVE LA FRANCE!

You can never surrender too early, or too often!. - Rule of French warfare

The French have always been something of an enigma to me. France is the country that gave us Napoleon, a man whose military exploits and thirst for conquest were legendary. Yet during the past century that same nation has fielded some of the most inept armies in history, and have depended on other nations to save their bacon on more than one occasion. So it boggled my mind when the French opposed a proposed United Nations resolution to oust Saddam Hussein for not complying with a directive to disarm, going so far as to threaten a veto in the Security Council. After all, they certainly had no objection when we sent troops to liberate *their* country during both World Wars, did they?

World War I was initially fought by the Army, but once Marines arrived in Europe they quickly made a name for themselves. The battle for Belleau Wood became one of the most famous in Marine Corps history, and the 5th and 6th Marine Regiments distinguished themselves with such valor the French renamed the area "Forest of the Marines." – and it was there we earned the nickname Devil Dogs.

The Marine Corps didn't fight in Europe at all during WWII, but I had a personal stake in the liberation of France nonetheless. My own father landed on the beaches of Normandy on D-Day in June of 1944. Tens of thousands of Americans died driving the Germans from French soil, but fortunately my Dad was not one of them. If he had been I wouldn't be here to write these words.

My feelings for the French can be best illustrated by something that occurred a few years back. A Marine colonel was attending a state dinner in a former French colony in North Africa on the occasion of Bastille Day, and naturally his Sergeant Major accompanied him. As per protocol the Sergeant Major was seated next to the French military attaché, who was a Colonel. As the evening wore on and the libations flowed (the Sergeant Major was not a temperate man) the Marine began eyeing the Frenchman with a growing amount of disdain. Finally, when he could stand it no longer, he turned and asked a question many of us have probably wondered about.

"So tell me Colonel, how many French troops does it take to defend Paris?" he asked.

After thinking about it for a long moment the Frenchman replied, "I do not know, monsieur."

The Sergeant Major smiled with thinly veiled glee. His prey had taken the bait.

"Of course you don't, because it's never been done!" He was of course referring to the French habit of declaring Paris an open city in the face of advancing German forces. The French Colonel was dumbstruck by the comment, and the Marine couldn't resist twisting the knife a bit more.

"But don't you worry, we'll always be happy to come on over and take it back for you *anytime*."

DON'T ASK, DON'T TELL

"The safest place in Korea was right behind a platoon of Marines. Lord, how they could fight!" - Major General Frank E. Lowe, US Army; Korea, 26 January 1952

There has been a great deal of debate in recent years over the role of homosexuals in the armed forces, and while I am totally against their admission I must say the toughest unit I've ever encountered was in a sense linked to that segment of our society.

Early in my career I was stationed at Camp Lejeune with 2nd Amphibian Tractor Battalion. In those days before the invention of Goretex we wore field jackets to ward off the chill of North Carolina winters, and since they were unit rather than individual property the word AMTRAC was stenciled across the back in bold letters. Other units of course did the same, and it was not uncommon to see TANKS, RECON and any number of other outfits on a given day - with one exception.

I soon noticed there was a group of Marines who absolutely refused to wear their issue field jackets, and they could be spotted shivering all over the base until it finally got so cold even they had to break down and put them on. They were the men of Field Artillery Group, and the moment I saw them wearing a garment prominently labeled "FAG" I could understand their compulsion for risking pneumonia.

Needless to say it was standard procedure for those poor fellows to be mercilessly taunted by Marines from other units, and they fought more often than a group of Yankee fans in Fenway Park. Over time they became so good at fisticuffs they were able to wear their FAG jackets with impunity, and no one would even *think* of starting any trouble. After all, what Marine wants to go back to the barracks and tell his buddies he got whipped by a bunch of FAGs?

COMMANDANT'S PARTY

The first time Chesty Puller was shown a flame thrower his only question was, "Where does the bayonet go?"

The Commandant of the Marine Corps, General Al Gray, was a crusty old "Field Marine." He loved his Marines, and often slipped into the mess hall wearing a faded old field jacket without any rank insignia on it. He would then go through the chow line just like a private. In this way, he was assured of being given the same rations that the lowest enlisted man received, and woe be it unto the mess officer if the food was found to be "unfit in quality or quantity."

Upon becoming Commandant General Gray was expected to do a great deal of formal entertaining - fancy dinner parties in full dress uniform. Now, the General would rather have been in the field eating cold "C-rats" around a fighting hole with a bunch of young "hard-charging" Marines. But he knew his duty, and as a Marine he was determined to do it to the best of his ability.

During these formal parties a detachment of highly polished Marines from the Marine Barracks at 8th&I were detailed to assume the position of parade rest at various intervals around the ballroom where the festivities were being held. At some point during one of these affairs a very refined, big-chested, blue haired lady picked up a tray of pastry and went around the room offering confections to the guests. When she noticed these Marines in dress blues standing like sculptures all around the room she was moved with admiration, because she knew that several of these men were fresh from our victory in Desert Storm.

56

She made a beeline for the closest lance corporal. As she drew near him she asked, "Would you like a pastry young man?"

The young Marine snapped to attention and replied, "I don't eat that shit, ma'am." Just as quickly, he resumed the position of parade rest. His gaze remained fixed on some distant point throughout the exchange.

The fancy lady was taken aback! She blinked, her eyes widened, her mouth dropped open. So startled was she that she immediately began to doubt what she had heard. In a quivering voice she asked, "W-w-what did you say?"

The Marine snapped back to the position of attention like the arm of a mouse trap smacking its wooden base when it is tripped. He said once again, "I don't eat that shit, ma'am." And just as smartly as before, back to the position of parade rest he went.

This time there was no doubt. The fancy lady immediately became incensed, and felt insulted. After all, here she was an important lady, taking the time to offer something nice to this enlisted man, (who was well below her station in life). And he had the nerve to say THAT to HER! She exclaimed, "Well! I never...!"

The fancy lady then remembered she had met "that military man who was over all of these soldiers" a little earlier. She looked around and soon spotted General Gray across the room. He had a cigar clenched between his teeth and a camouflaged canteen cup full of liquor in his left hand, and was talking to a group of first and second lieutenants.

The blue haired lady went straight over to the Commandant and interrupted. "General, I offered some pastry to that young man over there. And do you know what he told me?"

General Gray cocked his eyebrow, took the cigar out of his mouth and said, "Well, no ma'am. I don't."

The lady took in a deep breath, confident she was expressing with her body language her rage and indignation. As she wagged her head in cadence with her words, she paused between each word for effect. "He - said, I – don't - eat - that - SHIT- ma'am!"

The lieutenants standing there were in a state of flux. A couple of them choked back chuckles, and turned their heads to avoid having their smirks detected. The next thought most of them had was, "God, I hope it wasn't one of MY Marines!" as the color left their faces. General Grey wrinkled his brow, cut his eyes in the direction of the lieutenants, put his free hand to his chin and expelled a subdued, "Hmmmm…"

"Which one did you say it was, ma'am?" the General asked.

"That tall sturdy one right over there near the window, General," the woman said with smug satisfaction. One of the lieutenants began to look sick and put a hand on the wall for support.

General Gray seemed deep in thought, hand still to his chin and brow wrinkled. Suddenly he looked up, and his expression changed to one indicating he had made a decision. He looked the fancy lady right in the eyes and said, "Well, FUCK 'EM then! Don't give him any!"

BEWARE OF SNAKES

"When the eagles are silent, the parrots begin to jabber."
– Sir Winston Churchill

In the fall of 1988 my Force Recon detachment was based on eastern Long Island to conduct Special Operations training at several sites in the New York area. One night our objective was in the vicinity of West Point, which meant a long helicopter flight in each direction. The operation on the ground came off without a hitch, and by midnight we were "mission complete" and heading back to base. Our route took us south along the Hudson River and as we neared northern Manhattan we split into three groups, with the "Phrogs" (CH-46s) turning over the Long Island Sound, the "Snakes" (AH-1 Cobras) flying along the East River, and the "Hueys" (UH-1s) continuing on down the Hudson.

Our SOP at that time was to fly blacked out and low along the water to avoid detection, and this included flying *under* rather than over bridges whenever possible. As luck would have it on that particular night, and unbeknownst to us, a group of Greenpeace activists had suspended themselves from one of the East River bridges in boatswains' chairs as part of a protest against ocean dumping. The police had been trying to get them down for several hours with little success because the protesters had greased the ropes to prevent anyone from hauling them up.

It's hard to say who was more surprised, the pilots or the activists, when a pair of Cobra gunships passed beneath that particular span. But there is little doubt as to who was the most *scared*. Within seconds of their close encounter the "snakebit" protesters swarmed back up onto the bridge

59

where they were immediately arrested by waiting police, and minutes later police and news helicopters were airborne in search of our choppers. The duty officer back at our base of course disavowed any knowledge of the incident, but amongst those of us who knew the real deal the only question was how close those birds had come to making fish food out of a few save the whale advocates.

AIRBORNE MOUSTACHE

"We have two companies of Marines running rampant all over the northern half of this island, and three Army regiments pinned down in the southwestern corner, doing nothing. What the hell is going on?" - General John W. Vessey Jr., US Army, Chairman of the Joint Chiefs of Staff during the assault on Grenada, 1983

The three weeks I spent attending the Army's Airborne School at Fort Benning, Georgia were three of the longest of my life, not because the training was difficult, but because I was forced to experience the Army firsthand. I had heard prior to my arrival the course was a "Marine Corps Appreciation Program," an assessment that proved all too true. One thing that struck me as particularly odd from the onset was the Army's method of selecting Airborne students. While all twelve Marines in the class were Recon Marines or parachute riggers, an inordinate number of the five hundred plus soldiers in the class were in jobs or units that had no requirement for parachutists. Instead they were there at taxpayer's expense to get their ticket punched and pick up a badge for their uniform.

One individual who was particularly conspicuous amongst the various dentists, bakers, candlestick makers and messkit repairmen was PFC 'Miller,' a female MP. She was one of those women who are so prevalent in the military these days; the type who try their best to be a man. But she wasn't fooling anyone - despite an abundance of facial hair.

I first took notice of Miller when the class fell out for its inaugural PT session because as senior enlisted man in my "stick" I was responsible for ensuring all females in my charge fell out into a separate formation. This was because

61

the women were not required to run at the same pace as the men, were allowed to keep their heels on the ground while doing chin-ups, and so on (not exactly an endorsement of the myth women are equal to men physically).

The following morning we were notified no one with a moustache would be allowed to graduate, and I would have to part with the "cookie duster" I had worn for many years if I wanted to make it to jump week. I reluctantly complied, and was seething when I happened upon none other than PFC Miller. I told her I thought it was unfair she would rate to wear the same wings as everyone else despite not having to run as fast or do the same pull-ups as the men, and went on to say it was discriminatory for me to be required to shave off my moustache off – while she got to keep hers. Her reply, of course, was to burst into tears and immediately lodge a complaint with the duty "Black Hat," a Staff Sergeant named Fuller. After listening patiently for several minutes he said he could certainly understand why she was so upset and asked if he could offer a solution. When she said yes, he asked if she had ever considered trying electrolysis...

ONE FOR CHESTY!

"Don't you forget that you're First Marines! Not all the communists in Hell can overrun you!" - Colonel Lewis B. "Chesty" Puller rallying his First Marine Regiment near the Chosin Reservoir

Chesty Puller was the embodiment of everything a combat Marine should be. He fought in every conflict from the Banana Wars through Korea, won five Navy Crosses, and became a legend in his own lifetime. I won't cover all of Chesty's exploits here since it would take an entire book to do so, and since there is already an excellent biography entitled "Marine" by Burke Davis I won't have to try. Just suffice it to say Marines will defend his honor to the death if necessary.

Jump school, as I have pointed out elsewhere, is a USMC appreciation program. Marines *dream* about going back to a Marine Corps base after putting up with the Army's weak nonsense for three weeks. The Black Hats, as the instructors are known, could naturally sense it. Throw in our superiority as airborne students (Marines don't quit like some soldiers do) and it's not surprising they resent us.

The disciplinary tool employed by the Black Hats was the push up. Compared to the incentive PT Marine recruits do in boot camp it was a joke, especially since they were only allowed to make us do ten at a time. It wasn't even worth the trouble of getting down, so we added a few twists to make it more interesting.

The Army students did their level best to avoid being singled out for pushups, while Marines practically *begged* for them. If one Marine was "dropped" or sent to the "gig pit" every Marine in the class would immediately join him. It caused a lot of frustration for the instructors, and was a great source of amusement for us.

In the airborne community the biggest insult is to call someone a "leg," which is shorthand for a non-jump-qualified soldier. Whenever a Marine was dropped for pushups he would do the required ten, and then add one more accompanied by the exclamation, "And one for Chesty!" It drove the black hats batty when we did that, so they lashed out the only way they knew how.

"Chesty Puller was a dirty, nasty leg!" they would holler.

So we replied with the obvious response. "Yeah, and so was Patton!"

SOURPUSS AND THE HULK

"When someone discovers the center of the universe, a lot of people will be disappointed to discover they are not it!" – Bernard Bailey

Arrogance is a trait sometimes associated with Marines, and that is not necessarily a bad thing. It takes a lot of intestinal fortitude to do the things Marines do, and those who choose to swagger a bit are entitled. But it does have its limits.

Staff Sergeant 'Sourpuss' was an annoyingly cocky platoon sergeant who had recently come to 2nd Recon Battalion from the Drill Field. He thought he was God's gift to recon despite his limited experience, and never missed an opportunity to tell everyone how great he was. He was a moron.

One morning word came down from Battalion that a newly minted Second Lieutenant would be checking into Charlie Company, and Sourpuss decided to go over and have a little fun with the young shavetail. It was a perfect opportunity for him to be condescending and assert his self-perceived superiority, so he headed over and camped out in the company First Sergeant's office to await his prey.

The Lieutenant finally arrived. His broad shoulders filled the entire doorway. On his massive chest were pinned row upon row of combat ribbons and personal decorations, topped by gold jump wings and a scuba pin – he was obviously a mustang. He slowly surveyed the room and finally turned his steely-eyed gaze in the direction of Sourpuss, who was just beginning to realize that THIS was the new butter-bar.

The Lieutenant extended his hand and said, "Good morning Staff Sergeant, I'm Lieutenant Perrimore."

Needless to say, Sourpuss quickly shook the lieutenant's hand, mumbled "Welcome aboard, Sir," and went quietly on his way.

AN EYE FOR AN EYE

Payback is a Medevac!

The following story contains details of a clandestine operation that are only now being declassified. If I had divulged this information any sooner it would have been my regrettable duty to kill anyone reading it in the interest of national security.

2nd Battalion 25th Marines was conducting a weekend drill at Fort Indiantown Gap, Pennsylvania when an unspeakably heinous act of terrorism was perpetrated against the battalion commander, Lieutenant Colonel J. J. Cassidy.

Colonel Cassidy was the type of officer who commanded respect by his presence alone. A Silver Star recipient, he had a John Wayne persona and was very well liked by the troops.

One day Gunnery Sergeant 'Hardon' (aka 'The Pink Panther') of the I&I Staff decided it would be cute to launch a CS attack on the Colonel while he was eating his lunch. Keep in mind we were not in a tactical environment at the time, and the CO was relaxing and chowing down in his CP tent. It was totally uncalled for, and Hardon knew it.

The Colonel, being the warrior that he was, took the whole thing in stride. He never lost his bearing. But the Battalion S-4 Officer, Major Laroque, was outraged by the incident and asked if anyone would be interested in volunteering for a special mission. He wanted payback. My hand shot up so fast I almost dislocated my shoulder. I hated Hardon, and relished any opportunity to make his life miserable.

The Major took me aside and provided me with a canister of CS gas, and explained he would disavow any knowledge of my actions if I were caught or killed. I was on my own.

The I&I tent was located in the middle of a large field. It took quite a long time, but I managed to low crawl across the entire expanse without being detected. When I reached the back of the tent I slowly lifted the flap and peered inside. The entire I&I staff was in there, Hardon included. Even better, they were in the middle of changing uniforms and were in their skivvies.

I pulled the pin on the grenade, quietly slipped my entire arm inside the tent, and when they were all grouped close together let it fly. I was immediately rewarded with a storm of expletives, but for obvious reasons didn't hang around for an extensive BDA. I got up and ran down the hill as fast as my legs would carry me with one of the Staff Sergeants from the I&I, who had apparently escaped the carnage, close on my heels. I darted into the nearest treeline and took a circuitous route back to the main encampment, where I slipped into a tent and acted like I had been there all along.

Of course, no one had *any* idea what the I&I was screaming about up on the hill, but even so my compatriots bought me beers until my eyeballs floated upon our return to base!

FOOD BLISTER BLUNDERS

They will salute the rank, but they will only follow the man!

Back in the 1980's the CO of H&S Co, 1st Recon Battalion was best known to the troops as "Food Blister" because he never, ever passed up an opportunity to eat. He was a Captain, and a graduate of "Canoe U" - the U.S. Naval Academy at Annapolis. Now, many fine Marines have emerged from USNA, but Food Blister wasn't one of them. He was one of those guys who wore his ring in his nose - I'm sure you know the type.

One winter we were conducting a cold weather exercise up in the Sierra Nevada Mountains, and my team's mission was to set up a radio relay site on an 8000-foot mountain called Mean Peak. We were to be inserted by CH-53, which is the only helicopter powerful enough to fly at those altitudes. At least that's what the pilots told us.

Food Blister was assigned as the insert officer, and as such was responsible for seeing we were dropped off in the right place. Well, once we had landed I took one look around and knew we were *not* on the right mountain. It was obviously Lost Cannon Peak, which is close to *12,000* feet in elevation. I ran back up the ramp and told the Captain where we were, but he just pointed at his map and told me to get off the bird.

I have always said if it wasn't for bad luck I'd have no luck at all, and that held true on this day. As we attempted to set up camp a major windstorm sprang up, and as the sun began to set we worked frantically to finish before it got dark. Since there was no vegetation we were forced to use snowshoes to anchor the guy lines of our ten-man tent, and once the wind picked up they were ripped from the snow. We were out in the open.

Before long our tent and much of our gear had blown down the mountain, and there wasn't a thing we could do about it. We quickly dug a large "snow grave" and climbed in to break the wind and keep from being blown off the mountain ourselves. I kept our radio in my sleeping bag to keep it out of the elements, and stayed in contact with base camp throughout the night. You could hear the concern in their voices every time I checked in.

The weather grew worse and worse. It was almost surreal. The more the wind blew the deeper we became buried in snow, but that wasn't necessarily a bad thing. It acted as a blanket and provided the six of us with some much needed insulation.

Fortunately the weather eventually broke, and by morning the winds had died down enough to fly a helicopter to our location. The Battalion Commander, Lieutenant Colonel Baker, came up to get us personally. I think he was sweating our fate almost as much as we were.

And Food Blister, for his part, spent the rest of the deployment where he couldn't do any more damage – making mail runs between Bridgeport and Camp Pendleton.

GREEN BEANIES

"Why in hell can't the Army do it if the Marines can? They are the same kind of men; why can't they be like Marines?"
- Army General John J. "Black Jack" Pershing, US Army; 12 February 1918

Many people try to make comparisons between the "elite" units of each service, but they are trying to equate apples with oranges. Most of the time the units being compared have different missions. For instance, Army Special Forces' mission of training indigenous forces cannot be duplicated by anyone else, and they are the best in the world at what they do.

For years the U.S. Army has used unique headgear to differentiate special units from the rest, with the most famous being the Green Beret of Special Forces. Early in my career the Marine Corps even toyed with the idea of going to a beret like that worn by the Royal Marines, but fortunately we decided to stick with what we had.

One of the *worst* things the Army ever did was issue Black Berets for wear by all soldiers. In typical Army fashion they tried to boost morale and aid the recruiting effort by giving out a trinket to the rank and file, but when they did that it became *just another hat*. It was also an insult to the Rangers who had previously worn it. They are the closest thing to Marines the Army has, and such fine soldiers deserve better than that.

My first contact with "elite" headgear came while I was attending jump school at Fort Benning, Georgia. Soldiers in units where berets were worn, such as the Rangers and SF, were required to wear regular Army headgear until they

71

became jump qualified - so for them the acquisition of jump wings took on added significance.

Young soldiers from the 82nd Airborne would line up in front of mirrors shaping their 'raspberry' berets in anticipation of getting their wings. It was really quite pathetic. The worst of all was an Army SF reservist in my class who talked about nothing but his damn beret. I honestly don't ever recall him starting a sentence with a phrase other than "When I get my beret..." It got old rather quickly.

One night he was going on and on as usual when a classmate who shall remain nameless made it clear to him he would wipe his butt with the headgear in question if it was mentioned one more time. Naturally the "beret lover" couldn't keep his mouth shut for very long, and his antagonist made good on the threat. To our surprise, the loudmouth didn't lift a finger to stop him. I just can't imagine someone doing that to the cover of ANY Marine and living to tell about it, can you?

WINGS OF GOLD

**I don't know but it's been said, Army wings are made of lead...
And I don't know but I've been told, Marine Corps wings are made
of gold!** - USMC Recon cadence

The gold wings of a Naval parachutist are one of the most
coveted badges in the armed forces. Less than one percent of
all Marines earn them, and with good reason. All that is
necessary to get the curled up, pewter, basic jump wings we
like to call a "lead sled" is completion of the Army airborne
course. Cadets on summer break even go to jump school. To
be awarded the wings of gold, however, a Marine must be
serving in a paid billet where there is a requirement for
parachute insertion, and he must demonstrate a certain level
of proficiency as well. There are of course isolated cases
where "badge hunters" have managed to circumvent the
rules, but for the most part anyone who wears them is
deserving.

A time honored, but officially outlawed, Marine Corps
tradition is the pinning of gold wings. I realize it sounds
gruesome when described to an outsider, but when done
properly the ceremony is a highly motivating experience. It
involves standing the recipient against a wall, removing the
clutch backs from a pair of wings, and pinning them directly
into the chest of the Marine. Since a minimum of ten jumps
are required in order to be awarded gold wings, the recipient
must be "pinned" by a minimum of ten jumpers. It is
interesting to note that while getting "blood wings" is purely
voluntary, ninety-nine percent of eligible Marines opt to go
for it. I consider my blood wings to be one of my most
sacred possessions to this day, and I have gone so far as to

have them framed along with the blood-soaked t-shirt I wore for the ceremony.

While I was serving as the Communications Chief for 1st Force Reconnaissance Company I was thrust into the middle of an unfortunate situation that put the semi-secret gold wing ceremony into the public eye. A former parachute rigger from another unit had sold the videotape of two ceremonies to a television news magazine, and their exposé painted a very negative picture of the ritual. The only portions of the tape shown on the air were segments intended to sensationalize the story – literally, "if it bleeds, it leads." An investigation was started by the Marine Corps, and as luck would have it one of my communicators had a copy of the tape – which I was ordered to obtain.

The night before I turned the tape over I sat down and watched the entire thing myself. I was impressed by the way the Recon ceremony was conducted, and concluded that having it viewed by the investigating officer was the best thing that could happen. When he saw the true intent of the Marines involved he would have to conclude this was simply a harmless initiation. Unfortunately there was also a second ceremony on the tape that had been conducted by an Air Delivery platoon, and it was not carried out with the dignity I have come to associate with such events. There always seems to be somebody who goes too far and screws things up for everyone else.

One recipient of gold wings who didn't approach the ceremony in the proper spirit, in a different time and place, was a communicator at 2nd Force Reconnaissance Company named Corporal 'Jim.' Jim was a fairly competent radio operator, but suffered from a disease I like to call 'oral diarrhea.' He just couldn't keep his mouth shut! In the days leading up to his ceremony Joe talked trash nonstop, saying that no one would be able to hurt him, and needless to say that didn't sit too well with the gold-wingers in the company. He may as well have painted a bull's-eye on his own chest! So when the day of the ceremony arrived we decided to have a bit of fun with our loud-mouthed colleague.

One of the rules is those to be pinned are not allowed into the room where the ceremony is taking place until it is their turn. We made sure Jim was the last to be called, and he cooled his heels in the next room while we brought the other jumpers in one by one. Finally only Corporal Jim remained to be pinned. The Marine who had been initiated just prior to him was in cahoots with us, and he screamed at the top of his lungs - much like someone being interrogated by the Gestapo might sound. When we were finished with him he was carried out covered in blood and feigning unconsciousness, and you could see the color drain from Jim's face when he went past. I can only imagine what must have been going through his mind as we led him into that room...

DOC'S GREEN CARD

"It's no fun, being an illegal alien!"
- From the song "Illegal Alien" by the band Genesis

Corpsmen are in general the best sailors in the Navy, and the ones that serve with Recon are even better. The sailor who best illustrates this for me is an old pecker-checker named HMCS Fitzgerald. 'Doc Fitz' somehow managed to rise to the rank of Senior Chief despite being a tough, brawling, un-politically correct throwback to the days of wooden ships and grog. He was more Marine than Navy, and when the movie GI Jane came out he derived a great deal of pleasure from calling his SEAL buddies down at BUDS in Coronado and asking to speak with Demi Moore. Need I say more?

Inclusion into our fraternity came with all the privileges of being a Marine. It also came with all of the pitfalls. There was one Corpsman in 1st Reconnaissance Battalion named 'Hernandez' who learned this the hard way. He liked to give the Marines a difficult time whenever possible, and naturally we returned the favor.

Anyone who has driven the stretch of I-5 between Oceanside and San Clemente is familiar with the so-called "Mexicheck" station that is manned by the Border Patrol. One morning the Doc, who was of Mexican descent, was on his way to work and had forgotten his wallet and ID. To make matters worse he wasn't in uniform, and when he drove up to the checkpoint he was detained because he fit the profile of an illegal. Doc gave the agents the phone number to our barracks so we could vouch for him, but he should have known better. We told them to act as if we had never heard of him, and they were good sports and went along with our little joke. The agents even went so far as to prepare fake deportation paperwork, and put him on a bus purportedly heading for the border, before finally coming clean about our gag.

The next day several of our shot records 'disappeared,' requiring us to get reinnoculated, but Hernandez swore he had nothing to do with it. Sure, Doc...

LIBATIONS & LANDMINES

"Beer is living proof God loves us and wants us to be happy."
– Benjamin Franklin

When I was a brand new Private my first duty station was Camp Lejeune North Carolina, and it was a real eye opener for me. I was eighteen years old and out in the world on my own for the first time... and it wasn't long before I was fighting the "Battle of J'ville" on Court Street, which is the bar district in that particular berg.

Keep in mind prior to joining the Corps I did not smoke, drink, curse or use drugs of any kind. I guess I was an unusual teenager in that respect. I *still* don't smoke or do drugs, and I try to confine my swearing to the appropriate venues. But I *have* learned to feed the "wild hair that grows where the sun don't shine" when the occasion calls for it. I learned a lot about life and camaraderie in the barrooms of my youth, and no one got hurt in the process.

Since that time the powers that be have seen fit to raise the legal drinking age to twenty-one. I'm sure they based that decision on some sort statistical analysis, and believed they were doing a good thing. I have no problem with that. What I do have a problem with is the double standard applied to Americans who have not yet reached their twenty-first birthday. Consider the following.

On the MSG program every Marine in a detachment is assigned a collateral duty. The Mess NCO oversees food shopping and the preparation of meals, the Supply NCO orders and accounts for equipment, and so on. There is also a Bar NCO whose duties include planning detachment functions, organizing the Marine Corps Ball, stocking the bar, and selling drinks during functions.

In order to ensure fairness and give each Marine an opportunity to become well rounded it was my policy to rotate those duties periodically. As it happened I found myself in something of a predicament as a result. In the course of assigning a new Bar NCO I realized the Marine assuming that duty was not of legal age to consume alcohol. Talk about irony!

Eighteen is old enough to vote for the leaders of our nation. Eighteen is old enough to be responsible for the operation of multi-million dollar pieces of equipment. Eighteen is old enough to hold a security clearance and handle classified information. Eighteen is old enough to get married and raise a family. Eighteen is old enough to get drafted. Eighteen is even old enough to enlist in the military and possibly get shot or step on a landmine.

Admiral Nimitz said, "Uncommon valor was a common virtue" after the battle for Iwo Jima. So true, and yet many of the Marines about whom he spoke weren't yet old enough to *buy a drink* by today's standard. *Twenty-three thousand* of them were killed or wounded in that battle. Am I the only one who thinks a Marine should have the right to legally drink a cold beer before dying on the battlefield or getting his legs blown off?

SAY CHEESE!

"A Marine should be sworn to the patient endurance of hardships, like the ancient knights; and it is not the least of these necessary hardships to have to serve with sailors."- Field Marshal Sir Bernard Law Montgomery

For years the Marine Corps sent its divers to Navy scuba schools because there was no other option. Although the training was excellent, many of the things taught were not applicable to the mission of Marine divers. The Corps finally established its own combat swimmer course in the 1990s so the curriculum could be tailored to the use of scuba as a clandestine method of insertion, and it has worked out well for all concerned.

When I became a diver it was as part of an experimental class comprised exclusively of Marines. It was a prototype for the coming combat swimmer's course, and the dives were all compass swims rather than "working dives." When I say the class was entirely Marine I should point out there were in fact two Navy Corpsmen, but since they were assigned to 2nd Reconnaissance Battalion and had chosen to go "Marine regs" I think of them as Marines.

The course was conducted aboard the barge of Mobile Diving and Salvage Unit Two in Little Creek Virginia. The instructors were Navy divers, and didn't know what to make of us when we arrived. They were used to training out-of-shape sailors on submarine duty, and our class was filled with PT *studs*. That is because Recon Marines must first successfully complete a difficult Pre-Scuba course given by their command before being allowed to attend the formal school. The OIC was so impressed with the physical condition of the class he even waived the dreaded "Level-2" Physical Fitness Test for everyone, which was unheard of.

Our class had two Navy proctors, and they were as different as night and day. The senior of the two had a Spec War background and was very popular with the class. He had a good attitude about training, and didn't ask us to do anything he wasn't prepared to do also.

The second was named 'Kiley,' although we were referring to him as "cheese dick" by the end of the first week. He was the type who didn't like to get his hands dirty. Kiley also had a superiority complex, and his "do as I say, not as I do" attitude quickly alienated the entire class.

One morning the two of them took us out for a PT run along the beach. At one point the senior proctor led us into the cold ocean water, and we noticed that Kiley had decided not to join us. He had apparently purchased a new pair of running shoes, and chose to run on the hard packed sand while the entire class slogged through the surf. We'd had quite enough of him by that point. The class grabbed the wimp, carried him kicking and screaming out to the first line of breakers, and proceeded to throw him into the ocean.

When we returned the Senior Chief in charge of the class was furious at us for touching one of his instructors. He couldn't fail the entire class, so instead punished us with a "thrash session" at the pool. We were made to do thousands of repetitions of pushups, flutter kicks, and so on, but he ended up getting frustrated when the class seemed to *enjoy* it. Sometimes it really pays to be in shape!

On the day we graduated a class photo was taken, and our instructors joined us for the picture. When the photographer said "say cheese" one of our corpsmen hoisted up a sign behind Kiley that said, simply, "CHEESE!"

PUNCH OUT!

For years the most dangerous thing in the Corps was a Second Lieutenant with a map and a compass, but now we have GPS... so today it is a Major with a word processor and a fax machine!

Accidents involving military aircraft happen far too frequently, but ours is a dangerous profession and I suppose it is the price we must pay to ensure our training is realistic and aggressive. People sometimes confuse our accident rate with those of commercial airlines, but that is a case of comparing apples and oranges. I can't recall the last time I heard of jumbo jets strafing low level targets or flying wing abreast wearing night vision goggles, although come to think of it I have been on a few flights that *seemed* that way.

Most incidents can be attributed to mechanical failure or pilot error, but at least one accident was caused by simple confusion. One of the darkest days in the history of peacetime Marine aviation began with the crash of a Cobra helicopter gunship and a Sea Stallion heavy lift helicopter in unrelated incidents during a Combined Arms Exercise aboard the Marine Corps Air Ground Combat Center at Twentynine Palms California. Later that same day two fixed wing aircraft were to go down as well, but under far different circumstances.

On that particular day a section of Harrier attack jets was conducting live bombing runs at the "Stumps," as 29 Palms is often called. As is often the case during these exercises the fast movers were supported by two Forward Air Controllers, one down below on the ground and the other airborne in a Bronco observation aircraft. The story goes that as one of the Harriers made his run-in to target the ground FAC noticed the aircraft was on fire and screamed frantically over the radio for the pilot to eject, which he did. Unfortunately the observer in the back seat of the Bronco heard him as well, and you can imagine the pilot's surprise (some say it was none other than the squadron CO) when he suddenly went from flying a perfectly good airplane to hanging from a parachute.

Legend has it that General Al Gray, the "Warrior Commandant," was making one of his patented unannounced visits to that squadron's home base at New River Air Station a short time later when he decided to seek out the errant lad. The young Captain was understandably reluctant to meet the Commandant, and is reputed to have hidden in one of the stalls in the officer's head until the coast was clear.

I can't say as I blame him!

THE SLOP CHUTE

By Dick Overton

"We might be more eager to accept good advice if it did not continually interfere with our plans!"

One of the Marines in our unit was due to rotate back to the "world." He had orders, but no transportation to DaNang Airbase - so a few of us procured a "Six-by" and made the trip.

We found ourselves suffering from culture shock when we arrived on the airbase, since we lived in bunkers twenty miles up the road. We had to take in all the sights - the base was beautiful to us. Air conditioned buildings, the works. To this day I remember the designation over the front door of the officers club, "The 266 Gunfighters."

We checked our weapons at the base armory, and had to wake up the guard to do so. Since we had some time on our hands we found the enlisted club. It was terrific - open twenty-four hours, with a floor show going on when we arrived. The doorman said we could not enter, since we had no mess cards and were no one's guest. Looking past him to the band playing and all the food, we lingered and tried our best selling techniques on him to no avail. Just as we were going to give up, an Air Force Sergeant seated a couple of tables inside the door looked up from his hamburger long enough to say, "They're with me." Surprised but happy, we entered and asked no questions. We would learn later the Sergeant had served a first enlistment as a Marine.

After a couple of drinks some Airman a couple of tables away started the usual popping off, making cracks about our dirty fatigues and the IQ of Marines. I remember one of the guys with us smiled at one point and said, "Ah, jealousy rears its ugly head again." Soon, with a little false courage in his stomach, the Airman led a small group over to our table for a little close in action. As the conversation became somewhat pointed (in other words a fight was about to break out), the Air Force Sergeant who was acting as our host suddenly rose and gave a neat little speech. "Son," he said, "if you're looking for trouble, let me assure you these men will be glad to oblige. And if you've brought enough friends with you, you might even win this one. But, they'll be back. Tomorrow, maybe next week, but you can count on them coming back. With whatever and whomever it takes, they'll be back, and eventually you'll lose, and lose big. And about that time, you young man will not be a very popular individual, because you will be remembered as the dumb ass that said, 'let's mess with those Marines.' Now you think about that for a minute before you put your plane ticket home up for grabs."

The Airman retreated and we enjoyed a few more rounds, sang the Marines' Hymn with enthusiasm, and went back to our humble digs. I've always wondered whose side our host would have been on if we had gone to blows. I have my suspicions.

SEND IN THE MARINES!

By Colonel David H. Hackworth

"People sleep peaceably in their beds at night only because rough men stand ready to do violence on their behalf." - George Orwell

"If the Army and the Navy ever looked at heaven's scenes, they will find the streets are guarded by United States Marines." So goes the Marines' Hymn.

Maybe the heaven bit's a stretch, but as we enter 1998 the Marine Corps is the only outfit in Clinton's armed forces that can still fight the hard fight. The Army, the Navy and the Air Force have caved in to political pressure that has marginalized their fighting ability and made the often quoted statement that "America has the finest fighting force in the world" the biggest lie since the Pentagon said "Gulf War syndrome doesn't exist."

I'm an old Army doggy, not a Marine. So saying this is outright heresy and will cause a lot of Army loyalists to want to nail my dog tags to my forehead. But I'll take the risk. Because if our armed forces continue to slide down the gender-bending tube - which is destroying fighting spirit and driving out fighters – we'll lose future battles, wars and eventually our freedom.

The Marine Corps hasn't rolled over as much as the other services. For example, it hasn't allowed the women's liberation army, led by such advocates for women in the trenches as former Congresswoman Pat Schroeder and former Assistant Secretary of the Army Sara Lister, to have their anti-warrior ethic way.

Schroeder, Lister and thousands of others who have never spent a night in a front-line foxhole believe that GI Janes should have the same opportunity as GI Joes to fill bodybags. This way, they figure, women will have equality and can someday become Colleen Powells and Norma Schwarzkopfs. These misguided and tireless fighters for female equality-opportunity have become so obsessed with liberating women they've forgotten the purpose of our military is to defend America.

Defending America starts at the front lines, where it's always inhumanly brutal. And getting young women to the front lines as grunts has been their endgame. Since the Vietnam War the Schroeders and Listers have brilliantly picked away to get your daughter - not theirs - on the killing field. They have been far more strategic and effective than the weak-kneed politicians and the senior brass who swapped their souls for stars and went along with these fanatical hare-brained ideas. First the "femin-nazis" integrated Air Force basic training, then the Army went coed, while the Navy, in an attempt to deflect the bad press from Tailhook, surrendered in 1994.

But the Corps stood tall and said, "No way. Won't work." And now the Corps can say, "I told you so."

A panel led by former Senator Nancy Kassenbaum Baker recently concluded that the Army, Navy and Air Force should stop coed training because "integrated basic training is resulting in less discipline, less unit cohesion and more distraction." The Marines fought this wrong-headed thinking from the beginning. They said sex would get in the way. The liberating liberals counterattacked and said Marine leadership was prehistoric and out of touch with society.

The proof of the pudding that the Marines were right can be easily measured. Their morale and combat readiness are the best. Unlike the others, recruits are rushing to join and its quit rate is a fraction of the other services. For example, thirty-seven percent of all first hitch Army enlistees quit before their enlistment is up and male noncoms and junior officers are deserting squadrons, ships and battalions as if there were a post-war demobilization. This exodus of our best and brightest talent is gutting combat effectiveness and costing the taxpayers billions of dollars.

I receive over a thousand e-mails a week from service personnel. Most are rightfully grousing about bad leadership and conditions and lousy readiness. Few of these letters are from Marines. Dozens of times a week, young men ask me to recommend a branch of the service. My answer: If you want to be challenged and forge stronger values, better character and develop into a better person, join the Marines.

As the Marines say, they won't promise a rose garden, but they'll give you something you won't find in any of the other services - and that's being in an outfit with strong leaders who have the guts to stand up to confused crusaders in order to keep doing the right thing for the Marine Corps and America.

A FOGGY NOTION

"You miss one hundred percent of the shots you never take."
– Wayne Gretzky

Back when I went through Military Freefall School the instructors were a mix of military and civilian, on the theory the civilians would have more experience than their active duty counterparts. In fact, most if not all of the civilian instructors in my class were retired military. One of the problems that arose was some of those retirees tended to be *much* older than the active duty instructors, and a bit, shall we say, forgetful. I learned sometime after my departure that the man who had been my instructor was let go because he forgot to put on his parachute before boarding the aircraft for a jump. A minor detail, but important nonetheless....

The senior instructor for our class was a gentleman named Mr. Parker. He impressed me as being a capable and competent individual, and throughout the course he went out of his way to help us succeed. His job was to facilitate and oversee all of the training, and in addition to those responsibilities he had two students of his own to train. Another of his jobs was to present an axe, symbolizing a screw up, to the jumpmaster who made the worst "spot" on any given day and caused students to miss their intended target on the ground.

Classes progressed pretty much without incident, but on the last day of school we had a small problem. Our class had been plagued with a great deal of bad weather, and quite a few of the scheduled drops had to be cancelled due to rain or poor visibility – and since it is necessary to complete a minimum number of jumps in order to graduate we still

89

needed to make two in one night in order to meet that requirement. There was one night, O2, combat equipment jump on the schedule, but that was it.

Mr. Parker went to work and "locked on" a second aircraft so we could make that final jump. We made the first one of the evening from a C-141 without incident, and then moved to "green ramp" to board a smaller aircraft called a Casa 212. If you have never seen one picture a CH-46 with wings. Since a Casa is a relatively small aircraft and could only carry ten students and five instructors at a time it was necessary to go up in four separate lifts.

As we sat on green ramp waiting for the aircraft a bit of fog began to roll in. It was light at first, but as the first load took off it began to grow. I was in the fourth and final lift, and watched with some concern as it got progressively worse. When the plane returned from the third drop the fog had gotten so dense we couldn't see it land, although we could certainly hear it. We boarded the aircraft fully expecting not to jump, and I was amazed the pilot actually managed to take off under those conditions.

When the aircraft reached ten thousand feet the ramp went down, and we conducted our pre-jump equipment checks as usual. We then activated the chem-lite glow sticks that were attached to our legs and parachute risers to help us avoid collisions at night. It was a futile gesture, as we could see nothing but dense fog out the aircraft's windows. I was the last student in the stick, and heard the instructor behind me comment to the crew chief that there was "no way" we were going to jump. At precisely that moment Mr. Parker gave the signal to exit, and like a bunch of lemmings we dutifully dove off the open ramp one by one into the dark night.

While in freefall I made it a point to stay mindful there were fourteen other jumpers in the air, since one of the most devastating things that can happen is a mid-air collision. I fell flat and stable through the soup until I reached four thousand feet and deployed my canopy. Visibility was still zero. There was nothing I could do but fly at half brakes and hope for the best.

I was less than two hundred feet in the air when I finally broke through the cloud cover. Below me was what appeared to be a large field, but in the darkness it was hard to be sure. Then at the last minute I spotted what looked like a dirt road and angled over toward it. It was a good thing I did. The "field" I had seen from the air was actually a forest.

Once on the ground I checked my watch. It was four AM. I started to bundle up my gear and just as I finished packing my kit bag heard what sounded like a dog growling behind me. I turned in time to see a Doberman racing toward me with its teeth bared, and frantically looked for an escape route. There was a barbed wire fence about ten feet away, which I promptly dove over with the crazed mutt snapping at my heels.

I had no idea where I was, so I decided to just start walking down that dirt road and see where it took me. It was either that or try and get past that Doberman. After what seemed like forever my trail merged with a hardball road, and I decided to turn left rather than right based on a mental coin toss.

Several miles later I approached an intersection in the middle of nowhere and spotted a phone booth, and upon closer inspection saw there was someone in it. I knew it was one of our jumpers because there was a glowing chem-light attached to his leg. It turned out to be one of the instructors, and he was phoning in for a ride.

It turned out we didn't just miss the drop zone. We missed the entire *base*. A truck arrived to pick us up after a while, and we spent the rest of the night driving around looking for the rest of the class. Just before dawn the last two were found hanging in a tree, and once they were gotten down we headed for home.

By the time everyone made it back the sun was up, and plans for a formal graduation were scrapped. We gathered in the MFF classroom, unshaven and still in our jumpsuits, and were handed our diplomas. Most of us had planes to catch, so we said hurried goodbyes to our classmates and prepared to go. But there was one bit of unfinished business.

The instructors gathered in front of the room and presented Mr. Parker with the biggest axe I have ever seen!

CROSS EXAMINING...
A Cross Dresser

"Admit nothing, deny everything, and counter-accuse!"
– Clinton legal strategy

Major William Scott Bradley and I followed very similar paths in life, at least from a geographical standpoint. I first met him in New York when he was an enlisted man in the reserves, and later on he was my platoon commander in Okinawa as a First Lieutenant. But that wasn't the end of our encounters. Not by a long shot.

He and I crossed paths once again at Camp Pendleton late in my career. The Major and I worked together on a couple of field exercises, but most of our contact came through a running club to which we both belonged. More about that later.

One fine day I received a call asking me to appear as a character witness on Major Bradley's behalf. A WM in his command had charged him with sexual harassment. It was the holiday season, and a few of the females under his command had dressed in skimpy "elf" costumes to liven up the unit Christmas party. The Major's offense consisted of making the statement, "those sure are some sexy elves!" or words to that effect. That's all.

I ended up testifying at the Major's hearing because I, like the Major, was a member of the local Hash House Harrier chapter. I must explain that the HHH is billed as an "international drinking club with a running problem." The club itself is a harmless diversion, although on *that* day the prosecutor made it sound like something akin to the indulgences of Caligula!

At one point in my testimony I was asked if I knew the Major's "Hash Name." Those names are usually risqué, often take the form of a double entendre, and are bestowed upon a Hasher as part of his or her initiation. Some of them are actually quite funny. I answered in the affirmative, but didn't want to volunteer the name unless I was directed to. I was.

"Yes, Sir, the Major's name is Cross Dresser," I told them. As you can imagine there was quite a bit of snickering in the courtroom, and even the presiding officer was laughing out loud. I guess they don't hear that sort of testimony every day.

That name, along with the statement he allegedly made, was the entire case. Maybe it's just me, but there must have been *something* more constructive the dozen or so Marines in that courtroom could have been doing that day!

Not long after that episode I had the unpleasant but enlightening duty of sitting on a board considering charges of, you guessed it, sexual harassment. The allegation stated a male Staff Sergeant had rubbed the shoulders of a WM for a few moments while she was working at a computer terminal. She felt uncomfortable enough to mention the incident to a female officer she trusted, but didn't want to prefer charges. In fact she testified at the hearing the Staff Sergeant had done nothing else offensive, and that she admired his leadership and sense of fairness. Sounds pretty damning to me!

The only reason we were there was the WM officer to whom she confided had pressured the Corporal into coming forward and pressing charges. It made no difference that the defendant also was in the habit of doing the same thing to his *male* Marines. The Staff Sergeant was about to leave the Marine Corps to pursue a career in law enforcement, and the question that officer asked the young WM was, "How will you feel if you don't say anything and he *rapes* someone someday?" A bit of a stretch there!

What has happened to us? These incidents make me think of the General who had been nominated for a spot on the Joint Chiefs of Staff a couple of years earlier. During the confirmation process the General freely admitted having an affair *fifteen years earlier* while legally separated from his wife. Ironically, President Bill Clinton rejected the nomination based upon the *moral turpitude* of the nominee!

All of this was happening during a time in our history when the Commander-In-Chief of the armed forces was himself being accused of far more heinous things than shoulder massages and off color remarks. Talk about a double standard!

BOOM IN THE NIGHT

By Harrison Greene

"Improvise, adapt and overcome!"
- Gunnery Sergeant Tom Highway (portrayed by Clint Eastwood) in "Heartbreak Ridge"

Crawling on our bellies in the early morning hours of darkness, Lieutenant Jankorski and I slipped silently through the weeds and brush, concerned only about the deadly poisonous snakes which inhabit the island of Okinawa. We were on a mission. A mission of training good Marines to become better ones. We were part of the TECG, the Tactical Exercise Control Group, and were the men who put together wartime scenarios which Marines in combat might someday face. We were going to teach these Marines how to stay alive, for a dead Marine is no good to us in combat.

"Here!" Jankorski whispered, "Put one here, across this trail leading out of their tent." I reached inside my gunnysack and pulled out a grenade simulator - a "flash-bang" we called them. After taping the explosive device to a nearby tree, I strung a trip-wire across the path in front of the CP tent where four Marines were soundly sleeping. While doing that, I heard the lieutenant quietly snipping the communications line running inside the tent. "That'll do it, Lieutenant," I whispered. "Let's get their vehicle too."

We snuck past the darkened tent and approached the Hummer parked not quite fifty feet away. I raised the hood while the lieutenant rigged another flash-bang beneath the engine. We wired the hood so that when it was raised there would be a deafening explosion.

"Let's get the hell outta here Greene," the lieutenant ordered, "We're through here."

After clearing that team's area we moved on to the next, some five hundred meters away. There we repeated our performance, ensuring our grenade simulators were placed in such a manner that no one would be injured by them. But they *would* feel the blast if they did not practice good security in the field. An embarrassment to say the least, but they would still be alive - and will have learned something by it.

Then, onto the third team - another four hundred meters away in the darkness. Same procedure, same expected result. All team areas were now rigged for noise, confusion and chaos, and all communications lines had been severed. Just like it would happen in real life.

By 0415 we had only one flash-bang left. If we didn't use it we would have to fill out a mountain of paperwork to turn it back in to the ammo dump. Ones that were exploded were considered "expended" items and didn't have to be accounted for the way a returned one did.

Back on our feet now, the lieutenant and I walked quietly back towards our area and talked about where else we might be able to use the leftover flash-bang. We did not want to go through the paper drill to dispose of the extra device. There had to be somewhere we could set up just one more booby-trap.

As we walked across the training compound we passed the outhouse - the "head" - which had been centrally placed between all the team areas for use in the field. BINGO! It hit us both at the same time, as if it were a revelation.

We scurried over toward the head and quickly assessed the situation. Yep! One flash-bang beneath the four-holer oughta do it, we agreed. I took the dirty job and carefully placed the waterproof device inside one of the cans into which all the droppings fell, while the lieutenant ran the trip wire all the way around the outhouse to the inside. This particular head had a door that wouldn't stay shut, so we rigged the device for the modest individual - the man who wanted some privacy in his life - the decent guy who would try to close the door while inside taking care of business.

Content with our final surprise, we jogged back to the TECG compound and got into our bunks just before sunrise. Not able to control his emotions over the final surprise we had just set up, I heard the lieutenant giggling. Then he got me started. Dueling snickers in the night! We took turns almost laughing out loud at what was going to happen to some unlucky stiff.

Major Wildside was an outstanding leader and the commander of the TECG. He shared our tent with the rest of us. He was a "salt-of-the-earth" kind of guy. He was a modest man. He was a very private man. He was a decent man. And he was a man who needed to make a head call at 0515 on this particular morning. We heard him stirring in the darkness as he put on his boots to begin the long trek down the path to the head. In our defense, we did not know that it was the Major at the time. Three minutes passed. We heard him stumbling around outside trying to get his bearings in the darkness. Then the footsteps grew further and further away. Five minutes passed. Silence. Six minutes. Nothing. Then, out of the quiet stillness of the night, KAABOOMM!

The lieutenant and I just about rolled out of our bunks from laughing so hard. Our stomachs hurt. Our faces could hardly stand the stretching caused by the laughter. Others inside our tent started waking up and were asking what the hell was going on. Jankorski and I couldn't say a word. All we could do was hold our sides in hopes the pain would go away.

Then about four minutes later, as the Major re-entered our tent, we both stopped laughing. He was a sight to behold. Covered with some gooey wet stuff and toilet paper, the man was in a rage. I had never once seen the Major angry with anyone. He was a very mild-mannered sort of man. He was a good and decent man. But now he was a raving lunatic! He got all of us up out of our bunks and began the interrogation.

The lieutenant signaled me with his hand to keep my mouth shut. I willingly complied. I enjoyed life too much to throw it all away for the sake of a good laugh. Had the Major found out who set up the head there surely would have been a lynching that morning. Honesty, at this time, was not the best policy.

Things started going from bad to worse as the other teams in the area began waking up.

Off in the distance we could hear, KAA-BOOMMMM!

Then, KAAA-BOOOOOOOOMMMM! And, KAAAA-BOOOOOMMMM!

This went on for another eight or nine - we lost count. Our minds were clearly focused on our careers in the Marine Corps at that moment. As if that wasn't bad enough, I thought the Major was going to lose it completely when he tried calling in all of the teams to the TECG for interrogation. We had severed all the communications lines at the team areas. Our plan worked - but it also backfired!

No pun intended, Major, Sir!

Author's Note: A full confession was made to Major Wildside at his farewell party years later.

THE KING OF TONGA

"We're not here for a long time, so I'm here for a good time."
– Australian saying

Marine Mess Nights are in many ways unique, but we do not have a monopoly on such occasions. Australians, as well as other Commonwealth nations, have a similar occasion known as the Dining In. While it is different from our Mess Night in a number or ways, the protocol is very similar.

I was attending such a dinner at the Royal Military College in Canberra Australia when I was introduced to the new Regimental Sergeant Major, a fellow named Jack Selmes. Jack was quite the professional soldier. In fact he looked so much like a crusty Sergeant Major he was practically a caricature.

During the evening a few of the Aussies tried to convince me to "ask the RSM who the King of Tonga is." I thought better of it and asked around instead, and was glad I did. I had learned never to ask questions at the behest of others way back when I was a slick-sleeve Private, when one of my new "friends" had encouraged me to ask another Marine why he didn't buy his sister a bicycle for Christmas. When he answered that she didn't have any legs (it wasn't true) I felt about six inches tall. It was a cruel joke, but one that I have never forgotten. Fool me once shame on you, fool me twice shame on me.

I soon discovered the RSM had once been banished to some remote posting due to an incident that had occurred during a Dining In some years before - and that he was very touchy about it. The story goes that Jack had been imbibing rather heavily prior to the dinner, arrived late, and stumbled

100

to his place at the table just as the first toast was made. Keep in mind it is customary to toast the head of state of every country in attendance, followed by the "loyalty toast" to the Queen. Just as Jack took his place the President of the Mess raised his glass and proclaimed "the King of Tonga!" Jack had no idea there were Officers from that island nation present, and he had quite possibly never heard of Tonga, period. He belched loudly, and in his semi-inebriated state blurted out, "who in the *fuck* is the King of Tonga?" during one of those embarrassing moments of total silence that sometimes occur in a room full of people.

Unfortunately for Jack one of those silent people was a very unamused Australian General Officer!

DIFFERENT KIND OF DOPE

"Good judgment comes from experience. Sometimes, *experience* **comes from** *bad* **judgment."** – Christian Slater

During the 1980's the Drug Enforcement Administration ran a program known as Operation Snowcap, which involved sending teams of agents into the South American jungles to locate and destroy drug labs. It was a very ambitious program, and many of the skills needed to carry it out were beyond the scope of normal DEA training. As a result a group of agents were sent to Camp Lejeune to be trained by 2nd Force Recon Company in such things as patrolling, communications and insertion techniques.

Since these agents were the first to undergo this training they purchased a video camera with which to document each evolution for future review. It would prove to be well worth whatever they spent on it.

One of the most important things we taught the DEA was how to fast rope from a hovering helicopter. This technique is widely used by agencies such as the FBI, since its purpose is to rapidly assault an objective from the air. One morning the agents were practicing making a descent from a Huey while one of them taped each man as he went down the rope, and as soon as the last man hit the ground something unexpected happened.

For reasons that never became clear to me the helicopter crew chief suddenly decided he wanted to have a go at fast roping. He simply disconnected his comm cord, grabbed the rope, and started down without a word to anyone. If he had been paying attention he would have noticed each man descending the rope was wearing a heavy pair of welder's gloves, and he paid the price for not following suit. Friction burned right through the man's thin flight gloves, and after a few feet he was forced to let go. That knucklehead fell a good thirty or forty feet, and ended up breaking both of his ankles. To add insult to injury we captured the whole thing on tape.

That evening we sat around with the agents and enjoyed a cold beer while replaying the video over and over. Yes... once again, the DEA had located some "dope."

BLASTING HEADS

By W.D. Oz

"The deadliest weapon in the world is a Marine and his rifle."
- General John "Blackjack" Pershing, U.S. Army

During the Persian Gulf War I served with 1st Battalion, 8th Marines. Just prior to the war I attended an amphibious training school known as Coxswain School where I learned to conduct "over the horizon" and river raids from the sea. It was while I was in that school President Bush decided to go to Saudi Arabia with the intention of liberating Kuwait, and my classmates and I wondered when it would be our turn to deploy, as other units from Camp Lejeune were already enroute.

After graduation Boat Platoon was temporarily disbanded - since there was no need for boats in the desert. A "no-brainer" to everyone except Saddam Hussein, who was awaiting the arrival of Marines "from the sea." Our platoon was broken up and dispatched to different Marine companies. A real morale buster.

My story really begins in the middle of my tour in the desert just before the ground war started. There I was just finishing my chow, and since I was a young Lance Corporal I was available for any working party that came along.

"Oz and Brown," the First Sergeant called one day, "Get some fuel and burn the shitpile." The entire battalion put their trash into a pre-dug hole to be burned so wildlife would not stray into our area of operations. Brown and I went to the fuel depot and picked out two cans, and we poured the ten gallons of fuel onto the trash heap and tried to light it. Nothing happened. "That's funny!" we thought, "the fuel doesn't seem to want to burn." So being the Boy Scouts we were we twisted some paper like you do when you try to start a campfire and got a good flame started. Then we tossed it onto the trash heap. The trash started to catch in the dry areas. Satisfied, we started to walk away.

KA-BOOOOOOOOOOOOM!

We found ourselves about ten feet further away on our backs, flipped by the tremendous force of the explosion! Brown and I got up, brushed ourselves off, and pondered what had just happened. A couple of Corpsmen came rushing over to see if we were still alive, only to find us laughing and scratching our heads. Right behind them was the Company Commander, First Sergeant, Battalion Sergeant Major, and of course the Battalion Commander! We stopped laughing.

We explained that we did exactly what we were told to do, "Pour fuel over the trash heap, and light it." That's what we did. Brown and I had never pretended to be rocket scientists! Everyone knows, and even Brown and I *now* know, there were two basic types of fuel used in the Gulf War... MOGAS, and JP-5. As I look back on it, the physics are quite simple. MOGAS burns very slowly, and JP-5 is an explosive. This was a real learning experience for Brown and me. We had, of course, grabbed the explosive one.

The next day Brown and I were called for another working party. This time we were told to burn piles of *human* waste - my Battalion Commander wanted to see if we had learned our lesson about exploding fuel. This time we did it perfectly and didn't so much as spill a single drop of fuel. I did wear my gas mask though. That was the worst working party I had ever been on.

Shortly after the ground campaign ended Boat Platoon was reactivated and was preparing to go home. We were still in Kuwait awaiting orders for movement to the rear, and by this time were living with the Sniper Section. They had the neatest toy - a remote control scout plane. One day they had it out for training purposes and invited us to see how it worked, and some of us even had a chance to fly it. I was one of the lucky ones.

Now you have to understand in the desert there is no privacy, including when you go to the bathroom. Our head was located away from the Battalion area, and was a set of three sandbags spaced just far apart enough for the average man to sit on with a hole dug about three feet down in between.

So there I was flying the plane and watching the monitor when I saw a Marine looking up at the camera. He just happened to be relieving himself, so I went in for a closer look. As the plane flew by the man shook his fist at it. I thought to myself "this smart ass needs a lesson in manners." Being the "Top Gun" that I was I decided it was time to "buzz the tower," so I proceeded to go to full throttle and aimed right at the man on the crapper. The plane was now in a full nosedive, looking right down at the helpless target.

Buuzzzzzzzzzz!

All of us were laughing so hard we could hardly see anything because of the tears we were shedding - including the figure of a man coming towards us from the direction of the crapper. The plane operator took over the controls and landed the aircraft, and by now we were able to see the man coming toward us was definitely an officer. As he got closer we saw he was wearing silver.

"What do you think?" one of us said, "First Lieutenant, or... oh shit, it's the Battalion Commander - and he looks pissed!"

I am happy to report my Battalion Commander had a sense of humor. Instead of busting us to the rank of private he simply made sure we all knew the difference between MOGAS and JP-5... for the rest of our tour in the desert!

LE GRANDE CHEF

"With the help of God and a few Marines..."

I have never had an aptitude for languages. Just ask my high school German teacher, Fraulein Oetiker. I did fairly well with the vocabulary, but when it came to conjugating verbs and all that stuff I was lost. And I figured "who needed it" anyway...

When I first arrived in Brazzaville I encountered a number of roadblocks manned by the Congolese Army, and on more than one occasion thought that some drunken and undisciplined soldier was about to end my life with a rusty AK-47. It was at that point I decided it would be prudent to learn the local lingo, in this case French. While most language students start out with phrases like "my name is John," I memorized things more along the lines of "please don't shoot me!"

On the 4th of July in 1993 I celebrated Independence Day with some British friends, which I found to be quite ironic when you consider they were our opponent during the Revolutionary War. The Diamond Boys, as they were known to us, were a group of ex-pats living in the area, and as you may have already guessed by the name worked as quasi-legal diamond smugglers in West Africa.

Our outing was to be a picnic on a sandbar in the middle of the Congo River, and our mode of transportation was a couple of speedboats the Brits used to move their "inventory" across that same body of water. There were seven of us in all, including one of my Marines and his French girlfriend.

As we cruised down the river there were several bursts of automatic weapons fire in our general direction, but since gunfire was not unusual in Africa we ignored it and continued on to our destination. The picnic lasted three or four hours, and when we were finished playing "the Queen vs. the Colonies" we packed up and headed for home.

All was fine until a boatload of Congolese soldiers armed with AK-47s and an RPK pulled alongside and ordered us to follow, and we were taken to a remote island in the middle of the Congo River which served as some sort of military outpost. I decided to try out some of my rudimentary French in an effort to smooth things over, but from the reaction I got I must have insulted someone's mother – so I decided to let the French girl among us handle the negotiations.

After jabbering with them for a bit she confided that things were not going well. They knew who the boat belonged to, and wanted to know where the diamonds were hidden… but of course there *were* no diamonds. Just when I was beginning to go over my insurance coverage in my head the girl pointed to me and told them I was an American. They were unimpressed. She then added that I was a Marine, and their attitude changed visibly. I admit I was quite surprised these soldiers were familiar with U.S. Marines, because while the Corps certainly does have an unparalleled history of military accomplishment it wasn't the sort of thing you expect to be taught in Congolese history classes – assuming these guys had gone to school at all.

When she finally identified me as "Le Grande Chef," or big chief, of the Marine detachment those guys became downright friendly, and suddenly we were being treated like royalty. They not only let us go, they even offered to let me try firing their weapons. Talk about *respect*!

EQUAL OPPORTUNITY

"Our Country won't go on forever, if we stay as soft as we are now. There won't be any AMERICA because some foreign soldiery will invade us and take our women and breed a hardier race!" - "Chesty" Puller

A few years ago I attended the graduation of a class from the Basic Reconnaissance Course, which is the entry level school for aspiring Recon Marines. Back when I went through it was known as Amphibious Reconnaissance School, but aside from the name and a few new pieces of gear not much has changed. Much of the curriculum involves physical training, long range patrolling and ocean swims. It is not for the faint of heart.

The guest speaker that day, a Marine Lieutenant Colonel named Powers, wistfully proclaimed that Recon was one of the "last bastions of testosterone" in the Corps. Was he a Neanderthal who was out of touch with modern thinking? Or was he one of those rare individuals who dared speak his mind in today's politically correct climate?

Women Marines were first organized in order to "Free a Marine to Fight," and that concept still held true when I joined the Corps. Females were assigned to WM battalion and wore different work uniforms than we did. But over the last quarter century women have been "integrated" throughout the military – with mixed results.

My first real exposure to female Marines occurred while I was deployed to Uncheon, Korea for Operation Bear Hunt '86. The camp where we were billeted for several weeks consisted of dozens of GP tents, and conditions were quite primitive in most respects. For one thing there was only one shower tent for three thousand troops, and since there were no separate facilities for the twenty or so females in camp shower hours were set up according to gender. They were of course scheduled to go first, and what little hot water there was had been used by the time they were finished. Heat was a precious commodity during the cold Korean nights, and in every one of the tents there was a large kerosene heater, which we were required to shut down at taps as a precaution against fires. All of us, that is, except the WMs. They had a heater that ran twenty-four hours a day, along with a Marine posted outside to ensure no fires broke out.

In that same camp there were a total of four heads – two for the men and two for the women. Guess which one had the long line! You may be saying to yourself, "So, what's your point - you sound like a whiner!" Well here it is. Men are compelled to take care of women due to a combination of instinct, tradition and upbringing. Ever hear the term "women and children first?" That's not going to change just because we rewrote a few laws in the name of political expediency.

A couple of years later I was a student at the Staff Non-Commissioned Officer Leadership Academy, and for the first time was required to work directly with WMs. There were two female Staff Sergeants in the class, and the school treated them in a fairly even-handed way up until the day we fell out onto the PT field for some "team-building" drills. One such event was the fireman's carry. We were divided into two groups and formed single file lines on opposite sides of the field. The idea was to sprint fifty yards, pick up a prone Marine, and carry him back to the starting point as quickly as possible. It was luck of the draw who you carried, and naturally I ended up with the biggest guy in the class on my back. But the WMs didn't have to worry about that. They were only required to carry *each other*.

That was not the end of the double standard at the SNCOA. All of the leadership positions in the class were rotated daily in order to give everyone a chance at being platoon commander, platoon sergeant and guide. If you happened to be the guide on a day when we had PT, you had to carry the school guidon during the run. Well, the fickle finger of fate pointed to one of our female classmates one fine morning, and I swear she expended more energy frantically searching for someone to switch duty days with than she did on the run. Naturally, some gallant male Marine took pity on her and carried the stick in her place.

During the short time I was Company Gunny for H&S CO, 2nd SRI Group I suffered from culture shock. There were quite a few WMs in the company, and the first time I inspected the barracks I was confronted by racks made up with pink blankets and rooms filled with cuddly stuffed animals. I nearly blew a blood vessel. The organization I had joined was supposed to be a hell-for-leather expeditionary force whose sole purpose was to exterminate the evildoers in our world with extreme prejudice, and here I was looking for dust balls at Aunt Fannie's Finishing School.

On an operational level I was also responsible for ensuring everyone in the command turned out for unit PT each week. I soon discovered that an inordinately high percentage of the females failed to show up, and further investigation revealed such excuses as cramps and problems getting a baby sitter at 5 AM. Getting that to stop was an uphill battle, and I practically had to drag some of those women to formation kicking and screaming. And once they were there, when I treated the female run drops the same as the men by yelling for them to catch up with the formation, I was branded a sexist. My reward for doing my job was an unfounded allegation of "harassment," which is the silver bullet in the feminist arsenal.

My next assignment was as a student Detachment Commander at the Marine Security Guard School in Quantico. I had a nineteen-year-old WM Lance Corporal named Maddox in my group, and her presence was a thorn in my side. She was a nice person – and very pretty - so when it came to the smooth operation of the detachment she was a disruptive factor. The other MSGs expended a great deal of energy trying to get into her shorts, and I had to keep a tight rein on them in order to head off any problems. Easier said than done.

If someone would answer a few simple questions to everyone's satisfaction it would eliminate much of the controversy. Please explain to me why WMs, who are always complaining about a lack of equality, never seem to complain about not being held to the same physical standards as men. Wouldn't it "level the playing field" and help to deflect criticism if the same Physical Fitness Test was administered to both genders? Unfortunately the tendency has been to lower the bar in order to accommodate all, and that doesn't translate to success on the battlefield.

The same logic extends to the sporting world. If they were to integrate the NBA with the WNBA, and the PGA with the LPGA, and chose players based purely upon their athletic ability, how many female athletes would have a job? What about world records in sports such as track and field – is it *right* to have separate records for men and women if they are equal? If there was a woman who could play shortstop, or linebacker, as well as a man, don't you think the Yankees and Packers would be signing them? People sometimes forget combat is the *ultimate* contact sport!

The issue of sexual harassment is a political hot potato. Females must work in close quarters with a bunch of virile young men under difficult conditions for long periods. Gee, I wonder what's going to happen? Sergeant Major of the Army Gene McKinney was forced to retire because he supposedly harassed a female *Lieutenant General*. It seems to me we have a problem when someone wearing three stars can't deal with an enlisted man making a pass at her without resorting to the legal system.

Let's not forget pregnancy. The issue makes me think of a Staff Sergeant I knew in the 2nd Marine Division's Comm Company. He had a WM Corporal who was pregnant virtually the entire time she was in the Marine Corps, gave birth to four children in a span of four years, and each time was granted six weeks of maternity leave afterward. During that time she was exempt from PT, qualifying on the rifle range, going to the field, or making deployments. Even so she managed to get promoted along with her peers. Now I seem to remember signing a statement indicating I was "worldwide deployable and fit for duty on land and sea" every time I reenlisted. Hmmm.

I also recall having a spirited discussion with some British Royal Marines during which they called into question the toughness of our Corps relative to their own. I defended our honor and chronicled our battle history in great detail, telling stories of Puller, Basilone and O'Bannon. Just when it seemed like I had won the day a pregnant WM in a maternity uniform waddled on by. Given the fact that there are no women in the Royal Marines, there was little else I could say.

Finally comes my favorite question. If equality is really the issue, shouldn't *everyone* be required to register for the draft? I would think that feminists would be *enraged* by the draft registration pamphlets that say MEN over the age of eighteen must register for the draft. Shouldn't they say *Americans* over the age of eighteen? Where is the outcry of indignation over this disparity?

Do we dare put a set of uniform standards in place that correlate to the demands of serving in the Marine Corps, and grant admittance to all who meet those standards? Or shall we continue to operate with two sets of rules so that women can be treated "fairly" in their pursuit of a military career? Call me crazy, but the last time I checked there was nothing fair about combat.

Once upon a time black and white soldiers were segregated, and that was wrong. The only way we made desegregation work was to integrate the armed forces to where it is now the most color blind institution in this country. If women are to be part of the military, then we must follow suit and make it *gender* neutral. Not female friendly, but totally neutral. Same uniforms, same regulations, same PFT. You can't put apples and oranges into the same pastry and call it apple pie.

The term "equal opportunity" is a hollow one unless it is accompanied by equal responsibility and equal requirements. The Marine Corps is a martial organization charged with the defense of our way of life, not a laboratory for social experimentation. The next time a WM complains about being the victim of a double standard I suggest she take a look at USMC grooming and physical fitness standards. When those same women actually start complaining about not being required to wear their hair "three inches on top and graduated" or do pull-ups on the PFT, I will believe they are *sincere* in their pursuit of equality. Until that day they should just be quiet.

Bottom line – you can't have your cake and eat it too!

115

A CHANGE OF HEART

"I can never again see a United States Marine without experiencing a feeling of reverence." - General Johnson, U.S. Army

Politics are part and parcel of serving in the State Department. There's no getting away from it. We in the military, on the other hand, are trained to avoid becoming embroiled in politics - but sometimes you just have to speak up for what you believe.

As civil war heated up in the Congo there were no safe places in the city of Brazzaville, but some were less safe than others. Stray bullets would come through walls without warning, and there were roadblocks manned by armed soldiers everywhere. Even the Ambassador was in the line of fire, and one night he had a really close call. A firefight broke out near the Ambassador's Residence, and Mr. Ramsey and his wife had to take cover in an interior hallway. They waited there for several hours with nothing to drink but a bottle of champagne, which he had grabbed in a daring dash to the kitchen. When things calmed down some of us went down there to move Mr. and Mrs. Ramsey to an apartment near the Embassy, and upon entering the compound found that the brand new Jeep Cherokee he had shipped into the country was shot full of holes. I was glad it was the car and not the Ambassador!

The Administrative Officer of our Embassy at that time was a woman named 'Sandy.' She was third in the chain of command, but nothing at all like the Ambassador. Sandy despised the military in general, and Marines in particular. She had attended Berkley back in the 1960's, and as you might suspect her politics were just to the left of Fidel

Castro. I did my best to avoid confrontations with her, but she had a habit of taunting me about my politics every opportunity she got. As you may have guessed we were *not* friends.

Sandy lived on the edge of the Bacongo district of Brazzaville, which is precisely where government control of the city ended and rebel control began. One fine day it was her turn to get caught in the crossfire, and things quickly went from bad to worse. Rounds from Soviet-made 12.7 heavy machineguns were tearing through the walls of her house like they were made of paper maché, so Sandy lay down on the floor and radioed the Embassy for help.

When the call came in the Regional Security Officer asked me if I wanted to "go for a ride." He didn't tell me where we were going at first, probably because he thought I might join the rebels who were shooting at Sandy. We armed ourselves and headed for Bacongo in a hardened Suburban that belonged to the Defense Attaché - it wasn't an armored vehicle, but did have ballistic glass, a reinforced body, and self-sealing tires.

When we arrived at the gate to Sandy's residence we could see some rebel positions on the far side of the ravine, and there was an armored vehicle of the Congolese Army firing at them from a spot just up the road. Since there was incoming from the far side our driver pulled as close to the front door as possible, and I slithered out of the vehicle and low crawled inside in search of our Admin Officer. She was hiding under a bed in the center of the house when I found her, and since she was in tears and incoherent I simply drug her to the door, threw her in the Suburban, and told the driver to make tracks.

As we picked up speed and headed for home Sandy suddenly stopped blubbering and blurted out, "I've never been so happy to see Marines in my life!"

If there is one thing I hate it's a hypocrite, and if looks could kill Sandy would have died then and there.

THIRTY YEARS OF TRUTH
Up For Reconsideration

By Pat Conroy

"Freedom is the sure possession of only those who have the courage to defend it!"

The true things always ambush me on the road and take me by surprise when I am drifting along through placid days, careless about flank and rearguard actions. I was not looking for a true thing to come upon me in the state of New Jersey. Nothing has ever happened to me in New Jersey. But come it did, and it came to stay.

In the past four years I have been interviewing my teammates from the 1966-67 basketball team at the Citadel for a book I'm writing. For the most part, this has been like buying back a part of my past that I had mislaid or shut out of my life. At first I thought I was writing about being young and frisky and able to run up and down a court all day long, but lately I realized I came to this book because I needed to come to grips with being middle-aged and having ripened into a gray-haired man you could not trust to handle the ball on a fast break.

When I visited my old teammate Al Kroboth's house in New Jersey, I spent the first hours quizzing him about his memories of games and practices and the screams of coaches that had echoed in field houses more than thirty years before. Al had been a splendid forward-center for the Citadel; at 6 feet 5 inches and carrying 220 pounds, he played with indefatigable energy and enthusiasm. For most of his senior year he led the nation in field-goal percentage, with UCLA

119

center Lew Alcindor hot on his trail. Al was a battler and a brawler and a scrapper from the day he first stepped in as a Green Weenie sophomore to the day he graduated. After we talked basketball we came to a subject I dreaded to bring up with Al, but which lay between us and would not lie still.

"Al, you know I was a draft dodger and antiwar demonstrator."

"That's what I heard, Conroy," Al said. "I have nothing against what you did, but I did what I thought was right."

"Tell me about Vietnam, big Al. Tell me what happened to you," I said.

On his seventh mission as a navigator in an A-6 for Major Leonard Robertson, Al was getting ready to deliver their payload when the fighter-bomber was hit by enemy fire. Though Al has no memory of it, he punched out somewhere in the middle of the ill-fated dive and lost consciousness. He doesn't know if he was unconscious for six hours or six days, nor does he know what happened to Major Robertson (whose name is engraved on the Wall in Washington and on the MIA bracelet Al wears).

When Al awoke, he couldn't move. A Viet Cong soldier held an AK-47 to his head. His back and his neck were broken, and he had shattered his left scapula in the fall. When he was well enough to get to his feet (he still can't recall how much time had passed), two armed Viet Cong led Al from the jungles of South Vietnam to a Prison in Hanoi. The journey took three months. Al Kroboth walked barefoot through the most impassable terrain in Vietnam, and he did it sometimes in the dead of night. He bathed when it rained, and he slept in bomb craters with his two Viet Cong captors. As they moved farther north infections began to erupt on his body, and his legs were covered with leeches picked up while crossing the rice paddies.

At the very time of Al's walk I had a small role in organizing the only antiwar demonstration ever held in Beaufort, South Carolina, the home of Parris Island and the Marine Corps Air Station. In a Marine Corps town at that time it was difficult to come up with a quorum of people who had even minor disagreements about the Vietnam War. But my small group managed to attract a crowd of about 150 to Beaufort's waterfront. With my mother and my wife on either side of me we listened to the featured speaker, Dr. Howard Levy, suggest to the very few young enlisted Marines present that if they got sent to Vietnam, here's how they can help end this war: Roll a grenade under your officer's bunk when he's asleep in his tent. It's called "fragging," and is becoming more and more popular with the ground troops who know this war is bullshit. I was enraged by the suggestion. At that very moment my father, a Marine officer, was asleep in Vietnam. But in 1972, at the age of twenty-seven, I thought I was serving America's interests by pointing out what massive flaws, miscalculations, and corruptions had led her to conduct a ground war in Southeast Asia.

In the meantime Al and his captors had finally arrived in the North, and the Viet Cong traded him to North Vietnamese soldiers for the final leg of the trip to Hanoi. Many times when they stopped to rest for the night the local villagers tried to kill him. His captors wired his hands behind his back at night, so he trained himself to sleep in the center of huts when the villagers began sticking knives and bayonets into the thin walls. Following U.S. air raids, old women would come into the huts to excrete on him and yank out hunks of hair. After the nightmare journey of his walk north, Al was relieved when his guards finally delivered him

121

to the POW camp in Hanoi and the cell door was locked behind him.

It was at the camp that Al began to die. He threw up every meal he ate and before long was misidentified as the oldest American soldier in the prison because his appearance was so gaunt and skeletal. But the extraordinary camaraderie among fellow prisoners that sprang up in all the POW camps caught fire in Al, and did so in time to save his life.

When I was demonstrating in America against Nixon and the Christmas bombings in Hanoi, Al and his fellow prisoners were holding hands under the full fury of those bombings, singing "God Bless America." It was those bombs that convinced Hanoi they would do well to release the American POWs, including my college teammate. When he told me about the C-141 landing in Hanoi to pick up the prisoners Al said he felt no emotion, none at all, until he saw the giant American flag painted on the plane's tail. I stopped writing as Al wept over the memory of that flag on that plane, on that morning, during that time in the life of America.

It was that same long night, after listening to Al's story, that I began to make judgments about how I had conducted myself during the Vietnam War. In the darkness of the sleeping Kroboth household, lying in the third-floor guest bedroom, I began to assess my role as a citizen in the '60s, when my country called my name and I shot her the bird. Unlike the stupid boys who wrapped themselves in Viet Cong flags and burned the American one, I knew how to demonstrate against the war without flirting with treason or astonishingly bad taste. I had come directly from the warrior culture of this country, and I knew how to act.

But in the twenty-five years that have passed since South Vietnam fell, I have immersed myself in the study of totalitarianism during the unspeakable century we just left behind. I have questioned survivors of Auschwitz and Bergen-Belsen, talked to Italians who told me tales of the Nazi occupation, French partisans who had counted German tanks in the forests of Normandy, and officers who survived the Bataan Death March. I quiz journalists returning from wars in Bosnia, the Sudan, the Congo, Angola, Indonesia, Guatemala, San Salvador, Chile, Northern Ireland, and Algeria.

As I lay sleepless, I realized I'd done all this research to better understand my country. I now revere words like democracy, freedom, the right to vote, and the grandeur of the extraordinary vision of the founding fathers. Do I see America's flaws? Of course. But I now can honor her basic, incorruptible virtues, the ones that let me walk the streets screaming my ass off that my country had no idea what it was doing in South Vietnam. My country let me scream to my heart's content - the same country that produced both Al Kroboth and me.

Now, at this moment in New Jersey, I come to a conclusion about my actions as a young man when Vietnam was a dirty word to me. I wish I'd led a platoon of Marines in Vietnam. I would like to think I would have trained my troops well, and that the Viet Cong would have had their hands full if they entered a firefight with us. From the day of my birth I was programmed to enter the Marine Corps. I was the son of a Marine fighter pilot, and had grown up on Marine bases where I had watched the men of the Corps perform simulated war games in the forests of my childhood. That a novelist and poet bloomed darkly in the house of Santini strikes me as a remarkable irony. My mother and father had raised me to be an Al Kroboth, and during the

Vietnam era they watched in horror as I metamorphosed into another breed of fanatic entirely.

I understand now that I should have protested the war after my return from Vietnam, after I had done my duty for my country. I have come to a conclusion about my country that I knew then in my bones but lacked the courage to act on: America is good enough to die for even when she is wrong.

I looked for some conclusion, a summation of this trip to my teammate's house. I wanted to come to the single right thing, a true thing that I may not like but that I could live with. After hearing Al Kroboth's story of his walk across Vietnam and his brutal imprisonment in the North I found myself passing harrowing, remorseless judgment on myself. I had not turned out to be the man I had once envisioned myself to be. I thought I would be the kind of man America could point to and say, "There. That's the guy. That's the one who got it right. The whole package. The one I can depend on."

It had never once occurred to me that I would find myself in the position I did on the night in Al Kroboth's house in Roselle, New Jersey: an American coward, spending the night with an American hero.

SHANGRI-LA

"Yes, the President should resign. He has lied to the American people, time and time again, and betrayed their trust. He is no longer an effective leader. Since he has admitted guilt, there is no reason to put the American people through an impeachment. He will serve absolutely no purpose in finishing out his term. The only possible solution is for the President to save some dignity and resign." – Bill Clinton on President Nixon in 1974

The goings-on at Camp David have always been a microcosm of the administration in power at any given time. First founded by FDR as a sanctuary in 1942, the tranquil retreat in the Catocin Mountains of Maryland was originally known as Shangri-La. It wasn't until 1953 that it was renamed Camp David in honor of President Eisenhower's grandson.

Since the camp is not accessible to the public it has always been shrouded in mystery for the average American. I know I always wondered what was going on up there. I got my chance to find out when our First Sergeant, Kenn Capper, made arrangements for three of us to fly to Camp David to interview some of the grunts there for a possible future assignment with Recon.

We didn't get to see much of the camp on that trip in 1987, but in the ensuing years I have gotten to know a number of Marines who have served a tour there. They are all pretty closed-mouthed about specific things that occurred there, but when they talk about their impressions of the Presidents and their families their accounts are amazingly consistent. I think much can be learned from what they said, and from the different leadership style they encountered with each President.

Lesson number one is that loyalty from the military is not about politics. We are *all* Americans. It is more about the way members of the armed forces are treated by those in their chain of command. That is what determines how troops perceive a leader.

The Reagan years were remembered fondly by the Marines and sailors who were there during that time. They each felt they were treated like part of a family, and when the President left office he and Nancy said a teary and heartfelt farewell to everyone at the camp. He took care of the troops, and not just the ones at Camp David. We all loved him for it.

In later years an interesting contrast in styles occurred for some Marines whose service at Camp David spanned both the Bush and Clinton administrations. In each case it was a tale of two *very* different chief executives.

It was only natural for President George H. W. Bush to be automatically respected by the troops stationed at Camp David. He was, after all, a war hero. But after that point it became something he had to earn, and the fact that their respect for him continued to grow says a lot about the man. His wife was also highly thought of. A friend who served at Camp David once told me Barbara Bush actually baked cookies for the Marines on post!

President Clinton, on the other hand, needed to work extra hard to make the military forget his history as a draft dodger. Instead, he chose to further alienate those of us in uniform by violating practically every article of the UCMJ while in office. There he was, Commander-in-Chief to people who were themselves held to the highest possible standard, and he conducted him in a manner unworthy of the lowest private. What kind of example did that provide?

Unlike previous Presidents Mr. Clinton did not invite visiting dignitaries to Camp David, although that's not to say there were no guests staying there. As we have come to learn, the Clintons "rented" rooms at the White House and Camp David in exchange for campaign donations. In the wake of the subsequent fund raising scandal, information was released showing between the years '93 and '96 there were 938 guests at Camp David alone, and from '99 to 2000 there were another 404. It is ironic to note that among those to enjoy the amenities of the camp, and the protection afforded by the Marines guarding it, was none other than "Hanoi" Jane Fonda!

Respect should flow both up and down the chain of command. That is one of the precepts of leadership. The Clinton White House's obvious contempt for the military showed that members of his administration had no grasp of this very basic principle. Reports that the Chairman of the JCS was directed not to wear his uniform to the White House were appalling, and the open contempt displayed toward military personnel by Hillary and Chelsea Clinton was despicable.

It got so bad that the brother of a friend, who was a crew chief during the Clinton years on the Presidential helicopter known as Marine One, once stated that the act of saluting the President when he boarded and deplaned "sickened him."

It got so bad that in 1993, shortly after Mr. Clinton took office, a senior Air Force officer named Major General Harold Campbell was forced to retire and fined $7,000 after he described the President as a "dope smoking, skirt chasing and draft dodging" Commander in Chief at a banquet.

It got so bad that in an article published in the *Navy Times* in October of 1998 Major Shane Sellers called President Clinton "an adulterous liar." Major Sellers, an intelligence officer assigned to the Defense Intelligence Agency, lamented that Mr. Clinton was not held to the same standard as uniformed officers.

It got so bad that in that same edition of the *Navy Times* a Staff Sergeant named Taylor also questioned the President's fitness to lead, saying he should resign. "Is it too much to expect our President to be the last bastion of morality in a society where morality and values are ever declining?" he wrote. "What kind of message does it send when the Commander-in-Chief is not held to the same standard as the troops?"

It finally got so bad that the Assistant Commandant of the Marine Corps, General Terrence Dake, found it necessary to send a memorandum to every general in the Corps urging them to remind Marines of prohibitions against speaking contemptuous words against the President. "It is unethical for individuals who wear the uniform of a Marine to engage in public dialogue on political and legal matters such as impeachment," he wrote.

In response a White House spokesman issued a statement saying President Clinton did not believe the scandals had affected the morale of the armed forces, and added, "I think the President has enormous respect for the men and women in uniform in this country, and I think that respect is reciprocated."

He thought wrong.

THE PINK PANTHER

"He has the wisdom of youth, and the energy of old age."
– Excerpt from a fitness report

I will never forget Gunnery Sergeant 'Hardon,' not because he was a good Marine, but rather because he was such an improbable one. He was one of those rare individuals who somehow managed to incur the universal disdain of an entire company and yet remained blissfully ignorant of that rather dubious accomplishment.

Hardy was one of those guys who you just knew couldn't whip an old lady in a fair fight, yet he managed to menace the rank and file nonetheless. As training NCO for H&S Company 2/25, Hardon did his level best to ensure everyone in the command ran their annual PFT and re-qualified with the rifle each year. It sounds pretty admirable on the surface until you tried to remember the last time anyone saw *him* on the range or in PT gear. He was of course "pencil-whipping" his own scores, and everyone knew it. Things like that, along with an exceedingly annoying personality, led to his being ostracized by virtually the entire command.

Hardon eventually became a member of the Full Time Support (FTS) program, which meant he got all the benefits of being a regular while remaining a reservist and never having to worry about being transferred away from his hometown. It also meant he was a member of the Inspector-Instructor Staff, and as such was in a position to annoy even more people than before.

During the winter of 1983 the company went up to Ft. Smith NY for Annual Training, and when we arrived Hardon was there waiting for us. He was wearing one of the newly issued all-weather coats, but since none of us had ever seen one before we figured it was just a trench coat. His moustache was as always badly in need of a trim, and clenched between his teeth was his ever present pipe. I couldn't place who he reminded me of but later that evening, after decreeing that there would be no liberty, he crept around corners conducting bed checks - and had the name "Inspector Clouseau" hung on him by the firewatch.

The following morning we were in formation waiting for the First Sergeant to arrive when Hardon walked by, and at my behest the entire platoon launched into an impromptu rendition of Henry Mancini's "Pink Panther Theme." We didn't know it then, but we had just begun a tradition that would last for years. Every time he entered a room or passed by it became automatic for those present to sing his theme song, and for some reason he never caught on that it was for him. Not, at least, until I paid a saxophone player to dedicate it to him during the Marine Corps Ball one year. The look on his face caused Marines in dress blues to actually roll on the floor in hysteria, and he stormed over to our table not a little bit miffed. I explained to him that he was better off being known as the Pink Panther because it had eventually caused everyone to forget the old nickname he had carried, also unknowingly, for several years. After all what Marine, even Hardon, wants to be known as Mary?

FAST ROPE JOE

"Character is what we do when we think no one is looking."
– H. Jackson Brown, Jr.

One of the primary means of insertion for a reconnaissance patrol is via helicopter, but very often there are no landing zones in the area of operations. Either that, or the ones available are controlled by the enemy. A means of lowering troops into a forested area was needed, and several solutions proved to be practical.

Rappelling, which is a technique for quickly descending the face of a sheer cliff by sliding down a rope, was adapted as a means of reaching the ground from a hovering helicopter. It involves attaching oneself to a nylon climbing rope with a steel carabineer, and using the rope's friction to stop when necessary.

One of the big disadvantages from a tactical standpoint was the difficulty rappelers sometimes had in trying to disengage from the rope once on the ground. The delay left Marines exposed to enemy fire underneath the hovering helicopter, and additional troops could not descend until the man on the rope was clear.

Another idea was the SPIE, which stands for Special Patrol Insertion and Extraction. Despite the name, this it is used exclusively as a means of extraction. It involves wearing a harness and snapping into a "D" ring on a heavy line suspended from a helicopter. The bird would then pull the team through the jungle canopy by going straight up, and once the bottom man is clear the transition is made to forward flight. It's actually quite exhilarating.

A new method for descending from helicopters was needed for assault type operations, and during the 1980s the FBI came up with fast roping. A special, thick rope was suspended from a helicopter, and troops simply slide down like it was a fireman's pole. The key is there is no need to attach to the rope in any way. As a result it is a much faster means of insertion, and can put an entire team on the ground or the roof of a building in a matter of seconds.

As in most things there is some risk associated with techniques like SPIE rigging and rappelling. There was one period at 2nd Recon Battalion where there were two deaths as a result of rappelling accidents in a span of one week. We always took such things seriously, and the training required to become a Rope Suspension Training (RST) Master became even more stringent.

Now that I have laid the groundwork and explained the difference between rappelling and fast roping I can introduce you to someone I'll just call 'Joe.' When Joe first reported to our unit he was wearing Jump and SCUBA badges, which is usually a good indication of someone's training and experience - but not in this case.

In 1986 our company deployed to the Jungle Warfare Training Center in Panama, and while there parachute and scuba training were scheduled for the periods we were not out in the jungle. It was the first time Joe was to jump with the company, and looking back he seemed to have no idea how to suit up. Fortunately for all concerned the aircraft was a no-show, and that jump was cancelled.

Later that week a proficiency dive was conducted in the lagoon at Fort Sherman, and Joe was paired with Pablo Arroyo as his dive buddy. Pablo, or "Mr. X" as he was known, led something of a charmed life, having been one of the survivors of the Beirut bombing. He and Joe went to the bottom of the lagoon, but when Arroyo looked for his buddy to give him a thumbs up he was gone. If there is one thing a military diver learns it's to never, ever leave your buddy - but he had vanished. After a hasty search Mr. X surfaced to notify the dive supervisor, and when his head broke the surface the first thing he saw was Joe sitting on the beach claiming to have some sort of equipment problem. Hmmm.

The final straw came on a patrol near the banks of the Chagres River when Joe was attached to my team as a scout. All he had to do was walk along with the team and stay quiet, and he managed to do that without too much trouble. But as we moved to our extract point we encountered a steep cliff, and I decided it would be simpler to rappel to the bottom rather than search for a route down.

I secured the rope to a tree in such a manner that we could retrieve it, and rappelled down to act as belay or "brake" man for the other members of the team. One by one they descended, and finally it was Joe's turn. As the last one down he had to snap himself in, which involves wrapping the rope around a snap link in such a fashion that it creates friction. That is what enables you to make a controlled descent.

Joe bounded off the cliff and the fun began. In my capacity as belay man I saw him coming down at a high rate of speed and pulled the rope backward in an attempt to slow him down. He crashed into me and most of the others, and that cushioned his landing enough to prevent him from being seriously injured. I immediately had a look at his snap link and saw the rope was simply passed through it. He had not wrapped it around!

We later learned that he had never been to jump or dive school, and from that day on he was known as... what else... "Fast Rope Joe."

THE LINGUIST

"Actions speak louder than words – and speak fewer lies!"

The Army Special Forces (aka "Green Berets") are very misunderstood by the American public in that they were *not* organized to conduct raids and other types of direct action missions as many people believe. Instead their primary task is to organize, train, equip and lead strike forces comprised of indigenous troops. It is a unique mission, and one that they do well.

One of the things that make Special Forces unique is their language capability. Every soldier in an "A-Team" is expected to have a working knowledge of two languages in addition to English. That is particularly impressive in the United States. As the old saying goes: If someone who speaks two languages is bi-lingual, what do you call someone who speaks *one* language? An American!

So with that in mind, it happened that one day we had a Sergeant named 'Gordon' come to us via inter-service transfer. He had a chestful of ribbons to rival Audie Murphy, but explained most had been awarded while conducting classified operations while a member of Delta Force. He also claimed to speak Spanish and Russian, and we had no reason to doubt any of what he said.

Gordon's junior ribbon was the rainbow colored decoration I like to call the "Glad to be in the Army" ribbon. If you can believe it, the Army and Air Force actually award a ribbon for completing basic training. The Marine Corps, with a far more demanding boot camp, simply awards the right to be called "Marine." Words fail me on this one! They next thing you know they will issue every soldier a beret....

But I digress. Gordon often talked about bringing some of the troops over to Fort Bragg to tour the facilities of Delta Force and the JFK Special Warfare Center, since he had "connections" with his old buddies there. However every time he put something together an "operational crisis" of some sort would come up and conveniently limit access to those areas. On one occasion we *did* actually go to Bragg, but simply drove past a parking lot he claimed belonged to some of the ninjas stationed there. I smelled a phony.

Later that summer Gordon removed all doubt about his lineage. Our company was tasked with training a group of Mexican Naval cadets in such things as rappelling and handling inflatable boats, and the CO canvassed for Spanish speakers to act as translators. Fortunately there were several bi-lingual Marines of Hispanic descent in the company, and of course there was Sergeant Gordon.

I was in charge of running the rappel tower, and things went well until my assigned translator had to make a head call. Since we were in the middle of an evolution I waved Gordon over and asked him to tell the students to retrieve a rope. He hesitated for a moment, and then turned to the nearest Mexican.

He said, "You-o go-o get-o rope-o."

Heck, if I had known Spanish was *that* easy I would have put in for language proficiency pay a long time ago!

WATCH YOUR WALLET

"In the old days a woman married a man for his money. Now she *divorces* him for it!"

I read somewhere that Marines will fight with each other over a woman or a bottle of rotgut whiskey, but will share the last drop in their canteen with a thirsty buddy. How true. Integrity and camaraderie are what make the Corps what it is, but unfortunately other people don't live by those same ideals.

When I talk about the integrity of fellow Marines I love to tell the story of "my wallet." When I was a young devil pup we still lived in open squad bays – the "Holiday Inn" barracks of today hadn't yet been built. One summer I made plans to head out of town with some buddies over a long weekend, and in my haste to change into civvies left my wallet on my rack. It contained an entire months pay in cash, and I fretted about it the entire four days I was gone. I needn't have. When I returned it was right where I had left it.

The point of that story is twofold. The first and most obvious is the Marines in my unit were trustworthy, and they looked out for my welfare. The second is if the wallet had disappeared it would have been the fault of one person – me. Too many people in today's world fail to take responsibility for their own actions, or for their own lives. If something goes wrong it must have been someone *else's* fault, and they are quick to point the finger.

Take marriage for instance. Nobody gets married and has children in the belief they will get divorced someday. But it happens every day. Check the statistics. They show over fifty percent of all military marriages end in divorce! This means every married career military person has a 50/50 chance of losing a large portion of his or her military retired pay to a former spouse regardless of the circumstance that led to divorce. Of course during the blissful, or at least civil, years of a marriage many things are said with good intentions, but all of those words go out the window the moment an attorney or "well meaning" family member gets involved. I can still hear my ex-wife say "I would *never* go after your retirement pay; *you* earned that money, not me." Guess what – she did!

If you are wondering how this can happen it's time you became familiar with the Uniformed Services Former Spouses Protection Act. This is the law that says retired military members must in effect pay permanent alimony to their former spouses. It is actually an illegal law, having been backdated to the day *prior* to a Supreme Court ruling called McCarty v. McCarty, which said military retainer pay is not subject to division. Pretty sneaky, huh?

So who authored the USFSPA? None other than our old friend Pat Schroeder. Here is her rationale: "This bill recognizes that *both spouses contribute* to the service member's ability to earn a wage and receive a pension." Equal division would lead one to believe there was an equal contribution, wouldn't it? Let's see... is the spouse required to go on long, isolated deployments? Is the spouse asked to go in harm's way in time of war with the prospect of being killed, captured or wounded? Is the spouse subject to discipline under the UCMJ? Is the spouse subject to recall to active duty after retirement? Obviously, the answer is no in every case.

Another point to ponder. Enlisted service members - including combat veterans – can be honorably but involuntarily discharged, and commissioned officers may resign, with as many as nineteen years, eleven months, and twenty-nine days service without any compensation or benefits forthcoming. Not a penny. In the case of former spouses only one day of marriage is required to qualify for a portion of the service member's retainer pay. And how is that portion determined? Division of funds is not based upon need, merit or fault. It is based upon a formula. Period.

But wait, there's more! Let's say you were married the first five years of your career, and you got divorced at the rank of Corporal. You then decide to stay in and end up retiring from the Corps fifteen years later as a First Sergeant. Your ex's bounty will be based on E-8 pay at time of retirement, *not* the E-4 over five pay at the time of divorce. Your successful career translates into cash for your ex. Your former spouse can even *force* you to pay for a costly life insurance plan called SBP that guarantees a paycheck in the event of your death! Anything wrong with that picture? Child support ends when your offspring get old enough to care for themselves - at what point does your former spouse grow up and become self-supporting?

Think it stops when your ex gets remarried? Wrong again. Unlike alimony it goes on and on like the Energizer bunny. You will in effect be supporting his or her new spouse. If it looks like a duck, and walks like a duck, and quacks like a duck, it probably is one. Call it whatever you want, USFSPA is simply a euphemism for "alimony for life."

It's a pretty good deal if you ask me. Marry someone, live under the roof they provide, and have no responsibilities if you so choose. No oath to take, no military discipline to endure, no combat. What a deal! Want more? No humping twenty miles with a heavy pack, no sleeping on the ground in the rain, no eating MREs. And if your spouse should happen to run off with one of the neighbors while you are on a long deployment it's okay, since no-fault divorce will give them a piece of that pension no matter what.

I wish someone had told me about all of this a long time ago, and I say this now to all members of the armed forces who are contemplating matrimony. *Get a pre-nuptial agreement*, even if you don't plan to make the military a career.

If my wallet had disappeared that day many years ago it would have been no one's fault but my own, but it sure was nice knowing it was in the care of people who realized the money inside didn't belong to them. Don't leave *your* wallet unattended.

If you are one of the thousands who have been or will be affected by this illegal law and would like to put an end to this injustice visit usfspa-lawsuit.info on the worldwide web.

TOMCAT FOLLIES

"The Marines I have seen around the world have the cleanest bodies, the filthiest minds, the highest morale, and the lowest morals of any group of animals I have ever seen. Thank God for the United States Marine Corps!" - Eleanor Roosevelt, First Lady of the United States, 1945

Over the years there have been many politicians who have undermined the armed forces of our great nation, but one of the most despicable was former Congresswoman Patricia Schroeder of Colorado. Yes, *that* Pat Schroeder. The one who balled like a baby when she dropped out of the Democratic Presidential primary. As is too often the case these days Ms. Schroeder served on the House Armed Services Committee without the benefit of having ever served in uniform, and she used that position to further women's issue without any regard for how veterans would be affected.

Ms. Schroeder is a self-proclaimed "champion of free speech," but it's one thing to talk the talk and quite another to walk the walk. The First Amendment apparently doesn't apply when she gets *her* nose out of joint, and she is obviously not familiar with the adage, "sticks and stones, etc…" to boot.

Five Navy officers were relieved of command and sixteen others counseled in disciplinary action that resulted after a skit called the "Tomcat Follies" took place at the Miramar officers club in San Diego, California. A retired female Navy captain who saw the show protested a banner which contained a sexual message about Representative Schroeder, and her Congressional office later received an obscene message from a fax machine at the Marine Corps Air Station at New River, North Carolina. Waaaaa...

Keep in mind that Schroeder, in her days on the Armed Services Committee, had been very critical of the Navy's investigation of the 1991 Tailhook scandal. She wanted something more akin to a witch hunt. After all, it was a perfect opportunity to put those Neanderthal fighter pilots in their place. Let's be honest. What would have happened if someone had "inappropriately" grabbed a *male* fighter pilot? Probably a punch in the nose, and that's the end of that. Someone gets a black eye. But throw a female pilot into the mix and it turns into a federal case. Literally. And the entire Naval Aviation community gets a black eye.

As if that wasn't heinous enough, Schroeder's crowning achievement resulted in one of the greatest disservices ever propagated upon those who serve this country in uniform - the Uniform Services Former Spouse Protection Act. That law is an insult to everyone who wears a uniform!

Schroeder even wrote to Colin Powell and suggested his arguments against integrating homosexuals into the military were similar to the case made against breaking the color barrier in the armed forces decades earlier. To his great credit he replied, "'Skin color is a benign non-behavioral characteristic. Sexual orientation is perhaps the most profound of human behavioral characteristics. Comparison of the two is a convenient but invalid argument."

Is it any wonder she was the subject of ridicule? Twenty-one promising careers went down the drain because she got her feelings hurt.

I wonder if she cried?

Swift, Silent and Surrounded

DUST IN THE WIND

"It slips a-way, and all your money won't another minute buy..."
- From the song "Dust in the Wind" by the band Kansas

You never know when your time is up. Manila John Basilone earned the Medal of Honor on Guadalcanal, and then spent the next couple of years traveling around the U.S. on a War Bond tour – but there is only so much of that sort of thing a true Marine can stand, so he eventually requested to return to combat duty and was killed by an incoming mortar round shortly after going ashore on Iwo Jima. You just never know.

When I was a young corporal with Company A, 2nd Reconnaissance Battalion we deployed to the Marine Corps auxiliary airfield located in Oak Grove North Carolina to conduct patrolling and riverine operations. It was a great place to train because the terrain was unfamiliar to us, and a river ran right through the installation.

My team leader, Sergeant Jim Pechiney, was a strapping Marine who was a graduate of the Special Forces Underwater Operations Course in Key West. Anyone familiar with that school knows how physically demanding it is, and successful completion is a clear indication of superior swimming ability. He and Lance Corporal Velasquez were the only divers in the team at that time, and Pechiney liked to tease him about being "only" a Navy diver.

One night our mission was to conduct an area reconnaissance, which involved reporting anything and everything we found within our assigned sector, and it wasn't long before we located a group of aggressors located a few clicks from our base camp. It was easy to creep up on their position because they had a radio playing rather loudly, and we quickly made a detailed sketch of their camp.

Pechiney had of course heard the radio, and during the debrief at our objective rally point asked if anyone could remember what song had been playing. I answered immediately, and was quite proud of myself for knowing the answer. My team leader had never really cottoned to me, and it was nice to have his approval for a change – even on something as minor as that.

Once we had completed patrolling our assigned sector it was time to return to base, and our route took us to a point just across the river and a bit downstream from the rest of the company. Since we had to cross the river Pechiney decided to use a rope bridge in order to demonstrate our ability to construct one in a tactical situation. He opted to swim the rope across himself and scout the far bank for enemy activity, accompanied by the Lieutenant who was grading our patrol.

Each of the swimmers tied a sling rope around his waist and snapped into the end of the rope with a snap link so they wouldn't get separated in the rain and darkness. Off they went, and we huddled under a bush and waited for the signal which would indicate the rope was secured to the opposite bank. Several minutes later all hell broke loose. One of the swimmers began screaming for help, so we grabbed the rope and pulled it back in as quickly as we could. Within a minute we had reeled it all in, but the line seemed to be snagged on something - and the two Marines were nowhere to be seen.

I jumped off the steep river bank and found myself chest deep in the river, and when I couldn't see anyone dove underwater and followed the rope. The first one I found was the Lieutenant. He was gasping for air, and after unhooking him from the line I boosted him up onto the bank where the rest of the team was waiting. He was disoriented and had swallowed some water, but after a few minutes ended up being okay.

I dove once again, and after a few moments located Sergeant Pechiney. He was not moving. The rope had snagged something on the river bottom, and I yelled for PFC Satterfield to cut it. He unsheathed his K-Bar and cut the rope, but in his haste the knife sliced through the line and stabbed him in the forehead. He began to bleed profusely, but at the moment that was the least of our worries.

It took all of my strength to heave Pechiney's limp body up onto the bank, since his waterlogged uniform made him all the heavier. Once we had him on dry ground I began to administer CPR, and I will never forget the gritty taste that must have come from the river bottom.

Lance Corporal Velasquez got on the radio and called for help. Within a few minutes an inflatable boat was launched, and after a bit I could see them paddling toward us through the rain as I continued my resuscitation efforts. When they finally arrived I turned my charge over to the corpsmen, and they continued to work on him until a medevac chopper arrived.

I later learned that our efforts had paid off, but only temporarily. Doctors at the hospital managed to restart Pechiney's heart, but in the end he died. He was only twenty-three years old.

Sergeant James Pechiney was buried with full honors at Arlington National Cemetery, and the entire company drove up to Virginia for the funeral. As taps sounded over his grave I thought back to the song that was playing on the radio that night. Dust in the Wind...

THE NEO

"An imperfect plan executed immediately and violently is far better than a perfect plan next week." – General George S. Patton

The Non-Combatant Evacuation Operation, or NEO for short, is one of the most important missions assigned to our military forces deployed around the world. Marines train exhaustively to perfect their ability to evacuate an entire expatriate American community from a foreign shore on a moment's notice, and we have seen the fruits of our labor time and again in places like Liberia, Somalia and Lebanon. One of the lesser known NEOs to be conducted by the Marine Corps occurred in Zaire during the early part of 1993, and regrettably never got a catchy code name like operations "Eagle Pull" and "Sharp Edge." That was probably because it was smaller in scope than most - two Marines to be exact - but it was a NEO nonetheless.

Brazzaville, Congo and Kinshasa, Zaire (now the Democratic Republic of the Congo) are not only the capitals of their respective countries, they are the closest neighboring capitals in the world, separated only by the Stanley Pool portion of the Congo River. Because of their proximity to each other and the volatile nature of the region it was inevitable for the two nations to constantly become entangled in each other's affairs, and sometimes we had no choice but to get involved also. Such was the case in the early part of 1993.

I had assumed command of the Marine Detachment in Brazzaville only a few months earlier, and had taken it upon myself to refit and repair the Embassy's twenty-five foot Boston Whaler. It was intended to be used to evacuate

145

personnel in the event of an emergency, but the craft had fallen into disrepair due to a combination of abuse and neglect. Within a few weeks the fuel tanks had been purged, the outboard motors overhauled, and a two way radio was even installed. As it turned out the work was completed just in the nick of time.

Trouble had been brewing across the river in Zaire for weeks. President Mobutu, who had ruled the country since it gained independence from Belgium more than thirty years earlier, was a despot who also happened to be one of the richest men in the world. While the people of his country wallowed in poverty, Mobutu lived in opulence. One of the ways he maintained his lifestyle was by printing more money, which by the way bore his own likeness, whenever he was short on cash. While this certainly did fill his coffers, it also caused massive inflation and devalued Zarois' currency to the point it was literally not worth the paper it was printed on.

The most common denomination was the one-*million* note, and a stack of them was required to buy even the most inexpensive item. Mobutu's solution was to issue the new five million Z note, but when those new bills were used to pay the army all hell broke loose when shopkeepers refused to accept them. Many people were killed in the hours that followed, including a number of westerners.

Our Ambassador's wife, Luci Phillips, was unfortunate enough to be in Kinshasa when the fighting erupted. We all listened to her speaking with her husband on a hand-held radio while tracers and RPGs crisscrossed the night sky over the Zarois capital, and it was clear by the tone of her voice that her situation was rather precarious. Then the following morning we learned the French ambassador there had been shot and killed, and as the casualties across the river

146

mounted it became clear she had to get out of there ASAP.

The Deputy Chief of Mission, Bill Gaines, approached me and asked if I would be willing to cross the river and pick up Mrs. Phillips. I agreed to do it, but stressed that I would have to get permission from my Company Commander first. In the meantime I had Corporal Grantham, who had volunteered to go along, prepare the boat while I attempted to place a phone call to Company headquarters in Nairobi. The Ambassador himself came down after about fifteen minutes and said that if we were going it was now or never. It was time to make a tough decision, and I made the one I believe any good Marine would make under similar circumstances.

Shortly after we launched the boat our Army Military Attaché, Lieutenant Colonel Jacobs, showed up at the dock with a truckload of French paratroopers. I hadn't expected that. They were armed to the teeth, and were being sent to reinforce their Embassy. What the hell, I figured, the more the merrier.

We weren't too sure what to expect when we reached the other side of the river, but within a few minutes the personal protection team from Kinshasa radioed instruction on where to land. The landing beach was located in a small cove, and I landed the French and withdrew as quickly as possible. There were snipers on the hill overlooking our position, and every few seconds we would hear the *crack* of a round passing overhead.

While the first boatload of paratroopers set up a defensive perimeter on the beachhead I returned across the river for some reinforcements. We landed a second time, and Mrs. Phillips was ushered aboard along with several other evacuees. For some reason the one that stands out in my mind is an Italian national who had been shot in the foot. I probably remember him because he was bleeding all over my nice, clean boat. I also noticed that the Ambassador's wife was in a bit of shock, but when I jokingly said "thank you for choosing Congo cruise lines," she laughed and seemed to snap out of it.

Detachment Commanders are required to send out what is known as an "Operational Incident Report" whenever something out of the ordinary occurred, and there was no doubt our little operation fit that profile. I sent the required message, and as soon as the CO read it received a scathing phone call. All I could think was, 'Oh, *now* the phones work!' It went something like this: "What the hell are you doing down there Gunny! Do you realize that you illegally crossed an international border and for all intents and purposes *invaded* a sovereign nation?" I was in big trouble, at least until Mrs. Phillips wrote a letter praising all concerned for saving her life.

My CO, Colonel Duggan, was a big man in stature and even bigger in the ways that really matter. Once he had a chance to read Mrs. Phillips' letter and gave the matter a bit more thought he phoned to let me know he was calling off the dogs. Ever since that affair he liked to call me Gunny Highway, which I took as high praise – especially from him.

NICE KITTY

"Talent alone won't make you a success. Neither will being in the right place at the right time, unless you are ready. The important question is: 'Are you ready'?" – Johnny Carson

One of the strangest events to occur during my tour in the Republic of the Congo took place during the summer of 1993 while the post was under an evacuation order for all dependants and non-essential personnel. The city of Brazzaville had been a maze of armed barricades for several weeks, and a 1900 curfew was in effect in an attempt to limit the proliferation of running gun battles in the streets. One deceptively idyllic Sunday afternoon, while the guns were silent, some of the Embassy staff decided to take advantage of the lull and get out for a while.

One of those who ventured out was a communicator named Ann who went to the local zoo along with a visiting Diplomatic Courier to feed the lions. The Brazzaville Zoo in no way resembles the San Diego Zoo since the animals are given scarcely enough food to survive, with the "surplus" going to the families of the zookeepers. The courier, who was based in Frankfurt Germany, foolishly stepped over the low barrier that separates visitors from the cages and held out a piece of fish. When Ann called out to her she turned her head, and as she did so the lion decided that he would rather have *her* for lunch than the fish. He hooked the courier with his claw and pulled her arm through the bars of the cage - and proceeded to bite off most of her right shoulder as well as a chunk of her left forearm.

A local employee of the chimpanzee project which is collocated with the zoo beat the lion with a stick in an

149

attempt to get him to release his grip, and Ann got on her handheld radio and began to scream hysterically. I was at my residence several blocks away when the initial call came in and spent several minutes along with our Political Officer and the Marine on duty trying to get a coherent response out of her. Fortunately for the courier the employee who had wrested her from the lion's grasp had enough presence of mind to apply a tourniquet, and when we arrived we were able to take her by taxi to what passes for a hospital in Africa.

I then mobilized my detachment, and along with the Political Officer began rounding up surgical supplies and blood donors (the local supply was tainted with AIDS) via radio. The Embassy staff arranged for a medically equipped aircraft to come in from Johannesburg to fly the victim to South Africa, and later that night a military escort provided by the Congolese helped ensure our convoy got to the airport without incident despite the curfew.

Several articles were written in various publications about the incident, none of which were accurate, and the whole thing was largely forgotten save for the occasional lion joke. That is until the State Department, in a classic example of why it is one of the largest and least effective bureaucracies in the world, presented Ann with an award for *heroism*. We're still trying to figure that one out.

Everyone involved from the blood donors to the pilot of the medevac aircraft had done more than she, but if anyone truly deserved the label of hero it was the Congolese gentlemen who took immediate action and saved the courier's life.

CREATURE COMFORTS

"When in doubt, empty your magazine!"

In December of 1998 a Marine officer passed along a story told by then-Lieutenant General Tommy Franks of Central Command:

After all the briefings concluded, the General ended the meeting by relating a visit he had made along with the American Ambassador to Battalion Landing Team 2/4, just hours after a fatal Humvee accident. The General reminded the assembled officers that Marines live in holes and don't have a house to live in like "heavy forces." They had no tank or tents to sleep in - they carry their 'house' on their back and live in fighting holes. Although the Marines had just lost a buddy, their spirit was "uplifting."

He said a question by the Ambassador to a Marine Private drove the point home. The Ambassador asked a Private sitting in his fighting hole, "How is it here in the hole?"

The Private answered, "Kind of like the beach without water."

The Ambassador then asked, "If you could get something, what would you like to have?"

At this point General Franks related to the assembled officers how most troops would have answered, "a hot meal," or "a cot," or "a shower," but this Marine Private said, "I could use some more ammunition, Sir!"

DICK DINGLEHOFFER

"Lead, follow, or get the hell out of the way – but do *something*!"

During my time as a Detachment Commander on the Marine Security Guard Program I was required to work closely with members of the State Department, and it was an eye opening experience to be sure. I had always expected the people entrusted with formulating and implementing the foreign policy of the United States to be something special, and while there were a *few* who lived up to my expectations most of the members of State I knew were hypocritical, selfish prima donnas whose only interest was the advancement of their own careers. Whenever a decision had to be made their first thought would invariably be "how will I look" rather than "what is the right thing to do."

One of the Foreign Service's all stars of incompetence was the Regional Security Officer in Kinshasa, Zaire, who I will call 'Dick Dinglehoffer.' He was such a buffoon that virtually everyone in the Embassy, including his very own assistant RSO, invariably referred to him by using a number of decidedly unflattering nicknames when not in his presence. Dick had spent many years developing his reputation, with his crowning achievement being his inept handling of security in the Embassy in Moscow where he was largely responsible for the now infamous Lonetree incident. Why he wasn't sacked remains a mystery to this day, as anyone who is familiar with Diplomatic Security and has read the book *Moscow Station* will agree.

I am not inclined to believe a lot of what I hear because facts tend to get distorted in telling and retelling a story, so I gave Mr. Dinglehoffer the benefit of the doubt until I had the opportunity to judge for myself. Dick, for his part, wasted little time proving his reputation was not only well deserved, but had in fact been grossly understated.

Zaire, while not the most stable country in the world, was no worse than most of the other so-called African republics. Rife with disease, inflation (one million Zaires equaled about 12 US *cents* in 1993), and corruption, the country had been under the rule of the dictator Mobutu since gaining independence from Belgium thirty years earlier. So it was not the least bit surprising when civil war broke out.

The main reason we visited the Embassy in Zaire was they had a small commissary, and we didn't. The ferry between the two countries had stopped running due to the ongoing conflict, so it was decided I would cross the river in the Embassy boat to pick up supplies for our families. Easier said than done. What started out as a simple shopping trip turned into an odyssey filled with international intrigue.

Martial law was proclaimed in Zaire just about the time I shoved off from Brazzaville, and if I had known I wouldn't have gone. When I arrived the Zarois customs people kept my diplomatic passport, no doubt in an attempt to elicit a bribe in exchange for its return - and that just wasn't going to happen. I was told by the Kinshasa RSO to stay in Zaire until it was returned, but as time dragged on I grew more and more impatient. My detachment in the Congo was "down two," and the guy telling me it was "too dangerous to cross the river" had recently declared a state of emergency because someone heard a tire blowout. Dinglehoffer thought it was a gunshot.

Since the RSO had deemed a river crossing to be too hazardous a plan was hatched to smuggle us out on a small commercial airplane. We were each issued new civilian passports, but were prevented from boarding because they did not have an entry stamp. The Zarois Army arrested us as spies and took us to a holding area. I decided that NOW was the time for bribery, and slipped some money to a guard in exchange for our freedom.

A couple of days later I decided enough was enough. I had the detachment chauffeur drive my corporal and I down to the Embassy dock, and we casted off before anyone could stop us. We crossed the Congo River without incident, and the dangers the RSO had warned us about never materialized. Naturally Dinglehoffer raised hell when he found out we had left, and of course that led to an investigation.

My CO sent an investigating officer out from Nairobi to check into the RSO's complaint, but things worked out for the best in the end. The Captain who came thought Dinglehoffer was a moron, and understood why I had done what I had done. What's more, he had served in the Gulf as a platoon commander with 1st Force Recon, and we had a lot of mutual acquaintances. Of course, that had no bearing whatsoever on his findings…

That same officer eventually became part of the Marine Corps Congressional liaison office after his tour on the MSG program was over, and several years later accompanied a delegation of politicians to Camp Pendleton for a "dog and pony show." I was manning an exhibit of special operations radio gear, and had no idea he was in the AO. He was now a Major, and when he reached my display he took one look at me and exclaimed, "Holy shit. I heard you were dead!"

Fortunately *that* report of my demise was somewhat premature…

THE MARINE CORPS
And Psychotherapy

By Fred Reed

"That which does not kill you makes you stronger." – Friedrich Nietchze

Tell you what, I've had it with whiners. Furthermore, if I hear the phrase "self-esteem" again, I'm going to kill something. It'll happen. Just wait and see. Some New Age, psychotherapeutically babbling little parsnip is going to gurgle to me about how arduous his life is, when he probably doesn't have a life to begin with, and about how it's somebody else's fault, probably mine, and his self-esteem is all bruised and rancid and has warts on it. And I'm going to stuff him into a concrete mixer.

No, wait. I've got a better idea. I'll pack him off instead to Marine Corps boot camp at Parris Island, in the festering mosquito swamps of South Carolina. I spent a summer there long ago, in a philosophy battalion. All battalions at PI are philosophy battalions. The chief philosopher was named Sergeant Cobb, and he was rough as one. His philosophy was that at oh-dark-thirty we should leap up like spring-loaded jackrabbits when he threw the lid of a GI can down the squad bay. Then, he figured, we should spend the day at a dead run, except when we were learning such socially useful behavior as shooting someone at five hundred yards.

He didn't care whether we wanted to do these things. He didn't care whether we could do them. We were going to do them. And we did. The drill instructors had a sideline in therapy. They did attitude adjustment. If the urge to whine overcame any of us, Sergeant Cobb took his attitude tool - it was a size-twelve boot on the end of his right leg - and made the necessary adjustments. It was wonderful therapy. It put us in touch with our feelings. We felt like not whining any more.

I kid about it, but it really was philosophy. We learned that there are things you have to do. We learned that we could generally do them. We also learned, if we didn't already know, that whimpering is humiliating. The Marine view of life, which would eradicate American politics in about three seconds if widely applied, was simple: Solve your problems, live with them, or have the grace to shut up about them.

Can you imagine what this approach would do to the talk-show racket?

Fat housewife to Oprah: "My... I just won't... being so... heavy... hurts my self-esteem."

Oprah: "So stop sniveling and eat less. Next!"

The Corps believed in personal responsibility. If your life had turned to a landfill, it might be somebody else's fault. Maybe existence had dropped the green weenie on your plate. It happens. But the odds were that you had contributed to your own problems. Anyway, *everybody* gets a raw deal sometimes. Life isn't a honeymoon in the Catskills. Deal with it. I remember a coffee mug in an armored company's day room: "To err is human, to forgive, divine. Neither of which is Marine Corps policy." There's something to be said for it.

Nowadays everybody's a self-absorbed victim, and self-respect and strength of character have become symptoms of emotional insufficiency. Oh, alas, alack, sniffle, eeek, squeak, the world's picking on me because I'm black, brown, ethnic, fat, female, funny-looking, dysfunctional, dat-functional, don't use deodorant, or can't get dates. And sensitive? Dear God. If people suffer the tiniest slight, they

156

call for a support group and three lawyers. (Support groups: When I'm dictator, we'll use 'em for bowling pins.)

Whatever happened to grown-ups? It's incredible the things people whinny about. Go to the self-pity section of your bookstore. It's usually called "Self Help." You'll find books called things like, "The Agony of Hangnails: A Survivor's Guide." They will explain coping strategies, and assure you that you are still a good person, shredding digits and all. Other books will tell you that because you had an unhappy childhood (who didn't?) you are now an abused, pallid, squashed little larva, and no end pathetic. Other books will tell you how not to be toxic to your Inner Child. (I'm writing a book now: "Dropping Your Inner Child Down A Well.") We'd be better off if most people's inner children were orphans.

I once sat in on somebody else's group-therapy session, which was concerned about the morbid condition of the patients' self-esteem. I didn't understand the rules of therapy, and said approximately, "Look, maybe if you folks stopped feeling sorry for yourselves and got a life, things might be better." I thought I was contributing an insight, but it turned out to be the wrong answer. The therapist, an earnest lady - all therapists seem to be earnest ladies - told me firmly, and with much disappointment in me, that this was No Laughing Matter. The patients' self-esteems were undergoing cardiopulmonary resuscitation, and I was suggesting that they get a life instead of picking at their psychic scabs. She reckoned I was pretty terrible.

Stuff 'em into a concrete mixer, I say.

Fred Reed is a syndicated columnist and former Marine.

THE EXAM

"If you can find humor in anything, you can survive it." – Bill Cosby

One of the least glamorous things about being on jump and dive status is the requirement for frequent, stringent physical exams. I realize the environmental rigors associated with high altitudes require us to be in perfect health, but that doesn't make getting poked and prodded any less annoying.

An unfortunate requirement of those exams is the dreaded "digital rectal exam." It is designed to detect prostate cancer, and the older I get the more I understand the need for such exams in men over forty. It's *not* so easy for twenty-something Marines to accept, however. I can recall one young Marine in particular. When he returned from his appointment he had a thousand-yard stare - he was obviously taking things harder than most. When he finally spoke all he said was, "Staff Sergeant, I've been violated!"

A mean trick sometimes played on unsuspecting troops by Navy medical personnel involved the prostate exam. The examinee would drop his trousers, lean against the exam table, and steel himself for what was coming. The doctor would insert his digit and begin probing, and then casually rest his free hand on the patient's shoulder. While this was going on a corpsman would quietly enter the room in such a manner that the examinee was unaware of his presence, and then proceed to place one of *his* hands on the *other* shoulder.

At that point the Marine's mind begins to process data at the cyclic rate. "Okay - there in a hand on each of my shoulders, and the guy behind me is in the *Navy*. So what the hell is *that* in my rectum?"

And people wonder why we give squids a hard time.

UNFRIENDLY FIRE

By Mark Shields

"The bended knee is not a tradition of our Corps."
- General Alexander A. Vandergrift, USMC to the Senate Naval Affairs Committee, 1946

Press bias is an ugly thing. It really makes no difference if that bias is unintentional or even unconscious. Take the bias of the American elite - academic, financial and social - against the American military. Nowhere is that bias more obvious than the establishment press choosing to identify criminals and other anti-social misfits by their former association with the U.S. Marine Corps, as in: "Ex-Marine terrorizes shopping center." Have you ever seen a story that began: "Ex-draft-dodger convicted of bilking widows and orphans out of their life savings?"

This summer in Bristol, Connecticut a thirty-two year-old drifter "with a history of mental problems" used a church candlestick to murder a Catholic priest who had told him he could not sleep in the church. How did the New York Times describe him? That's right: "a former Marine."

And when Lee Williams, a twenty-three year-old student at Wayne State University in Michigan, sued a tattoo parlor for embarrassment and the cost of plastic surgery needed to cover up "villian" - instead of "villain" - on his arm, what did the Associated Press tell us about Williams (who had consented to the misspelling)? Of course: He was a "former Marine."

And now that the University of Texas has reopened its 307-foot-high clock tower, which was closed in 1975 after a series of suicides, we are reminded that Charles Whitman,

159

the psychopath who shot fourteen people dead and left thirty-one wounded there in 1966, was "a former Marine."

Bias is not simply ugly; it is stupid as well. Elitists never notice that the U.S. military imposes far higher standards of conduct and duty upon its officers than does either civilian life or the vaunted private sector on its members. Lying or adultery or sexual harassment can instantaneously end a military officer's career. The same cannot be said for a CEO or for the highest civilian federal official.

These are not easy times for military recruiters. Even with $6,000 signing bonuses and generous college tuition benefits to offer, the Army, Air Force and Navy have not been able to meet their enlistment quotas. This country's long economic boom and the lowest unemployment rate in the history of the all-volunteer service have made the military recruiter's task a tough one. Yet for fifty-one consecutive months the Marine Corps, alone of the services, has met and surpassed its recruitment quota. And to meet that quota, the Marines have not - as other branches have done - lowered their academic or intelligence standards. In fact, they have raised them higher than the Pentagon requirements.

Unlike their sister services, which woo recruits with tangible promises of travel, compensation, tuition and retirement packages, the Marines offer intangibles: the opportunity to belong to something bigger than the individual; a grueling challenge; the test of being held to a higher standard; sacrifice and self-reliance. As Captain Jeff Sammons, a twenty-year Marine and former enlisted man, explains, "We want you to join the Marine Corps for one reason and for one reason only - because you want to be a Marine."

What Marine service does for those fortunate enough to experience it is important. From the first day of boot camp a

Marine recruit learns that Marines never leave their dead or their wounded - their own - behind. Liberals especially ought to stand in grateful awe of this Marine Corps ethic, which contradicts the unbridled individualism that elevates personal well-being, comfort and profit above any obligation one might owe to his community or to his country.

American liberals may have led the good fight for civil rights, but the greatest civil rights victories have been won by the American military, including the Marines. Why is the American military the most integrated sector of American life today? Charles Moskos, the wonderful military scholar from Northwestern University, offers two reasons: no racial discrimination and no racial preference.

Up to now the 2000 campaign has been conspicuously silent and sterile on the subject of what we Americans owe to each other and to America. What are our duties as Americans that our would-be leaders ask of us? What sacrifices are we as Americans willing to make?

I don't know. But the Marines know.

This story originally appeared in the Washington Post in October of 1999

147 DEGREES IN THE SHADE

"In the snows of far off northern lands, and in sunny tropic scenes..."
- From the Marines' Hymn

The Marine Corps Air-Ground Combat Center at 29 Palms California, better known as "29 Stumps" or simply "the Stumps," occupies some of the most desolate real estate to be found anywhere in the United States. It is located in the Mojave Desert about midway between Palm Springs and Death Valley, and is an ideal place to conduct live fire Combined Arms exercises because it is in the middle of nowhere. It also has the dubious distinction of being close to where both James Dean and comedian Sam Kinison were killed in car crashes. What a *lousy* place to die!

I have gone there for training on a number of occasions and eventually came to the realization there are civilians living outside the main gate who actually *chose* to move to that God forsaken place of their own free will. These so-called "desert rats" are a unique breed who have literally, in my humble estimation, been out in the sun too long. They claim those of us who temporarily visit their desert paradise do not stay long enough to develop an appreciation for their way of life, but I seriously doubt that would occur if I was to remain for a hundred years.

The desert does funny things to people. Have you ever seen the commercial where they are frying an egg and say "this is your brain on drugs?" Well that's exactly how it feels out there. One summer we were out in the Delta Corridor and it was so hot, 147 degrees by one report, we were not allowed to do anything other than find a bit of shade and drink water by the gallon. The only responsibility anyone had was to fill up water bladders and hang them in the breeze.

One of the Marines in our platoon at that time was a Lance Corporal by the name of Smith. When it was Smitty's turn to fill the bladders he flatly refused, and the sergeant running the detail just snapped and started choking the life out of him. It took three of us to pry his fingers from around Smitty's throat. Like I said, the desert does funny things to people.

In fairness to that sergeant Smitty *was* a little bit "off," if you know what I mean. He had a habit of sitting on his rack aiming an M-16 at people as they walked by, and we were eventually forced to take it away from him. Not surprisingly, no one wanted to be in front of Smith during live fire assaults!

Then one day I was sitting around reading a book when some wise-guy tossed a mat of firecrackers into our hootch. It was almost comical watching everyone dive for cover. To a man we thought Smitty had gotten hold of some live ammo and had finally come undone...

HIGH FLYIN' TIMES

By George Kremer

"Blunt words often have the sharpest edge!"

We were in the middle of the ESPN "X-Games," which is kind of an extreme winter sports competition with skiing, snowboarding, snowmobiles and motor-cross motorcycles. One of the big sponsors of the event was the United States Marine Corps. They flew out some of their top recruiters for a working vacation, along with two CH-53E helicopters and two Cobra attack helicopters.

The choppers served as static displays at the event, and did a fly-over as well. Needless to say the Marines were giving rides to the muckity-mucks involved in the event and in the local government. Nice, round race-track patterns, and then back to the airport for another load.

Yours truly couldn't be held back with a team of wild horses, and I was taking pictures from the tarmac since I have an airport security pass. Did I mention I just happened to be wearing a certain black ball cap with the Third Recon logo on it, and the Eagle, Globe and Anchors on my uniform collar? Well, Captain Cambell with the Marine Corps contingent was shooting the breeze with me and asked if I would like to go up for a ride in a CH-53E.

WOULD I!

He asked if I was a "good flier," as they were now going to be doing some filming of the Cobras and of the event below for ESPN and for future Marine Corps events. He mentioned that the chopper may "move a little quicker" than what I had been seeing from the ground. Hmmmmm.

Off we went with all the doors off and the rear ramp open! We flew close to the terrain and made unbelievable turns while playing "chase me, catch you" with the Cobras! All in and out of the 14,000-foot mountains that surrounded us. I had no idea a big chopper like the CH-53 could do those maneuvers! I even got to go sit in the middle jump seat in the cockpit and watch the show from there. We did a fly-over of the event at about one hundred feet or so, and it was just great. Hard turns, dives and climbs were the order of the day for the rest of the morning until lunchtime.

I am not sure, but I think it was a week or so before the grin on my face wore off! The whole group of Marines were some of the sharpest, most squared away and professional I have yet to meet - a great example for the twelve thousand people who attended the games.

Later on, back in the "real" world, I was given a noise complaint call from one of the illustrious citizens who make Aspen their part-time home. Seems he wasn't happy with the choppers flying over his estate, and wanted something done about the noise. I'll probably catch Hell for it later, but I told him in no uncertain terms that "noise" was the sound of Freedom - and he had damn well better appreciate it!

I told him of my cousin Luke Kremer in his Hornet putting his life on the line over Afghanistan for this idiot so he could call up and complain. I told him of Rick Buesch's lifetime of giving so others could express themselves, and of my Dad's long walk out from the Chosin Reservoir so people like him could continue to make money - and then bitch when the very men who gave him that right, and who continue to protect it, happen to fly over his house in a show of patriotism, freedom and honor. Then I hung up!

MISTER ROGERS
Neighborhood

"Courage is endurance, for one moment more..."

One of the real characters I have known is my old friend Pat Rogers. I first met Pat when he joined 2/25 as a reservist in Garden City New York, and he wasted no time making an impression. He possesses a caustic wit, and is easily one of the most opinionated people I know. Just my kind of guy!

Like many reservists Pat was a cop, in this case with the NYPD. He is relatively diminutive in stature, but larger than life nonetheless. When someone asked if it was difficult for a small guy to be a city cop Pat commented that he had a black belt. We all nodded, duly impressed. After a short pause he added, "it's the one I hang my gun on."

It was Pat who organized my first parachute jump, along with half of the STA platoon, at the skydiving center in Lakewood, New Jersey. Freefalling was a passion with him, and if the weather was good there was a pretty good chance Pat was somewhere putting his "knees in the breeze."

Pat had served with 3rd Tank Battalion in Vietnam, and has many yarns to tell about that nasty little war. He always found a way to get into the middle of the action, and that didn't change much as he got older. During the Gulf War I happened to pick up a copy of *Marines Magazine* and to my surprise there was an article about Pat, now a CWO, training Marines in shooting skills prior to their deployment. He has since transferred his love of shooting to the private sector, and travels all over the world training special operations forces in the fine art of gunfighting.

One morning late in my career I was at our daily staff meeting when Colonel Coates informed us a "Mr. Rogers" would be training the company on the new M4 carbine out at Range 130. Someone made a joke concerning Fred Rogers from the children's television show, but when the CO added this individual was a former Marine Warrant Officer and retired NYPD detective I did a double take. It could only be one person.

We hadn't seen each other in many years, so I immediately drove out to the range to find my old friend. As I approached the firing line I could see a group of Marines gathered around one of the ready tables. It was easy to pick out Pat. He was holding court just like I remembered, and was engrossed in telling one of his patented tales.

When I was within about twenty feet I pointed at him, and with all the authority I could muster said, "I'm sorry, but you're going to have to leave." I then extended my arm to indicate a height of about five foot five. "You have to be at least this tall to fire on this range!" He peered at me more closely, and his eyes shifted to the name tape over my pocket. The expression on his face was priceless.

CODE TALKERS

By Bruce Watson

"Don't be afraid to go out on a limb. That's where the fruit is!"

During World War II Marines storming Pacific beaches used a unique kind of code machine. Each Marine Corps cryptograph had two arms, two legs, an M-1 rifle and a helmet. Their code name was *Dineh* – "the People." In English they were called the "Navajo Code Talkers," and theirs is one of the few unbroken codes in military history.

Like all Americans of his generation, Keith Little, who is a Navajo, remembers exactly where he was when he heard the news of Pearl Harbor. Little, then sixteen, was attending boarding school on the reservation in Arizona.

"Me and a bunch of guys were out hunting rabbits with a .22," he recalls. "Somebody went to the dorm, came back and said, 'Hey, Pearl Harbor was bombed!'

"One of the boys asked, 'Where's Pearl Harbor?'

'In Hawaii.'

'Who did it?'

'Japan.'

'Why'd they do it?'

'They hate Americans. They want to kill all Americans.'

'Us too?'

'Yeah, us too.'"

Then and there, the boys made a promise to one another. They'd go after the Japanese instead of the rabbits.

The next morning the superintendent of the reservation looked out his office window and saw dozens of ponytailed young men carrying hunting rifles, ready to fight. But the Navajo volunteers were sent home. No official call to arms had been issued, and besides, most of the men spoke only Navajo.

When the war broke out, a man named Philip Johnston had an extraordinary idea. Johnston, the son of missionaries, also grew up on the reservation and was fluent in Navajo. Early in 1942 he visited the Marine Corps' Camp Elliott, north of San Diego, and proposed to use the Navajo language as an up-to-date code, guaranteed unbreakable.

The Marines were skeptical at first. At the time, military codes were encrypted by high-tech black boxes that used rotors and ratchets to shroud messages in a thick alphabet soup. Still, Johnston returned with a few Navajo friends. For fifteen minutes, while the iron jaws of Marine brass went slack, messages metamorphosed from English to Navajo and back.

In the spring of 1942 Marine recruiters came to the Navajo Nation in the mile-high Southwest desert. There, among the sagebrush and sandstone, they set up tables, called them enlistment offices and began looking for a few good men fluent in Navajo and English.

Fewer than eighty years had passed since the Navajos had fought against the U.S. military. Kit Carson's scorched earth campaign had broken their resistance in 1864. Why would men volunteer to fight for a nation that had humbled their ancestors, killed their herds and wouldn't even let them vote?

Soldiers enlist for reasons of jobs, adventure, family tradition – and patriotism. Says one Navajo who fought in World War II, "This conflict involved Mother Earth being dominated by foreign countries. It was our responsibility to defend her."

Swift, Silent and Surrounded

Few Navajos had ever been off the reservation. Mostly, they had only met "Anglos" on trading posts. Soon they would fight across an ocean they had never seen, against an enemy they had never met. Yet they proved to be model Marines. Accustomed to walking miles each day in the high desert, they marched on with full packs after others buckled. When training was finished the first group of Navajos became the 382nd Platoon, USMC, and was ordered to make a code.

On the reservation the language was primarily oral, and the Code Talkers were told to keep it that way. There would be no code books, no cryptic algorithms. Navajo itself was puzzling enough. Germans deciphering English codes could tap common linguistic roots. Japanese eavesdropping on GIs were often graduates of American universities. But Navajo, a tonal language, was known to few outsiders. Its vowels rise and fall, changing meaning with pitch. A single Navajo verb, containing its own subjects, objects and adverbs, can translate into an entire English sentence.

To devise the code, the Navajos turned to nature. They named planes after birds: *gini* – chicken hawk (dive bomber); *neasjah* – owl (observation plane); *taschizzie* – swallow (torpedo plane). They named ships after fish: *lotso* – whale (battleship); *calo* – shark (destroyer); *beshlo* – iron fish (submarine).

To spell out proper names the Code Talkers made a Navajo bestiary, turning the Marines' *A*ble *B*aker *C*harlie… into Wollachee Shush Moasi… (*A*nt *B*ear *C*at). They also played word games. "District" became the Navajo words for "deer ice strict," and "belong" became "long bee."

The finished code was a hodgepodge of everyday Navajo and some four hundred newly devised code words. As a test, Navy intelligence officers spent three weeks trying, and failing, to decipher a single message. New Navajo recruits untrained in the code could not break it. Yet it seemed too simple to be trusted. And while codes normally took hours to translate, these Indians were encoding and decoding sensitive military information almost instantly. What kind of magic was this?

"In Navajo, everything – songs, prayers – is in memory," said William McCabe, one of the code's designers. "That's the way we was raised up. So we didn't have no trouble."

Two Code Talkers stayed behind to teach the next group; the rest were shipped to Guadalcanal. There, Code Talkers met skepticism in the flesh. One colonel agreed to use the Navajos only if they won a man-versus-machine test against a cylindrical gizmo that disguised words and broadcast in coded clicks. The Code talkers won handily. Still, other officers were reluctant to trust lives to a code untested in combat.

More than 3,600 Navajos served in World war II, but only 420 became Code Talkers. In boot camp Keith Little was just another Indian, and few cared from which tribe. Then a drill instructor took him aside and asked, "By any chance, are you a Navajo?" He was sent to Code Talkers school.

Eventually Marine commanders came to see the code as indispensable for rapid transmission of classified dispatches. Lent to the Navy, the Code Talkers kept the Japanese from learning of impending air attacks. On Saipan, an advancing U.S. battalion was shelled from behind by "friendly fire." Desperate messages were sent, "hold your fire,'" but the Japanese had imitated Marine broadcasts all day. Mortar crews weren't sure what to believe. The shelling continued. Finally headquarters asked, "Do you have a Navajo?" A Code Talker sent the same message to his buddy, and the shelling stopped.

During the first two days on Iwo Jima six networks of Code Talkers transmitted more than eight hundred messages without error. On the morning of February 23, 1945, the Stars and Stripes were hoisted on a mountaintop. The word went out in Navajo code. Cryptographers translated the Navajo words for "mouse turkey sheep uncle ram ice bear ant cat horse intestines," then told their fellow Marines in English that the American flag flew over Mt. Suribachi. A signal officer recalled, "Were it not for the Navajo, the Marines would never have taken Iwo Jima."

When the war ended, the Navajo headed home to their reservation. But the code itself remained top secret. Asked about the war, Code Talkers simply said, "I was a radioman." Finally in 1968 the code was declassified, and the secret was out.

In 1992 Keith Little was invited to the Pentagon, where he translated a prayer for peace phoned in by a Code Talker in Arizona. Then, Little and other Navajo vets helped dedicate a permanent exhibit on the Code Talkers.

"Most of us are common men," Little once said. But in school, all young Navajo learning native studies read about the Code talkers. The students all agree that without them, "We could have lost the war."

In code, the Talkers spoke of snipers and fortifications, but their real message needed no interpreter. Their heroes spoke of overcoming stereotypes and past conflicts for a higher cause, about blending tradition into the modern world. They spoke Navajo.

This story originally appeared in "Chicken Soup for the Veteran's Soul"

ROLLO THE CLOWN

"His men would follow him anywhere, but only out of curiosity." - Excerpt from a fitness report

The hills of Korea have been the scene of many great moments in Marine Corps history, but operation "Bear Hunt 86" wasn't destined to be one of them. Of that I was certain long before we ever set out from Okinawa aboard *USS Dubuque*, and looking back it's not hard to understand why. My sense of impending doom can be traced back to one particular moment in time, that being my introduction to one Staff Sergeant 'Rollo.'

Since my arrival on "The Rock" I had heard an inordinate number of rumors about Rollo, most of which I dismissed as being ridiculous. For some reason our paths had never crossed, so it was difficult to decide for myself if there was a grain of truth in any of the stories I had heard. That all changed the day I was assigned to "C" Company for Bear Hunt, since he was their company Gunny.

I've always considered myself to be a Marine who follows regulations, but sometimes situations arise that necessitate throwing away the book and applying a bit of common sense. Unfortunately for us, Rollo was forced to apply the book to *every* situation, because he did not possess one iota of common sense. If you doubt such a thing is possible, consider this: our company was operating in the field under conditions which can only be described as miserably cold. One fine and frigid morning Rollo suddenly appeared and ordered an immediate company formation. Based upon the urgency in his manner we all figured something the magnitude of the North Koreans crossing the 38th parallel must have occurred, but as it turned out the only one who considered it important was Rollo himself. He was furious because he had noticed some of the troops were wearing scarves wrapped around their necks in such a way as to ward off the bitter cold rather than draped in a "V" in the approved manner. Needless to say this prompted those of us who didn't already have scarves wrapped around our necks to do so right then and there, which of course had the desired effect and made Rollo all the madder. It was during this formation one of the troops hung the nickname "Rollo the Clown" on him, and it stuck.

Another incident that comes to mind occurred when we first arrived in the base camp area. Each unit was billeted in a series of GP tents, each of which was equipped with a kerosene heater. While our floor was frozen Korean real estate, the MAB headquarters and WM tents had the added luxury of a plywood floor. This prompted the camp fire marshal to issue a directive stating those tents possessing wood floors must place a dirt filled box under their stoves to soak up residual kerosene. This made perfect sense to us until Rollo showed up and insisted *we* must follow suit and place a box of dirt on top of our dirt floor. After losing the ensuing argument we dutifully constructed the box, and its presence served as a source of constant amusement for the remainder of our stay.

Yet another memorable confrontation occurred about a week later. The road bordering our area was a sea of mud during daylight hours, so we dug a foot wide drainage ditch along the shoulder to alleviate the problem. It did the trick, and everything was fine until Rollo approached me and said he wanted a footbridge built so the Captain wouldn't have to step across the ditch. I pointed out it was only a foot wide, and after a lively discussion (which I lost) set out to scrounge some lumber. I soon located some suitable wood scraps and the job was completed inside of twenty minutes - but that, of course, was not the end of that. Rollo insisted I make the bridge larger and move it a couple of feet closer to the head so as not to inconvenience the Skipper. Needless to say I was fit to be tied, but after fuming for a bit decided to follow his instructions to the letter. After enlisting the aid of a couple of troops, I got to work building what would soon be known as the "Rollo Memorial Bridge." A few sixteen foot 2x4's and a couple of 4x8 sheets of plywood later it was ready, complete with towers and suspension lines. I stretched some toilet paper across one end and waited with scissors in hand for Rollo to return so our bridge could be christened with a proper ribbon cutting ceremony. The ass chewing I took was well worth the look on his face.

These stories, along with dozens more which have yet to be chronicled, prompted a sort of cult following for Rollo amongst the "boys in Company C." Bets were placed on how long it would take him to top his latest directive, and to his credit he never kept us waiting long.

As our departure from Korea drew near we decided we had to do something to commemorate our stay, so some of us got together and went to town. There was little danger of running into Rollo out there because in the course of three months he had not ventured out the gate even once. What we came up with was a T-shirt that said "Rollo Busters," below which was a red circle containing a slash. Centered in the circle was a pair of "birth control" glasses, which had become Rollo's symbol because he always wore them, probably even while sleeping. On the day we left we wore those shirts under our field jackets and even replaced the company guideon with one. When Rollo saw them it marked the only time I can ever recall seeing him speechless.

175

O' CANADA!

"Marines are about the most peculiar breed of human beings I have ever witnessed. They treat their service as if it were some kind of cult, plastering their emblem on almost everything they own, making themselves up to look like insane fanatics with haircuts to ungentlemanly lengths, worshipping their Commandant almost as if he were a god, and making weird animal noises like a band of savages. They'll fight like rabid dogs at the drop of a hat just for the sake of a little action, and are the cockiest sons of bitches I have ever known. Most have the foulest mouths and drink well beyond man's normal limits, but their high spirits and sense of brotherhood set them apart and, generally speaking, the United States Marines I've come in contact with are the most professional soldiers and the finest men I have ever had the pleasure to meet." - An Anonymous Canadian

Back in 1979 the biggest news story in America was the Iranian Hostage Crisis. It was a long and painful episode in our nation's history, and one of the few bright spots occurred when the Canadian embassy in Teheran spirited a handful of American diplomats out of the country before they could be captured by the Iranians. In recognition of that act there were large billboards erected at many border crossings between our two nations proclaiming "Thank You Canada!" That incident really brought our two nations together.

That same year my unit went to Fort Drum, New York for a two week training period. The base, for anyone not familiar with it, is located just south of the US-Canada border near Watertown. We trained hard while in the field, and at the conclusion of the exercise my entire platoon decided to go out and 'kill a few brain cells.' We were leaving for home the next day, and the idea of a cold one was appealing. Unfortunately the Army owned the base, and didn't display a great deal of hospitality toward us. When we tried to get into the main Enlisted Club we were turned away because we didn't have "club cards." But we were still thirsty.

After scouting around for a bit we discovered a small, comparatively Spartan club in the far reaches of the base. It was not frequented by many Army personnel, and had been "adopted" by some Canadians who had come across the border for training. We made a beeline for the bar, and when we discovered the club was filled with Canadians one of us made a toast in recognition of what their government had done for our citizens. We backed that toast up with the purchase of several cases of beer, and before long we were all the best of friends. The Queens Own Rifles, as their unit was known, reciprocated by offering a toast to the Marine Corps, calling it the finest fighting force ever.

The Canucks had a bagpiper with them, and he got up on a table and began to play the Marines' Hymn. If you have ever heard that song played on the pipes you know the sound is almost spiritual. Every man, Marine and Canadian alike, stood at ramrod attention. When the last note sounded a cheer went up, and the club soon resembled the winning locker room after game seven of the World Series.

There was more beer than we could possibly drink, so some of the more inebriated members of the party began shaking cans and spraying everyone with the excess brew. After a short while we were all soaked to the bone, and it was something to see. Unfortunately the fun and games came to a halt when the Canadians discovered someone had stolen the dirk, or small ceremonial knife, that had been strapped to the piper's leg.

It was quickly decided by all present that the guilty party must be a member of the U.S. Army, and just like that a brawl broke out. I actually felt sorry for those doggies. It looked just like the beginning of the old F-Troop TV show!

Within minutes the sound of approaching sirens filled the air as the MPs descended on our little club.

We ran outside and soon realized there was no way to escape, since we had all arrived on foot. Just when it looked like the jig was up our pal Charlie Devine came through and pulled up in a six-by he had somehow 'acquired' - just in the nick of time. We piled aboard and he made a run for it. No one ever asked Charlie where he had gotten the truck, but he sure saved the day.

We were quite a sight at formation the next morning. All of our equipment and uniforms had been packed and loaded onto trucks to enable us to get an early start, and we were forced to wear the same uniforms from the previous evening. We stunk! Nothing smells quite as foul as stale beer, and our CO, Major Blaich, got a good whiff as he stood downwind of us. He kept his remarks short and to the point. "I don't know what STA Platoon was up to last night," he said "but it couldn't have been good. Let's get on the buses and get out of here before someone tells me something I don't want to know!"

MOOSE ON THE LOOSE

"An 'expert' is always able to create confusion out of simplicity!"

One of the most professional reconnaissance Marines I have known was a Sergeant by the name of Paul Moose. He and I crossed paths many times over the years, and every time I see him I can't help but think of an incident that occurred at Camp Lejeune during the eighties.

Moose's First Sergeant back then was named Mulligan. He was one of the absolute best, and was widely known and respected throughout the recon community. Like most colorful individuals there was a trait that set him apart from everyone else. Mulligan had a very distinctive, nasal way of speaking, and the troops loved to imitate him – but never, of course, to his face!

On the day in question Sergeant Moose's wife had apparently fallen ill, and the First Sergeant placed a call to the base day care center to let them know the CO's wife would be coming by to pick up the Sergeant's child in lieu of a family member. At least that's what he tried to tell them. The conversation went something like this:

"Do you have a baby Moose?" The First Sergeant didn't know the baby's first name, or the first name of either parent for that matter.

"Listen to me," he went on. We need to pick up baby Moose. Mama Moose is sick, and papa Moose is on a ship."

We lost it when he said that, and whoever was on the other end of the line must have heard us laughing in the background because the First Sergeant got frustrated and handed off the phone. One of the Sergeants present took it, and without missing a beat picked up the conversation where the First Sergeant had left off – in Mulligan's voice!

KICK TURN

"**The most dangerous man on the modern battlefield is not the one with the nastiest weapon. He's the one carrying the radio.**" - Todd L. Glen

One of the missions assigned to the 2nd Marine Division in the 1980's was the defense of northern Europe, and that meant we had to undergo a lot of cold weather training. First we went through a thirty day cold weather package at the Mountain Warfare Training Center in the Sierra Nevada Mountains, followed by an exercise against the Army called Alpine Warrior in Fort McCoy, Wisconsin. If you haven't operated in that sort of environment I'm here to tell you it doesn't get any tougher. The simplest task becomes more difficult simply because of the elements, and the demands of leadership become even greater.

Once we completed training, the MEB was deployed to northern Norway for a joint exercise called "Operation Cold Winter." If ever an exercise was well named, this was it. We were opposed by the Dutch and British Royal Marines, and they were formidable opponents. That was because they spend far more time conducting arctic training, and it showed in their skills.

My team was inserted into an area occupied by 45 Commando of the Royal Marines, and once we were on the ground traversed to the top of a steep mountain to set up our observation post. It was a great spot - we had a commanding view of the valley, and there was little chance of anyone stumbling across our position. Be that as it may, the best OP in the world isn't worth a damn unless you can communicate with higher headquarters. We constructed a NVIS antenna

181

called a horizontal loop, and soon had comm with the MEB via HF radio. If you don't understand what that last sentence was all about don't feel bad, unless of course you happen to be a communicator by profession. In layman's terms, we could talk.

After a couple of days we began to observe a steady succession of British helicopters flying past the OP, but couldn't see their destination because our view was obstructed by the treeline. But they were sure going *somewhere*, so I decided to take half of my six man team on a patrol to find the British LZ. We grabbed a short-range radio, donned our skis, and set off in search of the Holy Grail.

We had all become fairly adept skiers during our training in Bridgeport, with the notable exception of Lance Corporal Craft. Craft was without question the most intelligent Marine in my team, and quite possibly the entire company. He was a graduate of the Citadel, but had chosen to enlist in the Marine Corps rather than take a commission in the Army – but for all of his brains, Craft was one of the most uncoordinated Marines I had ever seen. In retrospect, I probably should have chosen someone else to go along.

After traveling a fair distance we finally came upon what looked like a toilet shrouded in white camouflage, but on closer inspection turned it out to be a Milan anti-tank weapon. Oops – danger close. The last thing we wanted was contact with the enemy. Right on cue a bunch of Brits appeared out of nowhere, and it was time for us to escape and evade. We all immediately executed a kick turn, which is a maneuver that allows a skier to turn 180 degrees, and began to ski down the hill away from the enemy position. All of us except Craft, that is. His feet became tangled, he fell down, and shortly thereafter he became a guest of the British Empire.

While our clumsy comrade was giving the Brits his name, rank and serial number, the rest of us were skiing down the hill like a bunch of madmen. It was like something out of a James Bond movie. I was never much better than a mediocre skier, but the two of us hurtled down the mountain at breakneck speed, dodging rocks and trees like Jean Claude Killy. It was exhilarating.

Once we had evaded our pursuers I grabbed the radio and called in an air strike by relaying the request through our OP. Within minutes a flight of F/A-18 Hornets appeared, and the British troops lined up waiting to board helicopters were sitting ducks. Craft had a front row seat for the bombardment, but unfortunately he was "constructively" killed by friendly fire. Such is war.

When the smoke cleared Lance Corporal Craft had earned the nickname "kick turn," and our team had once again demonstrated that a recon team with a radio is a formidable weapons system!

FIELD DAY

"Join the Navy and see the world - join the Marine Corps and police it!"

I've never really understood why people some use the term "field day" in a positive way, i.e. "we had a *field day* after we won the lottery." In the Corps the term denotes something extremely unpleasant, as every Marine knows all too well. The Marine Corps takes most everything to an extreme, and cleaning the barracks is no exception.

When I first arrived at 3rd Combat Engineer Battalion at Camp Hansen, Okinawa the barracks we lived in were so old they may well have been used by Archibald Henderson back in the day. But we were Marines, and no one had promised us a rose garden. But after I was there a few months things changed for the better, or so I thought. New barracks were being built nearby, and to a man we looked forward to moving into our comfortable new home. Big mistake.

A brand new barracks wouldn't be complete without brand new furniture, and it came in on a daily basis by the truckload. Many of us were assigned to a perpetual working party and we spent our days unloading, assembling and moving the seemingly endless stream of furniture. Even worse, our First Sergeant decided the new barracks should be field-dayed and inspected every single day.

Once most of the furniture was in place my roommate and I rented a small refrigerator from the PX, which we stocked with the usual assortment of bachelor food. It also held a couple of six packs of beer, which was a nice alternative to paying five dollars a can out in the town of "Sinville."

During room inspection the following morning the First Sergeant took one look at our icebox and went high and to the right. He ordered us to get rid of it by the following day. We were not happy, but of course complied. Then divine providence intervened. The very next day yet another furniture truck arrived, and it was loaded with... refrigerators! Bob and I raced to the CP, because each of us wanted to be the one to break the news to the First Shirt.

We now had refrigerators, but the field days went on. I was tired of scrubbing every night, and decided to change tactics the night before the battalion CO's weekly inspection. After setting up a sort of "booby-trap" I headed out to town for a couple of beers while everyone else in the barracks scrubbed away dutifully.

When the Colonel opened my hatch the next morning he tripped the micro-switch I had rigged, and a rousing rendition of the Marines' Hymn filled the air. Directly in front of the hatch was a large photo of the Marine Corps War Memorial, complete with the full complement of Marine Barracks 8th&I and the Marine Corps Drum & Bugle Corps. It must have been a motivating sight!

The Sergeant Major later related to me how the Colonel snapped to attention, and when the music had concluded spun on his heel and marched off without even inspecting the room. Just goes to show, sometimes it's better to work smarter than it is to work harder!

EULOGY
For the Great Santini

By Pat Conroy

"To the Corps elite, to that special breed of sky devil known and feared throughout the world, the Marine dogfighter, the bravest men who have ever lived. There is not a force that can defeat us in battle, deny us victory, or interrupt our destiny. Marines!" - Lieutenant Colonel W.P. "Bull" Meecham, aka "The Great Santini"

The children of fighter pilots tell different stories than other kids do. None of our fathers can write a will or sell a life insurance policy or fill a prescription or administer a flu shot or explain what a poet meant. We tell of fathers who land on aircraft carriers at pitch-black night with the wind howling out of the China Sea. Our fathers wiped out aircraft batteries in the Philippines and set Japanese soldiers on fire when they made the mistake of trying to overwhelm our troops on the ground. Your Dads ran the barber shops and worked at the post office and delivered the packages on time and sold the cars, while our Dads were blowing up fuel depots near Seoul, were providing extraordinarily courageous close air support to the beleaguered Marines at the Chosin Reservoir, and who once turned the Naktong River red with the blood of a retreating North Korean battalion. We tell of men who made widows of the wives of our nations' enemies and who made orphans out of all their children. You don't like war or violence? Or napalm? Or rockets? Or cannons or death rained down from the sky? Then let's talk about your fathers, not ours. When we talk about the aviators who raised us and the Marines who loved us, we can look you in the eye and say "you would not like

186

to have been America's enemies when our fathers passed overhead." We were raised by the men who made the United States of America the safest country on earth in the bloodiest century in all recorded history. Our fathers made sacred those strange, singing names of battlefields across the Pacific: Guadalcanal, Iwo Jima, Okinawa, the Chosin Reservoir, Khe Sanh and a thousand more. We grew up attending the funerals of Marines slain in these battles. Your fathers made communities like Beaufort decent and prosperous and functional; our fathers made the world safe for democracy.

We have gathered here today to celebrate the amazing and storied life of Colonel Donald Conroy, who modestly called himself by his nom de guerre, The Great Santini. There should be no sorrow at this funeral because The Great Santini lived life at full throttle, moved always in the fast lanes, gunned every engine, teetered on every edge, seized every moment and shook it like a terrier shaking a rat. He did not know what moderation was or where you'd go to look for it.

Donald Conroy is the only person I have ever known whose self-esteem was absolutely unassailable. There was not one thing about himself that my father did not like, nor was there one thing about himself that he would change. He simply adored the man he was and walked with perfect confidence through every encounter in his life. Dad wished everyone could be just like him. His stubbornness was an art form. The Great Santini did what he did, when he wanted to do it, and woe to the man who got in his way.

Once I introduced my father before he gave a speech to an Atlanta audience. I said at the end of the introduction, "My father decided to go into the Marine Corps on the day he discovered his IQ was the temperature of this room."

187

My father rose to the podium, stared down at the audience, and said without skipping a beat, "My God, it's hot in here! It must be at least 180 degrees."

Here is how my father appeared to me as a boy. He came from a race of giants and demi-gods from a mythical land known as Chicago. He married the most beautiful girl ever to come crawling out of the poor and lowborn south, and there were times when I thought we were being raised by Zeus and Athena.

After Happy Hour my father would drive his car home at a hundred miles an hour to see his wife and seven children. He would get out of his car, a strapping flight jacketed matinee idol, and walk toward his house, his knuckles dragging along the ground, his shoes stepping on and killing small animals in his slouching amble toward the home place. My sister, Carol, stationed at the door, would call out, "Godzilla's home!" and we seven children would scamper toward the door to watch his entry.

The door would be flung open and the strongest Marine aviator on earth would shout, "Stand by for a fighter pilot!" He would then line his seven kids up against the wall and say, "Who's the greatest of them all?"

"You are, O Great Santini, you are."

"Who knows all, sees all, and hears all?"

"You do, O Great Santini, you do."

We were not in the middle of a normal childhood, yet none of us were sure since it was the only childhood we would ever have. For all we knew other men were coming home and shouting to their families, "Stand by for a pharmacist," or "Stand by for a chiropractor."

In the old, bewildered world of children we knew we were in the presence of a fabulous, overwhelming personality; but had no idea we were being raised by a genius of his own myth-making. My mother always told me that my father had reminded her of Rhett Butler on the day they met and everyone who ever knew our mother conjured up the lovely, coquettish image of Scarlet O'Hara.

Let me give you my father the warrior in full battle array. The Great Santini is catapulted off the deck of the aircraft carrier, *USS Sicily*. His Black Sheep squadron is the first to reach the Korean Theater and American ground troops had been getting torn up by North Korean regulars. Let me do it in his voice: "We didn't even have a map of Korea. Not zip. We just headed toward the sound of artillery firing along the Naktong River. They told us to keep the North Koreans on their side of the Naktong. Air power hadn't been a factor until we got there that day. I radioed to Bill Lundin - I was his wingman. 'There they are. Let's go get 'em.' So we did."

I was interviewing Dad so I asked, "How do you know you got them?"

"Easy," The Great Santini said. "They were running – it's a good sign when you see the enemy running. There was another good sign."

"What was that, Dad?"

"They were on fire."

This is the world in which my father lived deeply. I had no knowledge of it as a child. When I was writing the book "The Great Santini," they told me at Headquarters Marine Corps that Don Conroy was at one time one of the most decorated aviators in the Corps. I did not know he had won a single medal. When his children gathered together to write his obituary, not one of us knew of any medal he had won, but he had won a slew of them.

When he flew back toward the carrier that day, he received a call from an Army Colonel on the ground who had witnessed the route of the North Koreans across the river. "Could you go pass over the troops fifty miles south of here? They've been catching hell for a week or more. It'd do them good to know you flyboys are around."

He flew those fifty miles and came over a mountain and saw a thousand troops lumbered down in foxholes. He and Bill Lundin went in low so these troops could read the insignias and know the American aviators had entered the fray. My father said, "Thousands of guys came screaming out of their foxholes, son. It sounded like a World Series game. I got goose pimples in the cockpit. Get goose pimples telling it forty-eight years later. I dipped my wings, waved to the guys. The roar they let out. I hear it now. I hear it now."

During the Cuban Missile Crisis, my mother took me out to the air station where we watched Dad's squadron scramble on the runway to their bases at Roosevelt Road and Guantanamo. In the car, as we watched the A-4's take off, my mother began to say the rosary.

"You praying for Dad and his men, Mom?" I asked her.

"No, son. I'm praying for the repose of the souls of the Cuban pilots they're going to kill."

Later I would ask my father what his squadron's mission was during the Missile Crisis. "To clear the air of MiGS over Cuba," he said.

"You think you could've done it?"

The Great Santini answered, "There wouldn't have been a bluebird left flying over that island, son."

Now let us turn to the literary of The Great Santini. Some of you may have heard that I had some serious reservations about my father's child-rearing practices. When *The Great Santini* came out, the book roared through my family like a nuclear device. My father hated it; my grandparents hated it; my aunts and uncles hated it; my cousins who adore my father thought I was a psychopath for writing it; and rumor has it that my mother gave it to the judge in her divorce case and said, "It's all there. Everything you need to know."

What changed my father's mind was when Hollywood entered the picture and wanted to make a movie of it. This is when my father said, "What a shame John Wayne is dead. Now there was a man. Only he could've gotten my incredible virility across to the American people." Orion Pictures did me a favor and sent my father a telegram; "Dear Col. Conroy: We have selected the actor to play you in the coming film. He wants to come to Atlanta to interview you. His name is Truman Capote."

But my father took well to Hollywood and its Byzantine, unspeakable ways. When his movie came out, he began reading Variety on a daily basis. He called the movie a classic the first month of its existence. He claimed that he had a place in the history of film. In February of the following year, he burst into my apartment in Atlanta, as excited as I have ever seen him, and screamed, "Son, you and I were nominated for Academy Awards last night. Your mother didn't get squat."

Ladies and gentlemen - you are attending the funeral of the most famous Marine that ever lived. Dad's life had grandeur, majesty and sweep. We were all caught in the middle of living lives much paler and less daring than The Great Santini's. His was a high stepping, damn-the torpedoes kind of life, and the stick was always set at high throttle. There is not another Marine alive who has not heard of The Great Santini. There's not a fighter pilot alive who does not lift his glass whenever Don Conroy's name is mentioned and give the fighter pilot toast: "Hurrah for the next man to die."

One day last summer, my father asked me to drive him over to Beaufort National Cemetery. He wanted t make sure there were no administrative foul-ups about his plot. I could think of more pleasurable ways to spend the afternoon, but Dad brought new eloquence to the word stubborn. We went into the office and a pretty black woman said that everything was squared away. My father said, "It'll be the second time I've been buried in this cemetery." The woman and I both looked strangely at Dad. Then he explained, "You ever catch the flick *The Great Santini?* That was me they planted at the end of the movie."

All of you will be part of a very special event today. You will be witnessing the actual burial that has already been filmed in fictional setting. This has never happened in world history. You will be present in a scene that was acted out in film in 1979. You will be in the same town and the same cemetery. Only The Great Santini himself will be different.

In his last weeks my father told me, "I was always your best subject, son. Your career took a nose dive after *The Great Santini* came out. He had become so media savvy that during his last illness he told me not to schedule his funeral on the same day as the *Seinfeld* farewell. The Colonel thought it would hold down the crowd. The Colonel's death was front-page news across the country. CNN announced his passing on the evening news all around the world.

Don Conroy was a simple man and an American hero. His wit was remarkable; his intelligence frightening; and his sophistication next to none. He was a man's man and I would bet he hadn't spent a thousand dollars in his whole life on his wardrobe. He lived out his whole retirement in a two-room efficiency in the Darlington Apartment in Atlanta. He claimed he never spent over a dollar on any piece of furniture he owned. You would believe him if you saw the furniture. Dad bought a season ticket for himself to Six Flags Over Georgia and would often go there alone to enjoy the rides and hear the children squeal with pleasure. He was a beer drinker who thought wine was for Frenchmen or effete social climbers like his children.

Ah! His children. Here is how God gets a Marine Corps fighter pilot. He sends him seven squirrelly, mealy-mouth children who march in peace demonstrations, wear Birkenstocks, flirt with vegetarianism, invite cross-dressers to dinner and vote for candidates that Dad would line up and shoot. If my father knew how many tears his children have shed since his death, he would be mortally ashamed of us all and begin yelling that he should've been tougher on us all, knocked us into better shape - that he certainly didn't mean to raise a passel of kids so weak and tacky they would cry at his death. Don Conroy was the best uncle I ever saw, the best brother, the best grandfather, the best friend - and my God, what a father. After my mother divorced him and *The Great Santini* was published, he had the best second act I ever saw. He never was simply a father. He was The Great Santini.

It is time to leave you, Dad. From Carol and Mike and Kathy and Jim and Tim and especially from Tom. Your kids wanted to especially thank Katy and Bobby and Willie Harvey who cared for you heroically. Let us leave you and say goodbye, Dad, with the passwords that bind all Marines and their wives and their children forever. The Corps was always the most important thing.

Semper Fi, Dad. Semper Fi, O Great Santini.

Pat Conroy, son of Santini, is the author of *The Great Santini*.

MANNA FROM HEAVEN

"The more Marines I have around me the better I like it."
- General Mark Clark, U.S. Army

The Drager LAR V is a closed-circuit diving apparatus that uses pure oxygen rather than compressed air, and whose main advantage is it does not emit a tell-tale trail of bubbles. It is a very difficult and potentially dangerous piece of gear to use, and divers require a great deal of specialized training in order to employ it.

In the days before the Marine Corps started the Combat Diver's Course there was no formal school which taught the LAR V, so each unit was responsible for conducting their own in-house training program. It was for one such package that we headed down to Key West, Florida.

Since expertise with closed-circuit systems was hard to come by in those days we were also tasked with training the Force Recon reserve unit from Mobile, Alabama - so our group drove down to Alabama to link up with them. From there we were slated to fly to the Keys. We all boarded a C-130 for the trip down to Florida, and parachuted into the ocean just off Key West. As we floated down to our watery drop zone there was little doubt we were on display for anyone who happened to glance up to the sky.

While in Key West we were billeted in Truman Annex, so named because it was the location of the "Southern White House" during President Truman's time in office. Today it is a naval installation, and has been used for a number of purposes such as drug interdiction and special operations training. One of the great things about the Annex is its proximity to Key West proper - just walk out the gate and you are right where you want to be.

As soon as we had stowed our gear everyone headed out to Duval Street, which is the center of Key West's entertainment district. The most well known nightspot is Sloppy Joe's, which is famous for being Ernest Hemingway's favorite watering hole. I wasn't in the mood for a big crowd that night, and since Sloppy's tends to attract a lot of tourists I opted to go across the street to a place called Rick's. The atmosphere there is much more laid-back, and I settled in for an evening of conversation and quiet imbibing to the strains of a reggae quartet.

Back in those days there were a number of well known special operations "groupies" on the prowl in Key West. These women kept themselves in tip-top shape, and would only "date" members of elite military units. I didn't know it at the time, but the woman standing next to me at the bar was one of them.

We struck up a conversation and talked about this and that, and as is often the case the subject eventually turned to the weather. A hard rain had begun to fall outside, and I commented that it might be awhile before we could leave without getting soaked. She replied that she liked when it rained. Then she smiled and added, "I knew today was going to be a good day, because when I looked up in the sky this morning it was raining *men!*"

GOOD TO GO

Roger Roy

"Keep your fears to yourself, but share your courage with others!"

The gas mask had hung at my hip for so long it felt almost permanently attached, and I'd gotten to where I'd reflexively reach down to make sure it was there, like checking for keys before locking the car door. But now I handed the mask and the rest of my issued gear to the Army captain, and he checked off his list: atropine injectors, pants and jacket to my chemical-weapons suit, rubber overboots and gloves. He marked off the list, slid it over the counter, and I signed it.

"You are now officially dis-embedded," he told me, and I'd been around Marines so much I was almost startled he hadn't said, "Good to go," the Corps' catchall phrase that means you're ready for anything, even if it involves bayonets and a beach that somebody else *thinks* belongs to *them*. I almost mentioned that to the captain, but I figured, he's Army, he wouldn't get it. A few weeks earlier, I wouldn't have gotten it myself.

For more than a month I'd been, in military parlance, "embedded" with the 1st Marine Expeditionary Force, traveling and living with the Marines as they pushed north from Kuwait to Baghdad. It was an experience that had swung dizzily from rewarding to exasperating to frightening, and now that it was suddenly over I was still sorting through its ups and downs. That night after turning in our Marine-issued gear at the military press headquarters in Kuwait City, I had dinner with a reporter I'd been with since before the

196

war started, Wayne Woolley of the Star-Ledger in Newark, N.J., who'd been embedded with the same unit. At the five-star Hilton looking out over the Gulf, we ate smoked salmon and fresh fruit and smoked Iraqi cigarettes. We wished you could buy alcohol in Kuwait, and managed not to feel guilty even though we knew the Marines we'd left in Iraq the day before were still eating MREs.

Over dinner, we rehashed our experience and came to a conclusion that would have stunned us if someone had suggested it a month earlier: If we were eighteen or nineteen again, neither of us was sure we'd be able to resist the urge to join the Marines.

The idea was troubling on several levels. First, practically speaking, we should have known better by then. Being with the Marines meant we'd been through the whole war without a hot shower, learned to consider ourselves lucky when we had a new MRE box for a toilet and occasionally worried we were about to be shot. We'd seen how the Marines had to make do with old or insufficient gear, some of it dating to the Vietnam era.

It's hard to argue that willingly subjecting yourself to such a thing isn't a sign of simple-mindedness. Beyond that, it was hardly a ringing endorsement of our ability to keep our distance from those we were writing about. I'd covered police, courts and politics without ever once wanting to be a cop, a lawyer or a politician. Fortunately, I'm old enough that our discussion that night was purely academic. But I think our reaction explains much about the Pentagon's decision to embed several hundred reporters for the war in Iraq, the first time the press has enjoyed such close war-time access to the U.S. military since Vietnam. Someone at the Pentagon had figured out what we now recognized: No matter what you think of the military as an institution, it's hard not to admire the actual rank-and-file troops.

Who would write glowingly about the Marine Corps bureaucracy for trying to push a convoy of 150 supply trucks through hundreds of miles of enemy territory with too little fuel, too few radios and not enough heavy weapons? But it's a different story when told from the seat next to a nineteen-year-old lance corporal at a wheel of a truckload of high explosives who hasn't slept in two days and is just trying to get the mission done.

Before the war, I'd never spent much time with the Marines, and I wasn't sure what to expect when I was assigned to them. I think I understand Marines better now, but I'm not sure I can *explain* them. They tend to do things the hardest way possible. They call each other "devil dog" and say "Ooo-rah." They are loud and rough. They have lots of tattoos. They'll ignore you or torment you if they think you're a fake. They'll do anything for you if they like you.

They'll believe the wildest rumors. One told me, early in the war, that he'd heard the Army, rather than the Marines, would occupy Baghdad because the Marines "break too much stuff." Marines tend to think and travel in a straight line.

They have a talent for complaining and swearing that I've seldom seen surpassed. I heard entire conversations between Marines that consisted of nothing but acronyms laced with profanity, something like:

"Where's your #&% NCO?"

"At the ^*&$ COC for *+$ CSSB."

"We need some #@* LVSs and a couple of *#% MTVRs."

"$*&#."

"Ooo-rah."

Marines get things done. They follow orders. They would sometimes do crazy things if they thought they'd been told to. Once, during a convoy stop, a young Marine begged us out of an MRE box we'd been saving for a toilet. When Woolley gave him the box he made a joke about bringing it back, but the Marine thought he was serious. Five minutes later the Marine was back, offering the no-longer-empty box back to a horrified Woolley. It had Gunnery Sergeant Kevin Mlay, who was standing there when the Marine brought the box back, shaking his head. Marines may not be the smartest, Mlay said, but you have to give them credit for following orders.

That doesn't mean they're afraid to point out that their orders may be, to politely paraphrase an often-used Marine term, messed up.

"That's (messed) up, sir," is a phrase I heard countless times. I'm sure it was the first thing the Marines said when they saw the reefs at Tarawa or the Japanese positions on Mount Suribachi.

There were endless variations of the phrase – "Sir, that's totally (messed) up," and "Sergeant, you won't believe how (messed) up it is."

But after complaining, the Marines would do what they'd been told, even if it didn't make any sense.

Most of the Marines were very young, most lance corporals only nineteen or twenty. That may be why I ran across so many of them who managed to have both a sentimental streak and a mean streak. I saw Marines who didn't have any extra food or water give what they had to Iraqi children begging on the roadside. But the same Marines laughed like crazy when they heard about a Marine who filled an empty MRE bag with sand, sealed it up and threw it to begging children. One Marine officer I knew liked to call his Marines "the most demented young people our society can produce." He wasn't really kidding, but he still admired them, and I did, too.

The Marines Woolley and I had been embedded with were in the Transportation Support Group, which included the Orlando-based reservists of the 6th Motor Transport Battalion. They were running convoys of ammunition, food, water and fuel, and fighting wasn't supposed to be their main job. They were ordered to more or less ignore civilians unless they were hostile. If they took fire, they weren't to stop: Getting the supplies to the front was more important than getting into a fight, especially since the fuel and ammunition trucks in a convoy would have been vulnerable targets. Their orders encouraged a sort of don't-mess-with-me-I-won't-mess-with-you policy. But if someone messed with them, they were inviting the worst. Marines return fire with a relish.

At a base south of Baghdad, I heard a young Marine reporting to an officer about how his convoy had taken sniper fire from a mud brick hut near the highway. "Did you return fire?" the officer asked, and the Marine told him casually that the Mark 19 gunner had gotten off "about a hundred rounds." The Mark 19 is a sort of machine gun that fires grenades, and one hundred Mark 19 rounds would be enough to level most villages in southern Iraq, let alone one mud brick hut. But the Marines figured anyone who messed with them had it coming.

Major Michael Yaroma, like all officers a dedicated student of the psyche of his Marines, told me how he'd found a young Marine tormenting a fly at their base south of Baghdad. The flies in the desert are big, ugly, biting things, and the Marine had caught one and pulled its wings off. As it tried to crawl away the Marine poked at it with his finger, asking, "How do you like it, huh? How do you like it?"

"What the hell are you doing?" Yaroma asked the Marine.

"He was (messing) with me sir, so now I'm (messing) with him," the Marine said, and then he went back to his fly.

When the Marines began pulling out of Baghdad last week, replaced by Army units, news reports noted how the Army tended to patrol the city in convoys of Humvees, while the Marines had been on foot and mixed with the locals. I'd seen it myself. There were times in Baghdad when a few Marines would be on guard at a busy intersection where there were hundreds, even thousands of Iraqis filing past. Many of those Marines seemed to enjoy the close contact, laughing, waving and joking with the Iraqis the best they could given the language barrier. But I also knew that none of them would hesitate to light up the crowd if it came to that.

A lot of the Marines I met recognized that their experiences in the war had changed them. After dark at a camp in Central Iraq, we were sitting with about a dozen Marines, and one of them of them was telling the group about his experience handling Iraqi prisoners, which the unit transported back to holding camps. The prisoners weren't treated gently, and the Marine was demonstrating how the guards would give them a string of contradictory orders the Iraqis didn't understand anyway, making their point by aiming their rifles at the prisoners' faces.

"We're like, 'What's your name!' 'Shut up!' 'Stand up!' 'Sit the hell down!'"

The Marine was waving his loaded M-16 around wildly and finally Sergeant Rob Anderson told him, "Put your damn rifle down."

The Marine sat down and, after a few seconds, he said, "When I get home, I'm taking an anger-management course." Everybody cracked up, mostly because they knew he was completely serious.

I found that even officers who had been studying Marines for years still scratched their heads over them. One fascinated by their quirks was Major Jeff Eberwein, an oil-company executive in civilian life who has a degree in medieval literature from Boston College. The books he'd brought to read during the war included Chaucer's *Canterbury Tales*.

Eberwein liked to joke about how Marines did things the hardest way. Since they'd arrived at Camp Saipan in January, the Marines had to wear their full battle gear - flak jackets and helmets and carrying their weapons - even to the mess hall and latrine.

I thought the conditions at Camp Saipan were bad, with tents that didn't keep out the dust storms and foul-smelling portable toilets. But it was luxury compared to conditions after the war started. And the Marines, who had assumed they would be using holes for toilets and eating standing up even in camp before the war, thought it was great they had toilets and a mess tent with chairs. Eberwein did a hilarious version of a sergeant's reaction to any Marine who complained about the mess hall food, which was actually awful.

"Do you think they had strawberry jam on Tarawa, Marine?! Did they have orange juice at Iwo Jima?!"

One day at the big Marine base south of Baghdad, Eberwein and I watched a Marine take a wrong turn with his LVS, a monster all-wheel drive truck, and come up to a ditch with a berm beyond it. The Marine could have backed up a little and turned to avoid the obstacle. But the shortest path was straight ahead, and after sizing it up the driver just gunned the motor and the big truck plowed over it, tires spinning and steel groaning.

Eberwein liked to say that Marines think finesse is a French sports car. But the truth is he admired their single-mindedness to getting the job done. That day as the truck disappeared through the cloud of dust, he just shook his head and said, "Mission accomplished."

But while Eberwein tended to be more reflective than most of the Marines, I came to realize he was one of them. We were at a camp late one afternoon when one of the Cobra helicopter gunships patrolling outside the Marine positions suddenly began firing. Marines grabbed their rifles and ran over the berm, hoping for a fight. In a few minutes, they all came back grumbling: The Cobra gunner must have been only clearing his weapon, and there was nothing out there to shoot at. Afterward, Eberwein joked about how only Marines would be disappointed that they couldn't get into a firefight. But he'd been the first one over the berm.

If we reporters often puzzled over Marines, there were things about us that didn't make sense to them, either. The first two questions Marines would ask us when they found out we were reporters were: Did you volunteer to come, and do you get paid extra for covering a war? They acted like we were crazy when we said we'd volunteered, even though they were all volunteers themselves, for the Corps if not for this particular war. They also thought we were crazy when they found out we weren't paid any more to cover a war than to cover a city council meeting. But I always pointed out that the extra pay the Marines were getting in Iraq was only a couple of hundred dollars a month, scant compensation for being shot at.

A surprising number of Marines, unaware that journalists were forbidden to carry weapons, asked if we were armed. When we told them the rules prohibited weapons for journalists, more than a few assumed our denials were just to make it seem we were complying with the rules, and that we really had some sort of weapons. Others seemed almost alarmed for our sakes that we were unarmed. Many insisted on showing us how to fire their M-16s.

After one long, scary night on a convoy in southern Iraq, Sergeant Joseph Gomez had asked me if I could throw. I knew Gomez played baseball last year on the Marine Corps team, so I answered that I could throw about like a girl, why? He held out a green ball printed on the side, *Grenade, Frag, Delay.* "You pull the small pin first, he said, then the larger pin, and throw it." I couldn't imagine ever using the thing, and tried to stay away from the spot in the bed of the truck where Gomez kept it tucked in between the sandbags.

At first, when we'd climb into a truck we'd wait for one of the Marines to move the weapons that were lying around. But after a while we'd just pick up the rocket launcher or M-16 and move it ourselves. Most of the Marines, after wed spent some time riding with them, would hand us their rifles to hold while they climbed in or out of the truck, and it became so second nature I never thought about it until later. Maybe that would have made us fair targets. But on the convoys one of the biggest dangers was snipers, and there was no reason to believe they'd have any idea we were reporters rather than Marines, or that they'd avoid shooting us even if they knew.

The reporters I knew, myself included, didn't expect any Geneva Convention niceties if we were captured, noncombatants or not. In any case, my sense of security was directly in proportion to my confidence in the Marines around me. We spent the first week of the war with Marines I came to trust completely - Gomez and his crew on a truck that provided security for the convoys - driver Lance Corporal Robert Kissmann and .50-caliber gunner Scott Stasney.

Gomez was only twenty-three, but the others on his squad had the same sort of confidence in him. "He's my daddy," was how one Marine in Gomez's squad described him. Gomez called his M-16 Marie, after his wife's middle name, and even his choice of wife I regarded as a sign of his bravery, since he'd married his platoon sergeant's daughter, a thought that made even the toughest Marines cringe.

I always figured nothing bad could happen until Gomez had fired his last round, but I was with him during my scariest moment of the war. On an Iraqi highway south of the Euphrates, during a blinding dust storm, our security truck stopped to guard a stalled truck full of ammunition and guided missiles while the rest of the convoy drove ahead. The dust and howling wind cut visibility at times to only fifty or sixty yards, and Iraqi trucks and cars would suddenly appear out of the dust, often turning to speed off. We felt like a whole Iraqi army could be a hundred yards away in the dust and we wouldn't know it.

The wind blew dust in my eyes even with my goggles on, and I was standing behind the truck, out of the wind. I wasn't particularly worried until Gomez came back and told me he couldn't see and asked me to take a look at his eye. That was when I realized all my confidence was tied up in him. His eye was bloodshot and full of sand, and I dug out the worst of it with my fingernail, then washed it out with a bottle of water. It still looked bad but he said it felt better, and he went back to the road.

The mechanics were still working on the truck, and a few more Marines had joined us, when we heard a loud squeaking clatter coming up the road behind us. We all knew what it was even before someone said it was tracks, which meant armored vehicles. A day earlier, American Cobra gunships or F-18s would have massacred any Iraqi tanks that dared to venture out, but now nothing was flying in the dust storm.

Eberwein yelled at a Marine to grab the AT-4 rocket launcher from one of the Humvees, but I had no confidence in the little rocket. Besides, you could tell there were several sets of tracks coming up the road. And I already had a vision of a column of Iraqi tanks coming up the road and was trying to figure whether it would be better to run north or south and how long it would take to get out of sight of the road in the dust storm. I was about to *dis*-embed myself on foot.

But when they clattered into sight, the tracks belonged to four U.S. Army Bradley Fighting Vehicles, which were as surprised as we were by the encounter. They stopped suddenly, backed up and crossed the road, keeping their cannons trained on us even as they rolled past and disappeared into the dust. I managed to snap a photo of the Bradleys just as they came out of the dust, but when I looked at it later the image was blurred, as if I'd moved when I took the shot. I don't think I could blame the wind.

Aside from the fact that the Marines' inclination was to fight and mine was to run, another difference between the press and the Marines is we tended to see things as black and white, sometimes in ways that seemed comical to the Marines. One night, some Marines had dropped me off after dark at an advance camp for our unit. I was fumbling around trying to unroll my sleeping bag when I startled a Marine who came walking around the command tent, which I was sleeping next to so I wouldn't be run over by a truck in the dark.

"Friend or foe," he asked me, and I had no ready answer. Technically, I was no one's foe, as a non-combatant. And while I'd made friends who were Marines, to call yourself a friend implies some compromise of objectivity. After a long pause I finally mumbled "Reporter," and when the Marine laughed I wasn't sure if it was because of my answer or how long it had taken me to spit it out.

To the Marines, the biggest difference between us was that we were more or less free to do as we wished. Technically the rules were that we would stay with our assigned unit, and that someone would keep track of us. Our press badges said "Bearer must be escorted at all times." But within a day of the war's start, we were pretty much free to do as we wanted, jumping on and off convoys and wandering around wherever we could get a ride and find Marines to give us water, MREs and a place to throw our sleeping bags. We learned to avoid unfriendly officers, and the friendly ones directed us to convoys that were heading closer to the action, even telling us when we should jump off to another unit.

Unlike the Marines, we could dress as we wanted and sleep until we wanted to get up. But the biggest difference was that we could leave whenever we wished. Many Marines told us they couldn't believe we would stay out there if we had the option to go home. I think it was the knowledge that we could pull out whenever we wanted that cemented our connection with the Marines.

Just before Woolley and I flew out of Iraq on a C-130 back to Kuwait, we were saying our goodbyes to the Marines at their base south of Baghdad. Staff Sergeant Charles Wells, a firefighter and EMT for Orange County Fire Rescue, made a point of pulling us aside before our flight. The Marines hadn't known what to expect when they heard reporters would be living with them, Wells said, and some had feared the worst, that we'd pry into personal details or try to portray them as bloodthirsty baby killers. But Wells told us his Marines appreciated how we'd lived as they'd lived, gone where they'd gone, eaten what they'd eaten, used the same MRE boxes as toilets and slept on the ground they'd slept on.

By then Wells knew we'd understand exactly what he meant when he told us, "You guys are good to go."

We considered it the highest praise.

This article originally appeared in the Orlando Sentinel on April 27, 2003

COMBAT SOCCER

"Always use a pile driver to crack a nut. The pile driver doesn't sustain much damage, and the nut stays cracked." - USMC axiom

I've never been a fan of competitive athletics programs in the military, although I've heard all the arguments about how they help the recruiting effort, promote physical fitness, develop teamwork, and so on. Don't confuse these programs with unit PT, because they're two different animals altogether. Unit athletics are just fine and deliver as advertised, but once you get into the rarefied atmosphere of team competition you lose my vote. The only ones benefiting from the teamwork or physical fitness aspects are the few athletes good enough to compete, and while those individuals are traveling around the country or the world boxing and playing basketball there are countless less athletically gifted Marines taking up the slack for them in far less glamorous jobs.

In my opinion athletics should be relegated to off-duty hours and not interfere with a Marine's regular duties, and any competition requiring travel should be entered in conjunction with annual leave. Anyone who disagrees with the foregoing needs to think back a few years to a Corporal by the name of Leon Spinks. During his time in the Corps Spinks got paid twice a month just like everyone else, but in return his only responsibility was to train and box. After making a name for himself in the amateur ranks he left the Corps and went on to become heavyweight champion of the world, a title he soon lost along with his money and self respect – and he became an embarrassment to the Corps in the process.

209

All of this is far removed from the average Marine who participates in a sport he loves to have some fun and get a little exercise, and even further from groups who are required to engage in sports they don't even understand. Just such a group was the first platoon of "A" Company, Second Reconnaissance Battalion during the fall of 1977. I was a member of that platoon, and while embarked aboard *USS Pensacola* for a Caribbean training cruise we pulled into Bridgetown, Barbados for some liberty.

As luck would have it our platoon pulled duty section instead of liberty the first day in port, but a golden opportunity to improve international relations would soon be ours nevertheless. On that particular day the Barbados national soccer team made the unfortunate mistake of challenging the visiting Americans to a game of their favorite sport. Since everyone else was ashore drinking and carousing when the invitation arrived the task of playing for the honor of the USA fell to our little band of cut-throats, reinforced by a grunt Captain and a Navy Lieutenant. It wasn't until we were enroute to the soccer field that we realized no one other than the officers had any idea how to play the game. Our only experience had come during a few long forgotten gym classes back in high school.

Eventually the game got underway, and the nimble home team scored a couple of easy goals the first two times they touched the ball. The next time they had possession, however, the forward dribbling the ball found himself sandwiched between two of our biggest players, Corporals "Big Bird" Wenke and "Dancing Bear" Blackburn. Each of them weighed in at well over two hundred pounds, and the sudden impact of their combined weight knocked the stuffing out of the slender soccer player and caused him to be medevaced to a nearby hospital. He was soon joined there by their goalie – who made the mistake of picking up the ball in the penalty area and was immediately tackled by a rampaging Sergeant named Blum. At that point we took a break to have the rules better explained to us while the broken body of the unfortunate goaltender was removed from the playing field.

The game eventually had to be called because Barbados no longer had enough healthy players to field a team, but since there was still plenty of daylight we decided to hang around for a while rather than return to the ship. Someone produced a football, and after tossing it around for a while it was suggested we challenge the surviving soccer players to a game where *we* knew the rules. A few of them were receptive at first, but that interest quickly faded once we demonstrated how to pass rush.

On the after-action report for that float some astute soul suggested that in the future all impromptu international competition be limited to a friendly game of darts at a local pub… and that's probably not a bad idea.

THE TEST COUNT

"The person who learns to laugh at himself will never cease to be amused." – Shirley MacLaine

If young Marines just graduated from boot camp are nothing else, they are well disciplined. An incident illustrating that statement which immediately comes to mind occurred when an NCO in my section put a new Marine into the front leaning rest (push-up) position as punishment for some minor infraction. A moment later he received a phone call from the 'head shed,' and after a short conversation went off to a meeting - totally forgetting about the young transgressor's predicament in the process. Since it is a long-standing tradition in Recon units that the only person who can recover someone from a punitive exercise is the individual who initiated the punishment, that particular PFC spent the better part of the afternoon contemplating the deck with his buddies stepping over and around him until that same NCO returned and gave him the word to get up.

Which brings me to PFC 'Morton' - long on discipline and short on common sense. Our communications section had just received a shipment of new PRC-68 squad radios, and we were assigned to check them for proper operation. The Lieutenant gave one to Morton and instructed him to walk to the other side of the battalion area while giving him a test count, and off he went. After a while we heard his voice coming over the speaker, *"one, two, three"* etc. We tried to acknowledge, but since he still had his transmit button depressed he couldn't hear us and continued on, *"fifty-one, fifty-two"* etc. It crossed my mind he might be a wise guy, until I remembered it was the middle of January and very cold outside. By the time he passed two hundred we agreed something had to be done, so I got on the phone with the OD and asked him to send our lost sheep back to the comm shop. A few minutes later he returned, shivering uncontrollably - but still counting dutifully into his radio!

THE FINAL FRONTIER

"I am here to turn you slimy civilian cesspool parasites into Marine Corps space aviators, invoking bowel wrenching fear into the dark hearts of your enemies."
- Mythical Sergeant Major Boguss (played by R. Lee Ermy) in the film "Space"

Anyone familiar with Marines knows that most of them are hams, and I guess I am no exception. When an opportunity to have our picture taken or get our name in the paper presents itself we are all "Hollywood" Marines at heart. I guess that's what prompted President Truman to once remark that a photographer was part of the T/O for every Marine rifle squad.

So I was quite pleased when the Air Attaché at our Embassy in Canberra, a Marine Major, asked me to field a phone call for him. The caller was a producer from the Fox television network, and he asked if I would be willing to work as a technical advisor on a movie about futuristic Marines. Naturally I said yes, with the caveat I would have to get permission from my Company Commander.

The CO was a bit cool to the idea at first, since two of the Marines from the Embassy in Bangkok had recently appeared in the Disney film *Dumbo Drop*. What had started out as a simple cameo turned into speaking roles, and each of the Marines had to fly back to LA to record voice-overs. I could understand the Colonel's reluctance to give the green light, and promised to keep things under control.

A couple of weeks later I was flown up to the Warner Studios on the Gold Coast of Australia, where my first task was to train a bunch of young actors to act like Marines. The first thing I noticed was every last one of them was in dire need of a haircut. I didn't expect high and tights, just something approaching regulation, but was quickly informed that each actor's contract prohibited things that were considered by them to be "extreme." I suddenly understood why so many military movies are full of flaws you could drive a six-by through.

The star of the movie turned out to be R. Lee Ermey. He was well known to most Marines, having appeared in such films as *Full Metal Jacket, The Siege of Firebase Gloria*, and *Purple Hearts*. Ermey had in fact been a real Marine prior to his acting career, and was medically retired after being wounded in Vietnam. Like most Marines, I am a big fan.

When Lee arrived at the hotel it was around dinnertime, and most of the cast and crew had gathered in the bar adjacent to the hotel's dining room. He appeared in the doorway, scanned the room for a few moments, and then walked straight over to where I was standing. "You must be the Gunny!" he thundered. I guess I stuck out amongst all of those slimy civilians.

He and I had dinner together in the hotel, during which I discovered that his on-screen persona is no act. When the waitress was slow to take our order he tactfully gained her attention by calling to her in the sweetest voice he could muster. "*EXCUSE* me, can we have some *SERVICE* over here!" I swear that poor girl jumped ten feet in the air, and from that moment on the service was great.

One morning after shooting had begun the producer pulled me aside and asked if I would be willing to play a small part in the movie. The actor they had contracted to play one of the assistant drill instructors was a bit overweight, and as a result didn't look very squared away in his uniform. I took one look at the individual in question and agreed he looked like ten pounds of manure stuffed into a five pound bag –

there was no way I could allow him to portray a member of my beloved Corps. If 'Gunny Hartman' had been there he would have no doubt told him "Son, you look like about a hundred and fifty pounds of chewed bubble gum!"

The part was something I had been rehearsing for my entire life. I just had to run around and scream at people, and even though I had never been a Drill Instructor it was a piece of cake. Any questions I may have had about my believability were answered during the scene where our new recruits arrived on a bus. When I got in the face of one of the female "recruits" she just sat down and began to cry. Shooting stopped so the director could remind the young lady I was only acting, and once she regained her composure we did it again.

Later on I received a call from Fox asking if I could train two of their actors to fold a flag for an upcoming funeral scene. I said of course I could, but suggested they use two *real* Marines instead. A couple of the Marines in my detachment idolized Lee Ermey - not only could they repeat dialogue from *Full Metal Jacket* word for word, they could do it in *his* voice. It would be quite a treat for them to meet their idol, and as a bonus they would get to appear in the movie with him. The studio agreed it was a good idea, and promptly flew my two devil dogs up to the studio.

They were in hog heaven!

THE TASTE TEST

"Mind over matter. If you don't mind, it doesn't matter!"

"Clear the head!" the Drill Instructor shouted. *"CLEAR THE HEAD!"* echoed seventy voices, and suddenly the doorway erupted in a stampede of bodies with each recruit doing his best to ensure he wasn't the last one out. Once the privates were locked up at the position of attention in front of their racks the DI checked the head for stragglers, and after what seemed an eternity reappeared carrying something in his hand. Upon closer inspection it became apparent that the sleeve of his immaculate Creighton shirt was wet up to the elbow, and the object in his hand was a recently deposited specimen of human feces.

"One of your ladies didn't flush the shitter, and I want to know who it was!" he roared. He then proceeded to parade the evidence the length of the squadbay, asking each recruit in turn if he recognized it as his own. When no one confessed he shook his head and walked slowly back to the quarterdeck, excrement still in hand, and said, "It doesn't look too goddamned good, does it?"

"*NO SIR!*" the platoon thundered in reply. He then held it to his nose and inhaled deeply. "It sure as hell doesn't smell too goddamned good either!" Several recruits were visibly pale by this point.

After a long moment he sounded off once more, "And I'm willing to bet it *tastes* just as bad as it *smells!*" With that the DI proceeded to bite off a large portion and began to chew with great relish. After a few moments he stopped and pronounced, "Just like I thought, it tastes like shit!" The recruit to his left had seen enough and vomited violently, and that set off a chain reaction throughout the platoon.

The DI then grabbed the guide and told him he had 'half a heartbeat' to get the mess cleaned up. As the platoon turned to he then spun on his heel and went inside the DI hut, an amused look on his face. The Senior Drill Instructor looked up from his desk and asked the young Sergeant what all the ruckus was.

"I don't know," he replied, "I've never seen anyone get so upset over a smashed candy bar and a little peanut butter before!"

CHEATING THE REAPER

"The Marines have landed, and the situation is well in hand."
- Richard Harding Davis

Having spent my entire career with ground units, I rarely had a good word to say about the Marine air wing. I knew, like all grunts knew, that "wingers" were long haired, undisciplined, and never, ever got mud on their uniforms. I harbored those feelings until the day I became acquainted with the Air National Guard, and on that day my respect for Marine aviation took a quantum leap.

I was scheduled to fly from Tarrytown N.Y. up to Ft. Drum to do an area study in preparation for a joint Marine/Army operation scheduled for the following month. When we arrived at the airport we immediately began to doubt that any of us would ever live to *see* Ft. Drum, let alone participate in the exercise. The aircraft assigned to fly us there was a military version of the old DC-3, and to say that it had seen better days would have been quite an understatement. One engine cowling was covered with oil, the starboard propeller was bent at a grotesque angle, and the fuselage was held together with bailing wire and bubble gum. It was so bad a Lieutenant Colonel in the group actually phoned his wife to make sure his insurance policy was up to date. We uttered a collective sigh of relief when a mechanic came over and told us the repair job was so big that a Marine Reserve C-130 had been dispatched from Syracuse to replace the aging craft – and not one complaint was heard about the ensuing three hour delay.

The trip up to Fort Drum was smooth as could be, and everything went according to schedule from that point on.

That ended, however, when we walked out of the operations building to board our flight home. An audible groan could be heard when we saw the very same DC-3 we had left behind in Tarrytown sitting on the runway before us. I hoped for another reprieve, but at the same time reasoned that she had somehow made the trip here in one piece and therefore must be airworthy.

I have flown hundreds of times throughout the course of my life, and as a rule don't give it a second thought. Such was not the case on that particular day. That old plane used every last inch of runway before it managed to get airborne, and I swore the landing gear brushed the treetops. I felt a little guilty about my sudden bout of paranoia, so I glanced over at my buddy for a bit of reassurance. Frank had spent two tours in Vietnam as a paratrooper and Green Beret and had hundreds of jumps under his belt. I hoped he hadn't noticed how nervous I was, but needn't have worried since he was gripping the armrests so tightly his knuckles were turning white. So much for my paranoia.

As luck would have it Mother Nature decided to put her two cents in that day, and we experienced heavy turbulence the whole way. We bounced around like a ping pong ball, and the plane shuddered so violently we were sure it was only a matter of time until the wings fell off.

One thing that struck me as odd was the pilot chose to fly with the door to the cockpit left open so we could all see him laboring at the controls. As we neared the runway at Tarrytown he came under some pretty intense scrutiny, because we weren't too happy with the way his approach was shaping up. We were coming in low over the trees and the wings were rocking back and forth to such a degree that some of the taller evergreens probably got a bit of pruning.

We finally touched down, and after bouncing back into the air several times rolled to a stop near the parking apron where the crash crew was awaiting our arrival. As the applause in the cabin died down we saw the pilot remove his headset, turn around and say, "Well boys, we cheated death again!"

ADVENTURES
In Fine Dining

"They say that in the messhall, the chicken is mighty fine. One jumped on the table, and started marking time!"

Military messhalls are about as far removed from Cordon Bleu dining as you can get, and are certainly amongst the most aptly named institutions in the world. A few years ago the same people who changed the name of the brig to "correctional facility" renamed messhalls "dining facilities," but to paraphrase the poet "a rose by any other name still tastes as bad." It didn't take long for the more descriptive (and more easily spelled) term 'messhall' to come back into official usage however, since we had all continued to use the unofficial term anyway.

In all fairness to those who perform the mundane and thankless task of cooking for thousands on a daily basis, the quality of fare has improved tremendously over the past couple of decades. My introduction to Marine Corps chow took place on Parris Island over twenty years ago and made an impression that has stayed with my gastrointestinal tract to this day. The pungent aroma of SOS and grits, mixed with the unmistakable smell of fear, greeted our newly formed platoon at the door. Rubber scrambled eggs, cardboard toast and hockey puck pancakes filled our trays, and our Drill Instructors expected us to eat every last morsel in short order... and it was all I could do to keep from visiting my old friend 'Ralph.'

That unfortunate experience notwithstanding, I have since learned to appreciate our messhalls - especially once I discovered there are far worse things in this world which are considered edible by some people. The first item that comes to mind is our field ration, the much maligned Meal Ready to Eat, or MRE. While many Marines swear the acronym actually stands for' Meals Rejected by Ethiopians,' they are in fact quite edible if drowned in a sufficient quantity of Tabasco sauce.

Far worse are some so called "native delicacies" that have distressed my palate in one way or another over the years. I have dined on everything from Korean kimchee to Congolese pili-pili for reasons that vary from fostering international relations to simply staving off starvation, and even our good and civilized friends from Australia have managed to come up with the culinary nightmare they call Vegemite. Amongst them all, however, one gastric misadventure stands out from all the rest.

While traveling from the US to Okinawa on a series of MAC flights I befriended a retired Vietnam-era Navy SEAL during a two day layover (i.e. the plane broke down) in Guam. Upon our subsequent arrival in the Philippines we had to endure yet another "layover," and my new friend offered to let me stay at the house he shared with a retired Green Beret Colonel until the Air Force aircraft mechanics at Clark AFB sobered up long enough to fix our plane. Having nowhere else to go I agreed, and soon discovered their Spartan existence included only those things deemed essential to sustaining life. The way they saw it that included popcorn, mountains of San Miguel beer, a dozen or so young girls, and little else.

At lunchtime we were replenishing the rapidly dwindling beer supply at the local sari-sari store when a street vendor appeared. He was selling something I had never heard of before, but which caused a great deal of excitement amongst the locals. They were called balut, but as far as I could tell they were nothing but ordinary chicken eggs.

As everyone began cracking them open a stench arose that made that nauseating Parris Island messhall smell like a Chanel No.5 factory. These particular eggs had been incubated close to the point of hatching and then buried in mud and allowed to rot. My revulsion must have been obvious because my companions taunted me by suggesting Marines were wimps who couldn't stomach such things. I responded by swallowing my pride along with a good sized balut, and somehow managed to keep a straight face in the process. When the moment passed I nonchalantly washed the vile thing down... with six or seven beers in a span of several minutes.

Someday I'm going to get my revenge on all of those third world connoisseurs - and bring them to the local Jack in the Box!

THE MESSAGE

"If you're going to be able to look back on something and laugh about it, you might as well laugh about it now." – Marie Osmond

One of the characters I had working for me when I commanded an MSG detachment in the Congo was a Marine by the name of Ruben Castillo. Sergeant Castillo was a tough Chicano from Chicago, and one of the most competent watchstanders in the detachment. He was also a bit of a wise-guy.

One of Castillo's pet peeves was the habit our Congolese "guardians" had of falling asleep on the job. The guardians were uniformed security guards hired by the Embassy to provide security for our homes, and there was one assigned to every American residence twenty-four hours a day. One such fellow was posted at the Marine House, as the detachment "dormitory" was known, and he had been seen snoozing on numerous occasions. The man always claimed he was simply resting his eyes for a few moments, so my sergeant decided to prove him a liar.

Late one evening Castillo covered his face with green camouflage paint and gained entrance to the Marine compound by slipping over the eight foot wall surrounding the residence. He crept around the side of the building and spotted the guard in his customary location – fast asleep in a chair on the front porch. To prove his point Castillo pulled a can from his pocket and covered the sleeping guard in shaving cream, after which he woke him up. When confronted with circumstances that could lead to his getting fired (jobs at the Embassy paid relatively well and were coveted by the locals) the man swore he was awake the entire time and had *allowed* himself to "slimed." Believe it or not that was his story, and he was sticking to it!

One of Castillo's personality traits was his stubbornness. He was worse than a mule. One day I decided it was time for everyone to change their radio call signs to enhance communications security, and being the nice guy that I am allowed each Marine to choose his own. I even gave them a week to submit it to me for inclusion in the Embassy list. But Ruben had some macho handle that he really liked, and I guess he figured if he didn't give me a new one he could just keep it. Wrong! So I assigned one *for* him, and designated his call sign to be "Plant Man" because it reminded me of how he had looked the night of the shaving cream raid. He initially refused to answer to it, but after a bit of 'counseling' we got *that* straightened out in a hurry.

Prior to coming to the Congo Castillo had served at the Embassy in Paris, and while there had met and become engaged to a lovely English girl. At one point she came down to visit him for a week or so, and we all decided she was *much* too good looking for him - and she was nice to boot.

As Sergeant Castillo neared the end of his tour in Brazzaville, and on the MSG program for that matter, he and his fiancé began making their wedding plans. When his tour in Brazzaville ended he was to fly straight to England for a big wedding, and from there they planned to go to Aruba for their honeymoon before he reported in for duty at Camp Lejeune.

When I heard the details of the wedding and honeymoon, and found out that the invitations had been mailed and everything paid for, I decided it was a perfect opportunity to give the sergeant a taste of his own medicine. Most of our official directives came via naval messages, which were processed upstairs in the communications center and placed in our box each morning. These messages have a distinctive format, and anything contained in one is treated as if it came from the burning bush. So I drafted a bogus message of my own, and had the State Department communicators run it through the system so it appeared to be legitimate. I then placed it in our in-box and waited for Castillo to take the bait when he picked up the morning traffic.

The message simply stated that any MSG who had less than a year remaining on his enlistment, and who had either not submitted a reenlistment request or had submitted one that had not yet been approved (Castillo fell into the second category) would be required to remain at their current post until approval was received or they reached their EAS – which meant he would miss the wedding.

When I arrived at the Embassy the next morning I knew the ruse had been successful, because Castillo was in what can only be described as a highly agitated state. I had barely walked through the door when he shoved a copy of the message in my direction followed by a string of expletives.

The Stone Age telephone service in the Congo was, for once, a good thing. Castillo had tried calling back to MSG Battalion, Headquarters Marine Corps, and even his Congressman. Fortunately he got through to no one, although he vowed to keep trying until he did. I sat in my office trying to keep a straight face while he paced back and forth on Post One ranting and raving. It was fun to watch, but I didn't dare leave him alone in such a state.

Finally I walked into Post One and asked him for the message. When he handed it to me I ripped it into small pieces and said "There, that takes care of *that* problem!" Castillo stared at me in disbelief, since he figured he would need the message as a reference. "You can't do that Gunny," he exclaimed. "I need that!"

As I headed out the door I tossed the message in the trash can and said, "Sure I can… I wrote it!"

OF ANTS AND MEN

"With self-discipline most anything is possible!" - Theodore Roosevelt

Some years back I was on patrol deep inside the jungles of a Central American country when I came to realize why the Marine Corps trains recruits the way it does. There didn't seem to be a purpose to a lot of the games Drill Instructors played when I was a boot, but one day an incident occurred which showed me there really was method to their madness.

While in the boonies I learned there were at least two types of ants common to the jungles of the Western Hemisphere. The first was the Leaf-cutter. They fascinated me. Those little guys would move in a column across the jungle floor to a bit of vegetation, and merge into a second column going in the opposite direction once they had picked up a bit of leaf. They were quite industrious. When one of us got bored we would sometimes put a line of bug juice across their path and watch the ensuing traffic jam. It was hilarious.

The second type of ant is called a Fallopian. They are far more sinister than their vegetarian cousins, the leaf cutters. These ants are comparatively large, and have stingers in addition to being able to bite. And they like to do *both*. Nasty little buggers.

Anyway, as we moved through the jungle the patrol leader signaled for a security halt. That is when everyone faces outboard, becomes motionless, and listens for any sound that could indicate there are enemy in the area. Most Marines took a knee, but I elected to rest against a tree instead since I was carrying the radio and my pack was especially heavy. Getting back up was just too much work.

What I didn't notice in the dim light of triple canopy jungle was the bark of the tree was moving. It was covered with Fallopian ants. They swarmed onto my pack, poured down the back of my neck, and began to sting me. I wasn't sure what was going on, but I knew it wasn't good. I quietly swung my pack to the ground and signaled for the next man in line to move up to where I was, and as I peeled off my uniform blouse he brushed the ants off of me without making a sound. There were already hundreds of bites on my back, and our doc must have used up an entire bottle of calamine lotion in treating them!

I couldn't help but think back to the day our Senior Drill Instructor caught a recruit slapping a sand flea during the First Phase of boot camp. A search party was formed to find the dead insect, and a burial detail carried the body out for proper disposition – much like in the movie *The DI*. The tiny corpse was placed in an empty matchbox. But just because the insect was tiny didn't mean the grave had to be. The detail dug a full size hole to inter the departed, using only e-tools and bare hands. Once it was complete the burial proceeded with full honors.

The lesson we learned that day stuck with me throughout my career. There are bugs out there. Let them eat all they want. If you scream and slap at them you will get yourself, and probably a lot of your buddies, killed!

TROOPING THE COLORS

"Proper Prior Planning Prevents Piss Poor Performance!"
– The Seven "Ps"

The Marine Corps Birthday is normally cause for great celebration, but the Corps' 208th was a bit different. With the memory of the Beirut bombing just two weeks old a somber mood prevailed throughout the Corps, particularly amongst those of us who had lost friends in the blast. I for one was looking for some special way to honor our fallen comrades, so when the opportunity to conduct a memorial color guard for the USMC/FBI Association arose I jumped at it. The ceremony was to be held at Camp Smith, NY and the guest of honor was to be none other than the Assistant Commandant of the Marine Corps, General P.X. Kelly.

Upon arriving at Camp Smith we immediately changed into our dress blues and began practicing for the ceremony and pass in review. About an hour later the General's helicopter landed in front of the reviewing stand and things literally began with a bang, in this case provided by a battery of National Guard 105mm howitzers. After General Kelly concluded his remarks a pair of buglers sounded echo taps, a detail of former Marine FBI agents fired a twenty-one gun salute, and finally we led the assembled formation of FBI agents past the reviewing stand.

With our mission complete we prepared to leave, but before we could do so a member of the Association approached and invited us to be their guests at the birthday dinner that was to follow. We accepted, and what transpired during that evening can only be characterized as a testament to the old adage "practice makes perfect."

231

Prior to the meal a keg of beer was rolled out and a cocktail hour of sorts was conducted. We all joined General Kelly and the Sergeant Major of the Marine Corps in hoisting a few, and then retired to the banquet hall for the main event. We had all worked up quite a thirst parading around under the hot sun, so as the meal progressed the entire color guard enjoyed a variety of wines and spirits topped off with some port wine for toasting and the traditional rum punch. To say that *we* got "toasted" would be a gross understatement.

It was at this juncture we were informed that, oh by the way, our services would be required for one more ceremony. This one had us preceding the birthday cake into the hall and executing a countermarch directly in front of the man with all the stars on his shoulders. It was with great trepidation that we unfurled our colors and prepared to march on, and our conversation focused on which articles of the UCMJ we would most likely face at our upcoming Court Martial. Our fears proved to be unfounded however, because once we stepped off we went on autopilot and proceeded to execute the ceremony flawlessly.

A memento of the occasion hangs on my wall to this day and serves as a reminder of the importance of practice, repetition and plain old good luck. It is a photo of General Kelly cutting a birthday cake with his Mameluke sword while in the background stand four Marines at ramrod attention. There is no clue as to the true condition of those Marines... unless you look very closely at our eyes.

THE FLYING BOAT

"To err is human, to forgive divine – neither of which is Marine Corps policy!"

For many years the mission of Marine Recon was exactly what the name implied - pure reconnaissance. In the 1980's things changed, and we took on the added responsibility of direct action missions such as destruction raids and hostage recovery. A lot of additional training and equipment was necessary in order to pull this off, but since we had the best troops on the planet the brass figured we could do it. To differentiate between the two missions we began to call the former a "green side op" and the latter a "black side op." I know it sounds somewhat sinister, but the names simply refer to the color clothing to be worn!

Once the Marine Corps had fully developed this capability we were invited to use it on occasion. In one instance our force was preparing to deploy overseas for a real-world mission, and conducted a full scale rehearsal to make sure everyone was on the same sheet of music. An R&S team was sent to the objective to gather intelligence, and we would follow with the assault element when the time was right.

The strike force was to be inserted by "hard duck," which involves pushing rubber boats mounted on plywood platforms out the back of a helicopter and following them out in a maneuver called a "helocast." We would then swim to the boats, mount the motors, don our gear, and move to the objective.

In order to load two boats into one helicopter it was necessary to "clamshell" them, which involves placing our gear in one and strapping the partially inflated second boat on top. The Marine in charge of making this happen was a Staff Sergeant named Bob Geer. Bob was one of the most experienced and well trained Marines in the command, and as I write this he is still one of the best recon Marines I have known. He had a lot of responsibilities and couldn't do it all himself, so naturally some tasks such as securing the boats inside the helicopters were delegated to others. That would prove costly. Like they say, you can delegate authority - but never responsibility.

After our briefing we took off in a pair of CH-53's. I was in the lead bird, and sat directly across from the strike force commander. The overall mission commander, Colonel Wheeler Baker, was up on the flight deck with the pilots. After about an hour in the air we were approaching the insert point and the aircraft began to descend to sea level. As the helicopters passed through about four hundred feet of altitude the ramp was lowered and we got our gear ready for the upcoming helocast. That's when "Murphy" added his two cents.

We felt the helo lurch and each of us looked around to see what had happened. It was then we noticed the boats were gone. Whoever had secured the bow line to the deck of the helicopter had apparently done it incorrectly, and the slight "flare" caused by our descent had done the rest. Bud Boney, who was in the bird behind us, reported he saw the boat slide out of our aircraft, and that it stayed stable all the way to the water below. He said it looked like it was flying.

Colonel Baker aborted the op and we searched for a place to put the birds down. I had always considered the Colonel to be an outstanding officer, but on that day my respect for him increased tenfold. While the strike force commander was cursing and throwing things, Colonel Baker gave no outward sign anything unusual had happened – he was cool as a cucumber. I remember thinking to myself, "he must be one hell of a poker player."

Our pilot soon located a corn field not far from the water and landed there. The local yokels came running from their homes to see what all the commotion was about and found a giant helicopter sitting in the middle of their field. I think a few of them thought it was an invasion!

We ran down the ramp and quickly found the spot where our boats had landed in the water. They had obviously impacted with a great deal of force. The gasoline bladders for our outboard motors had burst, covering our gear and filling the surrounding water with gallons of fuel. Everyone waded in and began to collect what was left. The satellite radio in my pack was smashed to pieces, and it too was filled with gasoline.

The Colonel instructed me to notify our command center what had happened, and since my radio had been destroyed I had to use an alternate means of communication, so I improvised and borrowed a cordless telephone from one of the locals. At first the duty officer thought my call was a hoax, since he knew there were no telephones on helicopters – and there were no cellphones in those days.

The next day there was an article in the local paper entitled "Helicopter Drops Raft in Woodville." It was hysterical. In one paragraph it said a resident "ran outside and blew a car horn out of fear in a futile effort to catch the attention of the pilots." What a hoot.

After this incident a lot of people had unflattering things to say about Bob Geer, but it was undeserved. It's amazing how quickly they forget all the great things someone has accomplished in the face of a setback. I guess the old saw that says "it takes ten atta-boys to cancel out one aw-shit" is true!

BART BONEHEAD

"A committee of Congressmen, who asshole to asshole couldn't make a beer fart in a whirlwind..." - Mythical Gunnery Sergeant Tom Highway (as portrayed by Clint Eastwood) in the film "Heartbreak Ridge"

One of the biggest problems with the Marine Security Guard Program is the requirement for experienced, professional Staff Non-Commissioned Officers with years of formal leadership training to answer to a series of State Department "Officers" who have *none*. They tend to think their lofty positions are all that is required to command respect, failing to realize it is a precious commodity which must be earned. That, along with the requirement to satisfy the needs of two parallel chains of command simultaneously, makes the job of a Detachment Commander far more complicated than it should be.

An example of such an incompetent, self-serving State Department employee was an individual who I will call 'Bart Bonehead.' Mr. Bonehead would be a perfect subject for a Psych 101 class because his problems are so transparent they would be easily identifiable to every student. A short, fat, one-eyed little troll, Bart no doubt became a Special Agent in the Diplomatic Security Service in an attempt to attain some degree of the manhood he had been denied by genetics. In the process he opened to question the entrance standards of DSS. He was such an insecure individual and possessed so little personality that he felt it necessary to create an artificial persona for himself in an attempt to impress others with his manliness. He thought by calling himself "Cowboy" and wearing a collection of pointy boots and ratty cowboy hats he would be macho, when in reality he became one of those people we've all known at one time or another who give themselves a nickname because no one else will. As a result he became a bit of a laughingstock in the process.

When Mr. Bonehead was first assigned to the American Embassy in the Congo he professed to be a big supporter of Marine Detachments and was initially welcomed with open arms. It wasn't until later that we figured out he liked to hang with the Marines because he figured by associating with, and dictating policy to, the tough guys at post he would be a tough guy too. He was assigned to Brazzaville as the Administrative Officer on an "excursion tour" outside of the security side of the house because he ostensibly had hopes of one day becoming an Ambassador - an aspiration even his friends considered laughable given his low self esteem, mediocre skills and lack of style.

During my tenure as Detachment Commander I had numerous occasions to butt heads with this walking advertisement for legalized abortion – and it is a testament to my self-control that he remained ambulatory throughout our six months together. It is because of people like him the Corps needs to review the agreement which assigns Marines to Diplomatic posts in support of the State Department. Too many decisions concerning the Marines are left to the discretion of the civilians working for State, and too often the Detachment is treated like a group of second class citizens. It is impractical to expect Marines to operate efficiently when they are subject to the whims of people who have no concept of professionalism, loyalty and integrity. What invariably happens is a confrontation the MSGs cannot possibly win occurs whenever the Marines do not automatically bow to the wishes of the State "officer" who happens to be in control at the moment.

The bottom line is I'd love to have the used car salesman who sold this concept to the Marine Corps working for me, since he could probably sell a glass of water to a drowning man!

THE MAIL BUOY

"To walk my post from flank to flank, and take no crap from any rank!" – Unofficial Twelfth General Order

My first deployment on a Navy ship was aboard *USS Barnstable County*, which is an LST. If you have ever been aboard a "T" you know they are most uncomfortable and cramped ships in the fleet. At least on an LPH embarked troops can go for a run on the flight deck or watch a movie in the hanger bay. On a T the only thing to look forward to is mail call, and that only happens about once per week. The boredom in between was palpable, and it was only natural for sailors to invent silly distractions to help pass the time.

One of the time-honored Navy traditions to be endured aboard ship is the rite of passage from "pollywog" to "shellback." For some reason crossing the equator is a big event for sailors, and anyone who hasn't done so is known as a "wog." All who are designated as such must go through an initiation which involves crawling through garbage, wearing bizarre outfits, and finally kissing the greased belly of Baby Neptune – in the person of a fat sailor wearing a diaper! At that point the former pollywog is admitted to the Realm of Neptune and designated a shellback. If you are trying to make some sense of all this don't look at me – I'm as clueless as you are. I can only guess it doesn't take much to keep our Navy brethren entertained when they are at sea for extended periods.

But most underway entertainment is not on such a grandiose scale. During our first week at sea there was an announcement that some "Sea Bats" had been captured, and anyone wanting to see them should lay (go) to the fantail.

239

Having never seen a sea bat I naturally went to have a look. It was in a cardboard box into which air holes had been poked. The guys who had caught the beast invited one of us to peek through one of the holes, and when the first one knelt down to peer inside he felt a sharp smack on his butt. The sailor behind him was holding a paddle, to which he pointed and said "See... bat!"

We were also required to stand "mail buoy watch" on the quarterdeck while at sea. Posted with binoculars, gas mask, radio and a boat hook, it was the duty of the man on watch to keep an eye out for buoys marked 'U.S. Mail' and snag them with the hook.

There is of course no such thing as a mail buoy. Mail actually was brought in by helicopter, but most no-rank fuzz-butts on their first deployment don't know such things. In the case of our ship it was dropped onto the flight deck from a hovering CH-46, because helos couldn't land there due to the due the large causeways strapped to the hull.

One day the helo delivering our mail was having a difficult time maintaining a hover over the flight deck due to a strong crosswind, and just as they dropped two bags from the "hell hole" the aircraft lurched out over the water. Splash! The mail began to drift away and slowly began to sink.

The Marine on mail buoy detail that day was one of the smarter guys in the platoon, and he was sure the whole thing was a crock. He was, of course, correct. But on that particular day his radio came to life with instructions to snag two bags of mail about to drift past his post. *Sure* there was! Even when the bags came into view he refused to try to grab them, figuring it was a setup. They sank moments later and were gone.

Needless to say, there was no mail call that week!

G'DAY MATE!

"Australia and the United States are two countries separated by a common language!"

On my first day in Australia I received a rather expensive education in linguistics from the locals. I had just reported in as the new Detachment Commander at our Embassy in Canberra, and the Gunny I was replacing suggested the happy hour being held at the Royal Military College Sergeants Mess would be a perfect opportunity to meet my counterparts in the Australian Army. I still smelled like jet fumes from the long flight over, but deferred to his judgment and went along.

The Aussies turned out to be the salt of the earth. They made me feel welcome from the very first moment, and bought me one 'Victoria Bitter' - which is a popular local beer - after another. I didn't realize it at the time but a "VB," like most Aussie beers, has about twice the alcohol content of an American beer, and was having a blast until one of my new found friends said, "Hey Yank, how about shouting the bar?" It sounded like some sort of game to me, and in my semi-inebriated state I said, "Sure, why not?"

It turns out that "shout" means buy a round, and shouting the bar meant buying one for *each* of the hundred or so who were present. The only thing that saved me from abject poverty was the strong US dollar, since the exchange rate was two-to-one in my favor. But to their credit I lost count of the number of times I heard one of those blokes say "It's my shout, Gunny" over the next two years, and that more than balanced the books.

That wasn't my last lesson in Aussie lingo, not by a long shot. A couple of weeks later I was in a crowded downtown pub watching a rugby match on the "telly." I was beginning to like and understand the rough sport, but hadn't yet developed an allegiance to any particular team. In an effort to learn more about the game I struck up a conversation with the young lady standing next to me at the bar, and at one point casually asked who she was rooting for. She slapped me right across the face and stormed off without saying a word. Needless to say, I was a bit perplexed!

The next morning I related what had happened to a couple of the Marines who had been in country a bit longer than I, figuring they might be able to offer some sort of explanation for what had transpired. They did… once they were able to stop laughing. "Root," I learned, is a versatile word which can be used as a noun, a verb, or an adjective, much like the "F-word" in the United States. I had unwittingly asked who she was sleeping with!

THE 34-FOOT PLF

"There are no secrets to success. It is the result of preparation, hard work and learning from failure." – Secretary of State Colin Powell

Anyone who has attended the Army's Airborne Course at Fort Benning, Georgia will be the first to tell you there is little, if anything, of an intellectual nature contained in the course curriculum. If you can follow simple instructions, perform basic tasks, and muster the courage to throw yourself out the open door of a C-130 you are pretty much a sure bet to graduate. Marines traditionally do very well at jump school in comparison to students from the other services, and I believe that is primarily due to our superior discipline, conditioning and esprit-de-corps. Members of our sister services differ with that opinion of course, and point to the misguided perception that little intelligence is required to be a Marine. They like to say that Marine stands for "Muscles Are Required, Intelligence Not Essential," but in reality the Corps requires higher ASVAB scores than the other services.

Jump school is divided into three phases, each a week long. Ground week mostly consists of practicing Parachute Landing Falls in a pit of sand, over and over and over. Next comes tower week, during which students execute door exits from a thirty-four-foot tower while wearing a harness and sliding down a long cable (remember that for later). Finally comes the actual jump week. The whole thing is pretty routine, but occasionally something occurs that makes you scratch your head.

Ed Sere was a New York City fireman, and a Chief Warrant Officer in the reserves. He once told me the story of how two young Marines in his class decided they wanted to quit jump school. Each of them was a burly country boy, and both were good, squared-away Marines. They approached Ed with the news on the Saturday after ground week, and naturally he tried to dissuade them from doing anything rash. When asked why they wanted to quit the two stated that the thirty-four-foot tower was just too high for them. He counseled them to go back to their room and sleep on it and come back to see him again on Sunday.

Keep in mind that while it was commonplace for *soldiers* to quit, it was unheard of for Marines to do so. Every morning at formation there was a call for quitters, and it was a source of tremendous pride that while there were usually a few takers there were never any Marines among them. So naturally Ed was fit to be tied.

When Sunday came the two returned and said they had made up their minds to quit. "Last night we went down to where those towers are to have a look. They still seemed kinda high, so we decided to try one out. Sergeant Sere, I damned near broke my legs when I hit the ground, and I was hanging on by my fingertips when I let go!"

THE EXTRA TESTICLE

"Don't take a butcher's advice on how to cook meat. If he knew how, he'd be a chef!" - Andy Rooney

Contrary to what some people think, being in Recon takes a lot more than the ability to "run long distances, clap hands, and count to four." In actual fact a great deal of training is necessary in order to perform complicated tasks such as hydrographic surveys, closed circuit diving, and land navigation. While a high level of physical fitness *is* important, the popular stereotype of a brainless PT stud is way off the mark.

With all the skills that are required problems sometimes arise when senior NCOs with no Recon experience are assigned to a reconnaissance unit. I have seen good sergeants come from the infantry and fail miserably as team leaders, at least initially, because they had no clue where to begin.

At the next higher level of command the situation is a bit different. Virtually every lieutenant assigned as a platoon commander has no recon background and must rely heavily on his platoon sergeant. That billet is normally filled by a former team leader who possesses a wealth of knowledge, but every now and then this is not the case and he is a rookie as well.

A good example of that less than desirable arrangement occurred while I was serving with 2d Reconnaissance Battalion during the mid 1980's. A new Staff Sergeant named 'Benson' was assigned to a platoon in my company and became Platoon Sergeant by virtue of his rank. His lack of experience was not immediately apparent, but his uncanny resemblance to the Extraterrestrial of movie fame *was* - and he was promptly dubbed ET. As we got to know him better it became clear he was one of those individuals who think they know everything, and it didn't take long for the definition of his nickname had evolved to the more descriptive "Extra Testicle."

A few months after ET joined our company we deployed to the Jungle Warfare Training Center at Fort Sherman, Panama for about a month. After receiving some initial jungle survival training we began preparing for a series of patrols, and ET was assigned to insert several teams, including mine, via inflatable boat. The only problem was he had never piloted one in his life.

Just prior to nightfall we boarded a truck for the trip to the pier where the boats were to be launched. Enroute ET asked a fellow Staff Sergeant to apply some camouflage paint to the back of his bald, light bulb shaped head, and his peer was eager to be of assistance. After writing "ET" in large block letters on the back of his skull the artist turned Benson's head so that we could inspect his handiwork. We all laughed so hard there were rivers of green tears running down our faces!

Once it was dark we boarded our boat and ET gave the command to cast off. Not until we were drifting on the swift current toward some jagged rocks did he decide to try starting the outboard motor, which of course promptly flooded. Our predicament was compounded by the fact that the mouth of the Chagres River is a prime breeding ground for sharks, and since the current was carrying us toward a rocky jetty we were seconds away from treading water.

Fortunately one of the experienced coxswains in the boat quickly sized up the situation and pushed ET aside, and managed to get the motor started just moments before we learned the true meaning of "rocks and shoals." With that, he turned over the tiller to ET and we headed upriver.

Tactical movement up a jungle river necessitates staying as close to the riverbank as possible in order to avoid detection, but that is quite hazardous due to a variety of obstructions such as trees leaning out over the water called "sweepers." The method used to avoid such things is for the Marine in the bow to direct the coxswain left or right by gesturing with his hands, and that works quite well – most of the time.

As we neared my team's insertion point the spotter pointed to the right, but ET steered left. Three of us were ripped from the boat's gunwales by overhanging branches and thrown into neck deep water. Since most of us were already out of the boat ET decided we were close enough to the proper insert point, and told us to move out. I of course pointed out that "close only counts in horseshoes and hand grenades," but he refused to be swayed.

We had to make the best of the situation, so I broke out my NVGs to get our bearings. We were up against a sheer river bank, and if we moved away from it the river got deep and the current swift. We had to climb up, so I held onto a tree root while another Marine climbed onto my shoulders. Then another Marine scaled us both and managed to get on top. We must have looked like the Flying Wallendas! All in all it took almost an hour to haul our gear to the top and figure out where the hell we were. Naturally, I was pissed!

I did of course calm down in due time… but even so, after the patrol had concluded, was disappointed to learn ET had not yet returned to his home planet…

A WALK IN THE WOODS

"I have only two men out of my company and twenty out of some other company. We need support, but it is almost suicide to try to get it here as we are swept by machine gun fire and a constant barrage is on us. I have no one on my left and only a few on my right. I will hold." - First Lieutenant (and future Commandant) Clifton B. Cates, USMC in Belleau Wood, 19 July 1918

One of the more unusual training exercises I have participated in came as the tenure of Captain "Hap" Holm was winding down as Commanding Officer of Charlie Company, 2nd Reconnaissance Battalion. The entire company hiked the Appalachian Trail through North Carolina and Virginia, and afterwards moved directly into a patrolling exercise in Quantico. It was without a doubt the longest hump I have ever been on!

The Company First Sergeant at the time, Kenn Capper, was right out of a recruiting poster – literally. I have lost count of how many of them include his image. I guess he just had that certain "je ne sais quoi" they were looking for. In any case he was someone who took Marine Corps history seriously.

While sitting around one evening on the trail the First Sergeant and I became engaged in an impromptu game of USMC trivia. We took turns trying to stump each other with questions about the history of the Corps, and he was clearly surprised by the extent of my knowledge. In fact he was so surprised that when he left us a few weeks later to take over as First Sergeant at Camp David he presented me with a book of Marine Corps history. It was a nice compliment.

After our field exercise concluded we showered for the first time in three weeks, put on our "Alphas," and were bused over to Marine Barracks 8th & I for the Evening Parade. Anyone who has not seen it at least once is missing out on one of the great thrills that come with being a Marine. If you can't get motivated watching the Silent Drill Platoon you have to be crazy, or dead!

On the drive back to Camp Lejeune we stopped at the Naval Weapons Station at Yorktown, Virginia to pay homage to Chesty Puller's medals. They were there on loan from his widow, and were in a large display case for all to see. We all felt like we were in the presence of the Holy Grail. He was a hell of a Marine, and a big part of our history!

That is relevant because one of the things that inspires the Marines of today to go forth and do great and heroic things is the legacy of those who have gone before. No Marine wants to be the one to bring discredit upon the Corps, or sully the names of Daly and Butler and Puller. I truly believe it is our sense of history, from Tun Tavern to the present, which makes the Corps different from the other services. To that end every leader of Marines owes it to his troops to teach them about those who have gone before. Not just the stuff in an EST book, but an in-depth history of the Corps.

After all, the very same Marines you are teaching today could well show up in the history books of tomorrow!

THE BIG SCARE

By Cameron McCurry

"One ought never to turn one's back on a threatened danger and try to run away from it. If you do that, you will double the danger. But if you meet it promptly and without flinching, you will reduce the danger by half." – Sir Winston Churchill

When you are a recruit training days are a blur. From the moment you first arrive at MCRD to the time that you are called a Marine you are moved at a pace many people would find inhuman. Your average day begins around 0400-0500 depending on what is on the training schedule, and you move around in what the DIs cheerfully refer to as the "Green Marine Blur."

Classes make up a large part of the first phase of training. Between assembling your M-16, managing your money or learning the history of the Marine Corps you get crammed full of knowledge in a short period of time.

One thing that you need to understand is not only are recruits on the move for a long period of time, they are also kept relatively ignorant of the outside world. What you know about life outside of MCRD is limited to letters from home and what the DI feels the need to tell you. In other words, nothing.

One morning we were sitting down for a Marine Corps History lesson, and the topic of the day was the Korean War. The instructor began speaking, but was interrupted about thirty seconds into the lesson by the arrival of our Commanding Officer. He came in, pulled the teacher aside and whispered something into his ear.

"Well recruits, it looks like your Commanding Officer needs the floor." The CO was a big man. He looked as if he could break the average recruit in half with little more than a harsh word. In his hand was a manila envelope that he held up high. "I have been authorized to read this to you by the Commanding General of MCRD San Diego." That got our attention. We listened silently as he began to read from the paper.

"At 0430 this morning Iraq launched another attack against Kuwait. The First Marine Division intercepted them. They have taken approximately four thousand casualties. Bow your heads in a moment of silence." He let us do that for a few seconds. "You're done. What this means to you is this: You will not be graduating in August like you thought. You will remain here for two more weeks, and then go to Camp Pendleton for two weeks of Infantry Training." At that point the CO's message was driven home rather painfully.

"How many of you are Reservists?" Those of us who were raised our hands. "From this moment, you are active duty. How many of you are in an MOS (Military Occupational Specialty for those of you not familiar with the term) that is not 0300 Infantry?" Again, those of us in that category raised our hands. "From this moment on you are Infantry. Your Drill Instructors are now your Platoon Sergeants. After your training at Camp Pendleton you will be sent to Kuwait as a part of the Casualty Replacement Platoon. You will be allowed a five minute phone call home to your families and you will be given time today to write out your last will and testament."

He walked out and we began to have our lives flash before our eyes. After allowing us to mull over what was going to happen to us for a few minutes the teacher announced that it was all a hoax. The point was to give us an idea of what recruits at the time of the Korean War went through when a similar announcement was made to them.

But for them it wasn't a simulation. It may sound like a horrid mind game, but it put what we train for into sharp focus that day.

Cameron McCurry is a Corporal in the Marine Corps Reserve.

SQUEALS FOR SEALS

"The Marine Corps has just been called by the New York Times, 'The elite of this country.' I think it is the elite of the world." - Admiral William "Bull" Halsey, U.S. Navy

President John F. Kennedy showed a great deal of foresight back in the 1960s when he realized the importance of unconventional warfare. It was he who brought Special Forces from the fringe to the mainstream, increased the budgets of such units, and even authorized the wearing of green berets.

While JFK made a leap forward by broadening the use of SF, he also made a huge mistake when he expanded the mission of UDT. Underwater Demolition Teams were an important part of advance force operations. They were responsible for surveying landing beaches and destroying obstacles prior to an amphibious assault, and they were good at it. Unfortunately the Navy wanted a piece of the Spec War pie, and came up with the idea for a Sea, Air and Land outfit. The SEAL team was born.

My first chance to see Seals operate in the field came during an exercise on the balmy Caribbean island of Vieques in the late 1970s. My Recon platoon was aboard *USS Pensacola* with a group of them, and while I admit we were envious of some of the gear they brought aboard we also had a good laugh watching them prepare for their mission. They didn't have a clue what they were doing!

The Seals were inserted by parachute prior to D-Day and were asked to blow up a bridge, execute a prisoner snatch, and extract by Zodiac to a waiting submarine. As I discovered for the first time during that op, land navigation is not a strong suit of the Seals. They couldn't even *find* the bridge, let alone blow it up. So they decided to try mission number two. Unfortunately they then ended up getting into a firefight with the exercise umpires, who were unarmed and wore white tape on their covers denoting them as non-combatants. With their missions incomplete, those hapless naval warriors loaded into a Zodiac and promptly ran it over a reef, ripping out the bottom and sending most of their gear to Davey Jones' Locker.

When my team came paddling ashore later that night we spotted the lot of them sleeping on the beach, but wouldn't learn the whole story until after our extraction a week later. It was then that I understood what my first platoon sergeant, who had done three tours in Nam with 3rd Recon, meant when he said Navy Seals should not be allowed beyond the high water line.

It's not fair to judge any group on just one little episode, so I kept an open mind about these guys. A few years later an organization called the Maritime Special Purpose Force was formed, and it gave us an opportunity to work with Seal teams on a regular basis. The MSPF consisted of a Force Recon detachment, Seal platoon, Recon and Surveillance element, Explosive Ordnance Disposal Team, and a few other cats and dogs. Its purpose was to provide a task force commander with a forward deployed spec ops element capable of conducting *in-extremis* missions, and overall it was a good concept.

During the late 1980s the MSPF I was attached to was in New York for TRUE training. The purpose was to practice missions in an urban environment. During a break in operations our platoon sergeant scheduled a HALO jump to help maintain our freefall proficiency, and he invited the Seals to "strap-hang" with us. They readily agreed to participate, but then opted out when they learned it was a combat equipment jump with packs, rifles and the whole nine yards. In those days Seal freefall training was done "in-house," and the order of the day for them was Hollywood jumps, i.e. no equipment. It was more like a skydiving club than a military unit. Fortunately someone eventually saw the light, and today Seals attend SF HALO School along with everyone else.

Part of the problem with these guys is their cowboy mentality. They actually believe their press releases, and act like a bunch of undisciplined hooligans. One example comes to mind. During a deployment to Panama we had a group of Seals going through the Jungle Operations Training Course with us. They didn't exactly distinguish themselves in the field, and when we all formed up to graduate their lack of discipline and professionalism was shameful. To a man they were unshaven, their boots were unshined and unbloused, and their idea of standing at attention was "base liberty."

But that was just training. In the real world, the Seals were tasked with securing General Noriega's personal plane during Operation Just Cause in Panama in 1989. They may as well have sent the Keystone Cops, and some of them ended up getting killed due to their own ineptitude. It was so unnecessary.

The assault on Grenada six years earlier was another fiasco. The Seals inserted by parachuting into the ocean, and four of them ended up drowning. I wasn't there, but from what I understand someone decided Seals were too macho to wear UDT vests or any other type of flotation device. If that is true, it is criminal.

More recently Seals landing on the beaches of Somalia were greeted by flood lights and CNN camera crews. While that's great for getting yourself on television, it's not generally considered good form for a clandestine operation.

If you've ever wondered about Seal Close Quarters Battle skills just watch the film "Navy Seals." Unless something has changed in recent years (and hopefully it has) they operate exactly as depicted in the movie. Upon entering a room everyone starts blasting away on full automatic, and while that certainly translates into dead bad guys it's also a cause for concern for any hostages who happen to be in the room. If you ever find yourself in a similar situation pray that Delta Force or Force Recon show up with their surgical shooting skills.

In all fairness I have to point out that I have known some very good individuals who happened to be Seals. If those guys had joined a different service I'm sure they would have been exemplary warriors, and they are not the ones I am critical of. It's the whole concept of NAVSPECWAR that is bad.

Why are the Seals flawed? It's simple. Those who apply for BUDS, the Basic Underwater Demolition School that trains Seals, have no infantry experience from which to draw. The Navy takes an assortment of rust pickers and boiler technicians and miraculously transforms them into 'special operations gurus' in matter of months. It's not a good formula. They enter training without any field skills whatsoever, and must start from scratch.

Marines applying to join Force Recon have already spent a few years in the infantry developing field skills such as land navigation, camouflage, and patrolling. Many have even spent a few years learning their craft in Reconnaissance Battalions. The fact is any *recruit* graduating from Parris Island has superior weapons handling skills, since the Navy does not conduct any significant marksmanship training.

256

The Navy needs to realize that you can't just throw a huge budget at something like this and expect it to work. The Seals sure do have some nice toys though. They also have to understand that selecting people based upon their level of fitness alone is not the answer, although there's no denying Seals do keep themselves in shape. The Navy just isn't the type of service that produces the type of raw material needed for Spec Ops. They should stick to what they do well – driving aircraft carriers, submarines and destroyers. Please leave land warfare to the grunts, and bring back the UDT.

A number of years ago there were a group of Seals aboard a Navy ship anchored off Camp Lejeune's Onslow Beach, which in those days was the home of the 2nd Reconnaissance Battalion. One evening they decided to come ashore and have a beer in our club, the "Eagles Nest." Their attitude immediately rubbed some of our guys the wrong way, and before long one of the Marines made a comment that I have never forgotten.

"You know," he began, " I took the test to be a Seal when I was in the Navy, but I didn't pass."

"Well, it is pretty tough," the senior Seal replied with a thinly veiled air of superiority.

"I'll say," continued the Marine. "No matter how hard I tried, I couldn't keep that damn ball on my nose!"

The ensuing fight was one for the books. The damage to the club was extensive, and the next morning there was a lump on my head from a pool cue someone had used as a club. And it was all good.

It's just a good thing my buddy didn't make that crack to Demi Moore!

THE ORACLE

"Knowledge is power!"

I don't have a lot of talent. I can't sing, I can't dance, and I sure as hell can't play a musical instrument. But I *have* always been a fountain of useless information. It started when I was a small child. I loved learning new things, and even read the encyclopedia up to the letter K before attending elementary school. I would have read the rest, but my family didn't have a complete set.

As the years went by my penchant for remembering insignificant facts became well known, and I began to receive lots of phone calls asking me to settle disputes over one thing or another. It's amazing how obscure some of the facts people argue over can be. I didn't always know the answer of course, and if I was stumped the contesting parties would be forced to go look it up.

During the time I worked in the 2nd Force Recon Communications Section computers were just beginning to come into the mainstream, and like most people over the age of thirty I was a bit leery of them. It all seemed so complicated - but since my job required their use I had no choice but to learn. That was when I discovered that you could also play games on a computer.

Gunnery Sergeant Joe Majewski was the communications chief back then, and at lunchtime every day he would fire up the computer and drag whatever hapless troop he could find into the office for a game of Jeopardy! The Gunny had a computer version of the popular game show, and loved showing the troops how smart he was. Then he made the mistake of challenging *me*.

If he had challenged me to a game of checkers, or darts, or even an arm wrestling match he more than likely would have won. But not trivia. I not only beat him, it was total humiliation. When I got up to leave he told me to sit back down for a rematch. Same result. He was fit to be tied!

Back then we shared a building with ANGLICO, probably because they were the only other unit with a parachute capability. They had a Navy Lieutenant assigned to them as custodian for classified material, and the vault he worked in was right next to our office. The Lieutenant was an Ivy League graduate and a member of MENSA, and I guess the Gunny figured he would be the perfect guy to take me down a few notches.

One Friday afternoon Joe arranged a match between our Navy neighbor and myself, and I was up for it because I wasn't getting much in the way of competition from anyone else. What I wasn't aware of at the time was bets were being placed on the outcome of the game.

The Lieutenant played a good game, although I had a slight lead going into Final Jeopardy. One thing I should point out about the computer version which makes it harder than the actual TV game is you not only have to know the correct answer, but must know how to spell it as well. As I write this it has been fifteen years since the day this happened, and I still remember the final question like it was yesterday. I had to spell 'cornucopia' in order to win.

I don't know how much he bet, or who he bet on for that matter, but you should have seen old Joe sweat!

GUNNY SCISSORHANDS

"She sets low personal standards, and then consistently fails to achieve them." – Excerpt from a fitness report

When I was selected for promotion to Staff Sergeant I was sent to Radio Chief School out in 29 Palms, California. That is the place where communicators with a few years of experience are transformed into the "duty experts" in their field and learn to run the show.

The senior student is always assigned as Class Commander, and in this case it was a female Gunnery Sergeant whose name eludes me. She had been an Air Traffic Controller until recently, but some sort of hormonal imbalance requiring medication made her ineligible to continue in that job. Since she would have sufficient service to retire in a couple of years HQMC decided to give her a lateral move to the communications field. Big mistake.

To say the Gunny had no background in communications would be a gross understatement. I honestly don't think she could tell an antenna from a pool cue, but in all fairness couldn't be blamed for her lack of expertise in communications since it was the Marine Corps' decision to reassign her. If she had been a man they would have more than likely put her in the infantry, since every Marine is theoretically a rifleman – but of course that was not possible in this case.

Whatever possessed HQMC to put someone like that into such a technically challenging field at such a senior rank is beyond me. As a Radio Chief the Gunny would be expected to take charge of Marines with years of experience in their

MOS, and it's not something you can fake. You either know what you're doing, or you don't.

She could, however, be blamed for her poor leadership and a general disregard for Marine Corps standards and regulations. As a leader she was an abomination. Each time the class fell out for PT the Gunny would take charge of the formation, give us right face, command double time – and promptly fall out and walk back to her room. It didn't seem to bother her in the slightest, but it sure bothered us.

She also had the longest, reddest fingernails I can recall seeing on *anyone* - let alone a Marine Corps Gunnery Sergeant. It was her defining physical feature. They were so far outside regulations that she was unable to properly key a radio handset, and every time she tried I couldn't help but wonder what had happened to the hard charging, hell-for-leather fighting force I thought I had joined.

As I said earlier, I can't for the life of me remember her real name - but it makes no difference. She will always be Gunny Scissorhands to me!

IN BED WITH THE ENEMY

**"I have neither the time nor the inclination to explain myself to a
man who rises and sleeps under the blanket of the very freedom
which I provide, and then questions the manner in which I provide
it. I would rather you just said 'thank you' and went on your way."**
- Fictional Colonel Nathan Jessup (portrayed by Jack Nicholson) in "A Few Good Men"

Benedict Arnold's name became synonymous with the
word traitor in this country when he conspired to turn over
West Point to the British during the American Revolution. I
think his legacy has suffered enough these past two hundred
plus years, and it's time to find a new turncoat to vilify. The
only problem is choosing the one who is most deserving,
since there are so many in the running.

One recent candidate that comes to mind is Peter Arnett,
formerly of CNN. He won a Pulitzer Prize for reporting from
Baghdad during the Gulf War, and a decade later resurfaced
in that same city during Operation Iraqi Freedom. I always
thought it strange that the Iraqis allowed a member of the
"enemy" press corps to remain in their capital during a war,
but it eventually became clear why they did so. Mr. Arnett
forgot he was there to report the facts, and instead granted an
interview on Iraqi state-run TV where he *made* the news. His
commentary that the coalition plan was failing was
interesting – I hadn't realized General Franks had personally
briefed him on classified strategy! Move over Benedict
Arnold, and make way for Benedict Arnett.

But the liberal media isn't the only culprit. A disturbingly
large number of entertainers have abused their celebrity
status, and need to learn being famous does not necessarily
make them smart. Exactly who appointed Sean Penn
Secretary of State, anyway? Of course the most celebrated

incident of the recent war occurred when Natalie Maines of the Dixie Chicks told a London audience they were "ashamed the President was from Texas." It's bad enough to say such things during a time of national crisis, but doubly so when addressing a foreign audience. They quickly changed their tune when their fans hit them right where it hurt – in the pocketbook. Ms. Maines, *I'm* ashamed that *you* are from the United States of America!

Jane Fonda is of course the benchmark by which all traitors are measured. She went WAY beyond voicing her opinions when she traveled to North Vietnam for a photo-op sitting at the controls of an active anti-aircraft gun. Bad as that was, it was nothing compared to what happened when she met with American POWs. As she shook hands with each man in line they slipped her tiny scraps of paper containing their service numbers so that their existence would become public knowledge. She immediately turned them in to their captors, and every man was tortured as a result. The last straw came when she spit in the face of a prisoner, and earned for herself the nickname "Hanoi Jane."

Martin Sheen of the television show *The West Wing* is another idiot with delusions of relevance. His "I'm not the President, but I play one on TV" mentality is scary. Someone needs to tell this man the foreign policy briefings he has been getting are *fake*. I'm amazed that he has no problem playing a fictional President who sends troops into combat on TV, but criticizes a President who must make such difficult choices in real life. Like most actors Sheen's life is an illusion, and like his cohorts he thinks fame gained making believe he is someone else entitles him to a "bully pulpit" from which to vilify those who are making a real difference.

I was particularly saddened when Senator Kerry of Massachusetts called for a "regime change" in the United

States. I suppose he thought his choice of words was clever, but I sure didn't. The Senator was a Naval Officer in Vietnam, and should know better than to criticize the Commander-in-Chief during time of war. His rhetoric was a transparent effort to further his own Presidential aspirations, and it ended up backfiring on him.

You may ask why the average ass-in-the-grass grunt should be concerned with the actions of these people. It's simple - they are the ones making the sacrifices necessary to ensure free speech. The First Amendment not only applies to liberals who speak out against the government, but to those who call them traitors as well. If anything, grunts have *more* of a right to it since they are the ones who put their butts on the line! I'm just glad the troops in the field have been too busy doing their jobs to hear a lot of this nonsense.

If there were any justice in this world Fonda, Arnett, Sheen, Maines and the rest would have put their money where their mouths were and moved into Saddam Hussein's bunker as "human shields." It would have been the mother of all targets!

TAKING CARE OF OUR OWN

By Ellen Gamerman

"Semper Fidelis works both ways - we are always faithful to the Corps, and the Corps remains faithful to us."

John Ripley's worthless liver had left his skin a sickly yellow. Toxic fluids were collecting in his system, causing his lean frame to bloat. Once a robust one hundred seventy-five pounds, he now weighed in at four twenty-five. His kidneys were failing. An incision glared from his abdomen, closed with staples in case surgeons had to rip it open fast. Eighteen IV lines fed into his unconscious body.

One of the Marine Corps' greatest living heroes was dying. In the intensive care unit at Georgetown University Medical Center, a son of the retired colonel, Tom Ripley, sat vigil. It was seven AM when the phone rang. A donor liver had been found, but his father might not live long enough to get it.

That's when the Ripleys understood that the delivery of the liver, from a sixteen-year-old gunshot victim in Philadelphia to the dying veteran in Washington, would take too long if left in the hospital's hands. Their only thought: Call in the Marines.

Over the next hours on that day, saving John Ripley's life became a military mission. It would involve the leader of the Marine Corps and helicopters from the president's fleet. Support teams would come from police in two cities, a platoon of current and former Marines, the president of Georgetown University and even a crew of construction workers.

"Sir, this is my dad's last chance," Tom Ripley said in a call to the Marine Commandant's office. "I'm measuring my father's life in hours, not days."

The extraordinary efforts to save the sixty-three year old Ripley, recovering from transplant surgery at Walter Reed Army Medical Center in Washington, shows how far the Corps will go to protect one of its own.

Marines will say they'd do this for any fallen comrade. But Ripley is no ordinary Marine. In a messy war with few widely recognized heroes, he is a legend. And at his moment of need, the Corps treated him like one.

"Colonel Ripley's story is part of our folklore - everybody is moved by it," said Lieutenant Colonel Ward Scott, who helped organize the organ delivery from his post at the Marine Corps Historical Center in Washington, which Ripley has directed for the past three years. "It mattered that it was Colonel Ripley who was in trouble."

On Easter Sunday in 1972, then-Captain John Walter Ripley - swinging arm over arm to attach explosives to the span while dangling beneath it - almost single-handedly destroyed a bridge near the South Vietnamese city of Dong Ha. The action, which took place under heavy fire over several hours as he ran back and forth to shore for materials, is thought to have thwarted the onslaught of twenty thousand enemy troops.

His tale is required reading for every Naval Academy plebe. In Memorial Hall Ripley, a 1962 academy graduate, is the only Marine featured from the Vietnam War. A diorama shows him clinging to the grid work of the bridge at Dong Ha.

Ripley received the Navy Cross, the second-highest award a Marine can receive for combat. That decoration is surpassed only by the Medal of Honor which, many in the Marine Corps vigorously argue, Ripley deserves.

But on this July morning, three decades after surviving combat wounds, Ripley was facing death from a transportation problem. His doctors tried four civilian organ transportation agencies and could not immediately be guaranteed a helicopter by any of them. The Ripleys said they were told that a civilian helicopter would not be available for at least six hours. Driving to Philadelphia was not an option because doctors worried that any traffic delays would ruin the organ.

Tom Ripley saw only one solution. From his father's hospital room, he called the office of the Marine Corps Commandant, James L. Jones, and secured the use of a CH-46 helicopter, which is part of the presidential Marine One fleet. The plan: The chopper would ferry the transplant team to the University of Pennsylvania hospital to remove the donor liver and then transport the doctors back to Washington.

Marine lawyers instantly approved the use of military materiel for Ripley, including nearly three hours on a helicopter that costs up to six thousand dollars an hour to operate. The Commandant considered this an official lifesaving mission for a retired Marine still valuable to the Corps as a living symbol of pride.

Action was swift. The doctors rushed to Anacostia Naval Air Station, where the helicopter was waiting, rotors spinning. The chopper took off before the surgeons were even strapped in. By about ten that morning, just three hours after learning that a new liver would be available in Philadelphia, the transplant team was swooping into that city. On the landing pad an ambulance and a Philadelphia

Highway Patrol car, both summoned by the Marines, were waiting. The motorcade took off, sirens blaring.

"When you're in a situation like this, and an organ becomes available, you use the fastest resource to get it," said Dr. Cal Matsumodo, a transplant surgeon from Walter Reed who flew on the helicopter to retrieve the new liver. "This turned out to be the swiftest and best-organized effort that I've ever seen."

Ripley's original liver had been ruined by a rare genetic disease as well as a case of Hepatitis B that he believes he contracted in Vietnam. After a year-and-a-half of hospitalizations and infections, Ripley had received a new liver from a D.C. area donor July 22. But within hours of the surgery, that donor liver began to fail.

Medical professionals say the organ donation process is safeguarded to keep powerful people from skipping to the top of the waiting list. It was Ripley's critical condition - caused by the failure of the first donor liver, his doctors said - not his personal story, that put him first in line for another liver that July 24. Still, most new organs are never granted military escorts.

"It was clearly extraordinary, what they did," said Roger Brown, manager of the Organ Center at the United Network for Organ Sharing, a clearinghouse for organ procurement and allocation. Sometimes, Brown said, patients will die because available organs cannot be transported to them in time. "There's a lot of work that goes into matching a donor with a patient," he said. "If you can't find that one piece of the puzzle, it's just devastating."

In Ripley's mind, the mission that day reflected the strength of the Marine Corps fraternity. As he convalesced at Walter Reed, where he went after his operation and was listed in stable condition, he summoned his booming voice long enough to insist that Marines would do the same for even an unknown grunt.

"Does it surprise me that the Marine Corps would do this?" Ripley said from his hospital bed, his dog tags still hanging around his neck. "The answer is absolutely flat no! If any Marine is out there, no matter who he is, and he's in trouble, then the Marines will say, 'We've got to do what it takes to help him.'"

In Philadelphia though, the Marine pilots knew exactly whom they were helping, and they called it an honor. On the helipad, the flight crew stood ready as the transplant team rushed back with a box marked "HUMAN ORGAN: FRAGILE." Moments later Tom Ripley, traveling with the doctors, got an update from his oldest brother, Stephen, who was at his father's bedside. Their dad's condition was worsening. The organ had to get to Washington, fast.

Tom and Stephen, both former Marine captains, debated the quickest "RTB" - return to base, which in this case meant the Georgetown hospital. In pager messages fired off like battlefield dispatches, the chopper became "the bird" and the doctors the "pax" - slang for passengers. As the day wore on, the brothers drew from their military roots, comforting each other with the Marine motto, Semper Fidelis.

Their father, meanwhile, lay still. His dog tags, fastened with the same tape he'd used to keep them from clanking on secret missions in Vietnam, had been removed. Twice, the family had summoned a Catholic priest to deliver last rites. Now, the Ripleys wondered whether a third might be needed.

The hours ticked away, and the family learned that the Marine helicopter was too big to land on the Georgetown hospital helipad. But the doctors feared getting stuck in traffic on the drive from the Anacostia helipad to the hospital.

A well-connected Marine buddy of Ripley's called the president of Georgetown University and got permission to land on the school's football field. A construction crew standing nearby was soon ripping down fencing to make room. But the Marines rejected that makeshift helipad after sending another helicopter to survey it. The area was deemed too crowded for a landing. At one point, the Ripleys suggested landing at the Marine Corps War Memorial, across the river from Georgetown, by the statue that depicts Marines raising the flag at Iwo Jima. But that fanciful notion went nowhere.

The answer finally came in the form of a D.C. police helicopter pilot – Sergeant Thomas Hardy, a former Marine. A Corps official found him and asked whether he would take the team from Anacostia to Georgetown on his smaller chopper.

"This was a Marine Corps mission," said Hardy, a Vietnam veteran who agreed to fly without hesitation. "Once a Marine," he explained, "always a Marine."

The organ delivered, the surgery could finally start. The next day, Ripley's recovery began.

The sons who orchestrated this rescue operation called it a culminating moment in their father's military life. John Ripley was shot in the side by a North Vietnamese soldier, and during two tours of duty was pierced with so much shrapnel that doctors found metal fragments in his body as recently as last year. After Vietnam Ripley continued to serve, losing most of the pigment in his face from severe sunburns while stationed above the Arctic Circle.

The Marines, his family believed, repaid a longtime debt. "Dad gave thirty-two years of his life to the Marine Corps," said Stephen Ripley. "When he really, really needed the Marine Corps, they were there for him."

Swift, Silent and Surrounded

Even from the quiet of his hospital room, the Marine Corps still defined Ripley. His family packed a cabinet by his bed with copies of a book that John Grider Miller wrote about Ripley's heroics, and Ripley gave complimentary copies of *The Bridge at Dong Ha* to the medical staff. Not long ago a military color guard held a bedside ceremony for him, placing in the room the Marine Corps colors that normally hang in Commandant Jones' office. Ripley was urged to keep the flags in his room until he left the hospital. One afternoon, Ripley looked past his IV machine, past the uneaten hospital lunch, past the plastic cup of pills, to the flags. He was at that moment John Ripley, grateful warrior, awed by what his sons, and the Marines, had done.

"They reached over the side," he said, "and they pulled me back in the boat."

This story originally appeared in the Baltimore Sun on August 16, 2002

WHAT A MESS!

"Take courage then, seize the fortune that awaits you, repair to the Marine Rendezvous where, in a flowing bowl of punch, and three times three, you shall drink." - From a Revolutionary War era recruiting poster

If you have never attended a Mess Night, or worse yet have never heard of such an occasion, you are missing out on one of the finest traditions the Marine Corps has to offer. It is an evening of camaraderie which, when properly run, can evoke many emotions in even the hardest of men. One of the best accounts of a Mess Night I have ever read is contained in the book *The Great Santini* by Pat Conroy. I suggest you read it.

The Marine Corps Mess night is an occasion which has its roots in the British practice of a formal gathering of men in an atmosphere which contributes to the unity and esprit of a unit. The uniform for such an event is Mess Dress, blues, or black tie for civilian guests. The affair is always stag, and is presided over by the President of the Mess. His word is final on all things, and there is no appeal.

The evening begins with a cocktail hour, followed by a formal dinner. When it is time to serve the main course the chief steward "parades the beef" to the head table, accompanied by a drummer and fifer playing "The Roast Beef of Olde England." Once the President pronounces it "tasty and fit for human consumption," dinner is served.

Once the dinner has concluded port wine is passed to each member of the mess, and formal toasts are proposed. That is followed by a final "bottoms up" toast with traditional 1775 rum punch to the words "Long live the United States, and success to the Marines." At that point the mess is adjourned to the bar, and the evening progresses in accordance with the impulse and ingenuity of the members.

There are many rules that must be observed within the mess, not the least of which is a prohibition on the topics of politics, religion and women. "Charges" of improper behavior may be brought against any member of the mess, save the President and Guest of Honor, by any other member. Proper etiquette is enforced through the practice of fining, and the imposition of such fines can be quite enjoyable to watch when done with a bit of humor. All fines collected go on the bar at the conclusion of the evening to defray the cost of after dinner drinks.

I have been fortunate in that I have attended numerous such occasions, and even had the privilege of hosting a few. One particularly enjoyable Mess Night took place in Canberra and was attended by representatives of all services and several nations. As President it was my duty to make some opening remarks, and I didn't want to spout off with the same old politically correct drivel that tends to be the norm at international functions. In preparing my remarks I realized it is a well known fact Australia was originally a penal colony for the British, and I thought that would be an appropriate subject to begin the evening with.

"When I applied for my visa to come to Australia I was asked if I had a criminal record," I began. "Now, I'm certainly aware of your history... but I didn't realize it was still a requirement for admittance!"

From that point on the evening just got better and better. But it is not *all* fun and games. An important part of the Mess Night tradition is the Fallen Comrades table. No one sits there. It is symbolic of our comrades who have fallen in battle, and is covered in a black tablecloth and adorned with the cover, gloves and sword of a Marine - lest we forget.

273

SEMPER FI
In Oklahoma City

In the American heartland, a stunned nation stood paralyzed by the face of domestic terror. For rescuers who clawed at crumbled concrete, time lacked importance. The search for hope slipped quietly beyond reach as efforts shifted to the recovery of bombing victims - and dead children. Buried beneath the surface of shock rested hundreds of humbling stories of simple men, one unknown to the other, who bonded in a common, virtuous struggle spawned by an evil act.

April 19, 1993 was a very bad day for America. For Marines, the bombing of the Alfred P. Murrah Building struck a painful nerve. The Corps mourned two lost Marines while four other were injured by the blast. When television first broadcast the images of the catastrophic explosion, one could hear the Corps gasp.

"It looks just like the Embassy in Beirut!" was the common comment, referring to the April 18,1983, terrorist car-bomb detonation in Lebanon, a prologue to the disaster that would claim two hundred and forty-five Marine, soldier and sailor lives in the barracks that October.

It was difficult for Michael Curtain, a New York City police officer, to remember exactly what happened. The psychological trauma of the explosion, still felt by most of the rescuers, had to be set aside in order for them to tackle the ordeal of rescuing those who may have still been alive beneath the rubble. For the first forty hours there was no rest.

Sometime on the morning of April 21st Curtain, almost spent of energy and only using adrenaline to keep moving and save lives, came upon a familiar sight. Deliriously scrambling across and through the wreckage of the Federal building, Curtain saw a body covered by the rubble... and he recognized the material of the trousers.

The trousers were deep blue with a broad red stripe - the Corps calls it a blood stripe. It was a Marine.

Police Officer Curtain knew immediately. He, too, was a Marine - a Reserve First Sergeant.

"It was like I was driven," said Curtain, who had been a reservist for five years after serving on active duty for fourteen. "Somehow, I knew what I had to do," he said.

After the First Sergeant found the dress blue trousers, he cut away part of the fabric and saw that the man was Caucasian. He knew that it had to be Captain Randolph Guzman, the Recruiting Station Executive Officer. The other Marine still unaccounted for was Sergeant Benjamin Davis, known to be of Asian heritage and darker-skinned.

"After I found the Captain, I started asking around to see who among the rescuers was a Marine," Curtain said. "I found three former Marines who were part of the rescue effort."

Curtain found Manny Hernandez and Juan Garcia, both New York City policemen. But Curtain needed another man to complete the team. Ray Bonner, a paramedic, stepped forward. First Sergeant Curtain now had a fireteam.

Because of the inherent danger involved with the unstable structure, most of the recovery efforts were focused in other areas of the building at that time. However, Curtain approached the FEMA chain of command and told them he and a team of former Marines were taking a special interest in the recovery of Guzman's remains. Permission was granted to the Marines to accomplish this special mission, but they only had a four-hour window of time to work.

"It was something I had to do," said Hernandez, a Vietnam veteran who has been a police officer for twenty-two years. "I had a squad under me in 'Nam and whenever we lost a Marine, he was never left. We have this tradition. We take care of our own."

The excavation took five hours and involved a great deal of risk. The team was operating on the sub-ground level, with a lot of concrete and steel debris. There were apparently two major structural columns, one vertical and one horizontal, which were the primary obstacles to their recovery. However, removal was not possible because the beams were the only support for the heavy debris above and around the Marines.

"We had to use an electric jackhammer to chip the concrete away from the Captain," Curtain said. During the effort, the columns dangerously shifted twice before they were able to get Guzman free. Kneeling beside the Captain, former Corporal Hernandez covered Guzman's face with his hand.

"I closed his eyes," Hernandez said. "For the glory of God and the glory of the Corps. It was just a little thing. We had to keep the tradition alive. The Captain deserved the honor and respect - like all Marines."

After Guzman's remains were placed in a body bag the word spread throughout downtown Oklahoma City that the Marines were bringing out one of their own. With the help of Dennis O'Connor, also a New York police officer, Peter Conlin, whose father served as a Marine in World War II, and Steve Smalls, a structural engineer from New York City, the Marines prepared to take Guzman home.

An unidentified Air Force Colonel, upon hearing of the Marines' mission, found an American flag and sent it into the building.

"Before we lifted Guzman up and away from the rubble and carried him out, we draped the flag over him," said Curtain. "When we came out of the building I couldn't believe what I saw."

"Everything had stopped," he said. "You could have heard a pin drop. Cranes had stopped. It was completely quiet. Rescuers stopped and looked. People had lined the street outside the building. Everyone was watching in silence as we brought our Marine out."

"We were in a highly visible location... engines were turned off... people removed their covers... bowed their heads... covered their hearts. You could tell the veterans," Curtain said. "They were the ones saluting with tears in their eyes."

For Curtain, Garcia, Hernandez and Bonner, the scene filled them with pride, but was almost too much for them to emotionally handle. "When we came out with the flag-draped Captain, I saw why I was once a Marine. It is because I know I wouldn't expect anything less from any other Marine if it were me in that body bag," Hernandez said. "It revalidated the esprit and brotherhood that I remember being taught to me in boot camp years ago. It lifted me up. It was overwhelming. We are a Band of Brothers."

Once Guzman's remains were carried from the building two long lines of rescue workers and bystanders formed, without any order or direction, to make a corridor leading to the recovery vehicles taking remains to the makeshift morgue.

"It was one of the most emotional experiences of my life," said Curtain. "People had taken their hard hats off and were offering respect any way they knew how. It was symbolic of all the emotion everyone was feeling. Whether they were a

Marine or not, we were all involved. The compassion for all the lost just seemed to surface all at once."

Just like the 1983 bombing in Beirut, when Lance Corporal Jeffery Nashton, after blindly feeling the four stars of General P.X. Kelly, scribbled "Semper Fi" on a piece of paper as he lay on life support in the hospital in Germany - the enduring ethos of the Corps is alive in Oklahoma City.

"It was just a simple thing. But it had to be done," Hernandez said. "Once we saw the blood stripe on Captain Guzman's trousers, and we knew it was a Marine - we had no choice. It was simply - Semper Fidelis."

WE NEVER LEAVE
Our Brothers Behind

Major David C. Andersen

"Greatness is not found in possessions, power, position or prestige. It is discovered in goodness, humility, service and character!"

Pain shot through my back in the late night hours of March 6th, 2002 from the weight of the stretcher, but Marines always complete the mission. With Sergeant Major Michael Curtin, USMCR (Ret) & NYPD, in my left hand and his wife and daughter only feet in front of me, sense of duty led the way as it has for many men better than I for hundreds of years.

As we picked up the Sergeant Major, I thought back to only hours ago when my U.S. Marine Corps Public Affairs Office in Midtown Manhattan received the call that we had stood ready for since September 11. In fact, I received four calls in about three minutes from numerous Emergency Services Unit men - better known as "E-MEN" throughout the famed New York City Police Department. The messages were all the same, "Dave, get down here - we found the Sergeant Major."

We proceeded down from a small plateau on the north side of the dig, which probably would have put us in sub-level five (five stories underground) of Tower One. My mind wandered to the Sergeant Major's wife Helga, a former Marine, and his three daughters Jennifer, Heather, and Erika. The native of Rocky Point, New York had become a folk hero in the NYPD as he ran his Truck like a platoon - a platoon of Marines.

"TRUCK-2" is located on 125th Street in Harlem, and upon entering one might think they have entered a company office at Camp Lejeune or a barracks at Camp Schwab as proud men go about their business with Marine Corps haircuts and squared-away uniforms. Sergeant Major Curtin had obviously been here.

Leveling out at about sub-level seven in a pool of soupy mud heading south toward the exit ramp, I glanced back over my shoulder and saw the Ground Zero flag I had grabbed out of our office on the way downtown. It had been signed by the victim's families months prior and we were able to get it to the 26th Marine Expeditionary Unit aboard *USS Bataan*, who then took it ashore to fly in the face of terrorism over the Kandahar Airport in Afghanistan. Who gave it to us? E-Men that Curtin knew. Curtin had loved the American Flag, his family had told me, and it was fitting that he lay next to me covered in the flag he had raised in Kuwait City a decade ago. That flag had been waiting for him in a box in the ESU Headquarters that I had noticed on occasion, marked "THIS FLAG IS FOR SGT MIKE CURTIN ONLY!!!!!!!!" And of course to make it complete the Marine Corps colors were also present, and were carried by two of his TRUCK-2 E-MEN.

As we started up the bridge the voice of what had to be a former Marine rang out throughout the sixteen-acre complex – "*PRESENT...* arms!" The exit ramp was lined with hundreds of proud members of the NYPD, ESU, PAPD, FDNY and Steel Workers with the night lit up by thousands of flashing emergency-vehicle lights. As we pushed forward keeping step with former Marine and Police Commissioner Ray Kelly I thought of the infamous story that made the Sergeant Major a Marine Corps folk hero. It was not the story of his rescue efforts at the first Trade Tower's bombing in 1993, but rather the story of him spotting the red stripe of Captain Randolph Guzman's dress-blue trousers in the rubble of the Oklahoma City bombing. He located a group of former Marines and then took approximately seven hours to pull him out as he said, "We never leave our brother's behind." He managed to free the "Skipper," who was probably watching this procession waiting to thank Mike one day. They carried him out draped in an American flag with his dress blue trousers sticking out and with his shined shoes pointing toward heaven's gates. All was quiet. No talking. No machinery. Only the sound of a million thoughts - much like I could hear at this very moment heading out of the hole.

As we approached the top I noticed that an ESU Truck was waiting for him - his truck...TRUCK-2. We hoisted the Sergeant Major up high - hands reaching with fingertips outstretched - and I wondered if anyone shared my thoughts at that moment. It was reminiscent of the outstretched fingers of another famous group of Marines years ago on a small island in the South Pacific. Finally, with one last adjustment needed to secure the stretcher, a body was needed to jump up and climb to the top. Who scrambled to the top of the huge truck? Who else - Helga, his wife. In front of hundreds of tough cops, she made the last adjustment to take care of her husband - much like I imagine he had done for her for many years. That simple act was breathtaking - an act that the Sergeant Major represented for years - selflessly helping other people and NOT wanting to be recognized for it.

We then headed north on the FDR. The motorcade was long and bright as we approached the 0100 hour mark. All traffic was stopped and civilians stood outside their halted cars lining the roads with hands over hearts and hats off. Motorcycle cops at every intersection had salutes at the ready. At the morgue, my Gunny and I folded the flag under many watchful eyes. Suddenly, TRUCK-2 members and other E-MEN stepped forward to aid us. We presented the colors to Helga and then took care of the Sergeant Major.

My ride home was long. Covered in mud I never wanted to wash off, I hoped and prayed we had done the Curtin family proud - as well as our nation. I think the Sergeant Major would have been proud. I also thought that although my Marines and I have seen the pile shrink on a daily basis, it is still there – and it will always be there. The billions of tears that have fallen on this earth will never be washed away and we cannot forget. The mangled iron, the smell and the feeling is still lurking in that hole and I feel it every day. You just cannot see, hear or smell it on television.

I shed a tear coming out of "the pit" that night as I held my head high. I also felt like there were a band of brothers waiting at the top all dressed in our Corps' uniforms from days gone by. Then it really hit home that the bridge was symbolic. It was a long steep trek up seven stories, but Sergeant Major Curtin made it out of that hellhole led by his wife, carried by the entire Corps, and by the rest of his country that he loved so much.

POLISHING THE EMBLEM

By Tad Lincoln Palmer

"Actions, not words!"

I have visited Washington, D.C. at least four times since I was fifteen years old. The last trip I took while I was still in the Corps, and it was with the woman who was my wife at the time. She had never seen D.C., so I wanted to take a trip and show her the sights... with one of those sights being the Vietnam Memorial. I was not born until 1971, but have the utmost respect for everyone associated with that war regardless of their branch of service.

It's a known fact that when a Marine is visiting the Wall he must pack along some Brasso to polish the Marine Corps brass at the base of the U.S. Flag. So on the day we went to the Wall I dressed myself up in my Dress Blues, with a final uniform inspection by my ex-wife to ensure all was in order, and we were on our way. It was a quiet and solemn visit. She didn't even say a thing the whole time... it was as if she automatically understood the importance of the Wall.

Upon reaching the Flag I immediately knelt down and began to polish the brass Marine Corps emblem. I must have spent a good fifteen minutes polishing away, and all the while people were passing by. I got many strange looks - but it's a Marine thing and they just wouldn't understand. Some even took pictures, and a few older Devil Dogs stopped and thanked me.

But what stands out most in my memory was a Park Ranger who stopped and said, "It's amazing...."

I said, "What's that?"

283

He replied, "I just don't get it. Every day there is at least one of you in your Blues stopping and polishing your emblem. I don't think I have worked a single day when the USMC emblem didn't shine. I have not *ever* seen any of the other services do what you guys do!"

I explained, "It's a long and proud tradition steeped in pride, honor and commitment. It's a Marine thing... so you wouldn't understand!"

He thanked me for my service and wished me luck on my future service. It's nice to know that I am not the only young Devil Dog out there who still finds time to show his appreciation for those who have gone before.

TO HONOR MY COUNTRY

By 'Anonymous'

"Some people *wave* the flag, and then *waive* what it stands for – but none of them are Marines!"

A foreign diplomat who often criticized American policy once observed as a United States Marine performed the evening colors ceremony at an American Embassy overseas. The diplomat wrote about that simple but solemn ceremony in a letter to his country:

"During one of the past few days I had occasion to visit the U.S. Embassy in our capital after official working hours. I arrived at a quarter to six, and was met by the Marine on guard at the entrance to the Chancery. He asked if I would mind waiting while he lowered the two American flags at the Embassy. What I witnessed over the next ten minutes so impressed me that I am now led to make this occurrence a part of my ongoing record of this distressing era.

The Marine was dressed in a uniform which was spotless and neat. He walked with a measured tread from the entrance of the Chancery to the stainless steel flagpole before the Embassy and, almost reverently, lowered the flag to the level of his reach where he began to fold it in military fashion. He then released the flag from the clasps attaching it to the rope, stepped back from the pole, made an about face, and carried the flag between his hands - one above, one below - and placed it securely on a stand before the Chancery. He then marched over to the second flagpole and repeated the same lonesome ceremony.

285

On the way between poles, he mentioned to me very briefly that he would soon be finished. After completing his task he apologized for the delay - out of pure courtesy - as nothing less than incapacity would have prevented him from fulfilling his goal. He said to me, 'Thank you for waiting, Sir. I had to pay honor to my country.'

I have to tell this story because there was something impressive about a lone Marine carrying out a ceremonial task which obviously meant very much to him and which, in its simplicity, made the might, the power and the glory of the United States of America stand forth in a way that a mighty wave of military aircraft, or the passage of a super-carrier, or a parade of ten thousand men could never have made manifest.

In spite of all the many things that I can say negatively about the United States I do not think there is a soldier, yea, even a private citizen, who could feel as proud about our country today as that Marine does for his. One day it is my hope to visit one of our Embassies in a far-away place and see a soldier fold our flag and turn to a stranger and say, 'I am sorry for the delay, Sir. I had to honor my country.'"

LEST WE FORGET

By Harrison Greene

"You cannot exaggerate about the Marines. They are convinced to the point of arrogance, that they are the most ferocious fighters on earth - and the amusing thing about it is that they are." - Father Kevin Keaney, 1st Marine Division Chaplain, Korean War

The hill in front of us was lit up like daylight on this particular November morning in Vietnam. We could see an occasional burst of our artillery hitting its target off in the distance. The three of us sat peering out of the slits in our bunker. Despite being able to see an occasional flash from an enemy rifle, we did not open up with our secret weapon... a .50 caliber machinegun. We chose not to do so since the enemy had not yet figured out where all of our heavy guns were located. After all, we had only just moved into position on the side of this small hill late the night before and our bunker had not yet been dug very deeply. Things had been quiet most of the night, and now at 3:30 AM the enemy chose to wake us up. We had 105mm howitzers behind us cranking off illumination and high explosive rounds at a rate of one every fifteen seconds. It was getting quite noisy, and the three of us had to nearly shout in order to carry on a conversation.

Things were beginning to get busy out in front of us. The grunts were starting to rock 'n roll. We could hear the familiar sound of M-14s cranking off semi-automatic fire, as well as the reports of the enemy's M-1 carbines and an occasional AK-47 assault rifle.

Earlier that evening while things were still quiet Gunnery Sergeant Tchaikovsky had called all the outposts on the field phone and told us intelligence reports were predicting an enemy probe sometime during the night. He told us that there was reportedly a battalion-sized Viet Cong unit moving towards our position. He ordered a 100% alert! He didn't have to order that, believe me. We were all more than a little nervous about finally being baptized under fire. This would be our first battle since arriving in country several weeks prior.

Gunny Ski (affectionately known as "Gunny Godammit") was a big, lanky Pennsylvanian with a curious bit of wit about him. We gave him the respect he deserved for having been a veteran of the Korean War, but not much else. Just about every sentence he spoke would include the word "godammit" in it. I can still hear him in front of our morning formations back in California, "Alright, godammit, FALL-IN!" One afternoon the Gunny called a special formation. He had heard a complaint that several Marines in our unit had only been issued one wool blanket. "Alright, godammit," Gunny Ski bellowed, "some of you Marines have been issued two wool blankets, while others have only been issued one. So, I want the ones who have two blankets to give the guys with only one blanket one of their blankets, and then everyone will have two." I'm still wondering where the logic was in that one! Like an idiot, I gave one of my blankets to Lance Corporal Jimmy Jones. Gunny Ski was certainly tough on us, and he was a Marine that all of us loved to hate.

Jimmy was my A-gunner on the .50 caliber machinegun. The other Marine in our outpost was Jake Barnes, a Louisiana man who spoke very slowly and deliberately… and with a strong southern drawl. We heard Gunny Godammit off in the distance behind us yelling some obscenities. "Alright, godammit," he yelled, "keep your heads down up front." As soon as he said that we began getting clobbered by 40mm M-79 grenades, which were landing all around our bunker. About five or six of them landed to our right, and one hit the back of our bunker. We wondered if the gunny had been drinking. Jones picked up the field phone and tried calling back to our HQ to let them know that the Gunny's aim was off. Our phone was dead, the line probably severed by the rounds that landed in our vicinity. We started yelling back to the Gunny to cease fire, but the rounds kept coming. Finally, after another dozen rounds were fired in our direction, we couldn't hear each other talking anymore - but then the bombardment stopped. We breathed a little easier for the moment, but then things began picking up momentum in front of us.

TAT-TAT-TAT-TAT-TAT-TAT-TAT-TAT-TAT-TAT!

"That was an AK!" said Jones. We all agreed that it was very close to our position. TAT-TAT-TAT-TAT-TAT-TAT-TAT-TAT! A spray of dirt from the sandbags in front of us filled my eyes. TAT-TAT-TAT-TAT-TAT! ZING! My head felt like someone hit me with a sledgehammer, and I fell backwards against the rear wall of our bunker. I reached up to wipe my eyes and feel my face, and it was all wet. At the same time I felt a huge weight slump against my shoulder. It was Barnes. At first I couldn't see what was wrong with him. I heard a gurgling sound, and another sound like he was trying to talk. The cannons behind us grew more intense, and the weapons fire to our front was now murderous. I yelled to Jones, telling him that I thought I was hit. I told him that something was wrong with Barnes, but I still couldn't see clearly what was happening.

The illumination rounds being fired from the 105's kept the night sky lit and we were finally able to see Barnes, who was now lying on the floor of our bunker. He was bleeding badly from the face, and his hands were clenching his throat.

Still in a state of shock from having my own bell rung, I dug around in the darkness looking for a first-aid packet on one of our cartridge belts. Got it! I felt like I was all thumbs as I opened up a large field dressing and began working with Barnes. Still unsure of my situation, I asked Barnes if he could hear me. He nodded in the affirmative, and then started to cry. Things were getting seemingly worse out in front of us, and Jones reported he could see more rifle flashes pointed in our direction. He wanted to fire the machinegun, but I told him not yet.

Barnes was shaking violently, and was obviously already in shock. He was conscious of what was happening, yet there wasn't anything we could do to make the hurt go away. Jones tried the field phone again to get a corpsman down to us. The phone was still dead. He started calling back to the rear area where the cannons were still firing away. We could hear Gunny Godammit yelling down to us to answer our field phone, but it was apparent he had no idea what was going on with us at that moment. "POST TWO, ANSWER YOUR GODAMNED PHONE, GODAMMIT!" he yelled.

I told Jones that one of us had to get back to the CP and get help. Barnes needed a corpsman before he bled to death. Jones volunteered to stay with him while I crawled back to get HM2 "Doc" Stewart.

Crawling out the back of our bunker, I followed the comm wire towards the battery CP. Shortly after leaving the safety of our bunker I felt very vulnerable to the rounds that were landing around me, so I crawled as fast as I could up the side of the hill. Holding onto the wire, I came across the break - it had been severed by one of the 40mm grenades Gunny Ski was laying on us. After searching around for the other end of the break and finding it, I twisted the wires together and crawled back down the hill to the safety of our bunker and tried the field phone.

"Battery CP, Lance Corporal Toomey speaking," I heard the voice say. "This is post two… Barnes is hit pretty bad… send Doc down here NOW," I shouted into the field phone. Barnes' field dressing was completely soaked in crimson red, and he was still whimpering and shaking uncontrollably. I reached over to him and told him Doc was on the way.

Just as I was doing so I turned around and saw this huge figure of a man come sliding into our bunker. "Alright, godammit… let's get this Marine outta here." Never before was I ever so glad to see Gunny Ski. He was the veteran Marine. The Marine that all of us sometimes hated – and yet secretly admired because he was a seasoned combat veteran. Somehow we knew we were going to be all right now. The Gunny came to our rescue. And he brought with him a replacement for Barnes, who was now being carried back to the CP in the arms of this big, lanky, tough, dim-witted, loveable Gunnery Sergeant of Marines.

It was now about 0530, and the fighting began to taper down. The morning dawn was creeping over the hillside on which we were entrenched, and we could barely make out the outline of several water buffalo which were casually strolling across the meadow beyond.

"Time to check-in, isn't it, Greene?" Jones asked. "Exec Pit, this is post two… all secure," I reported.

I never saw Gunny Tchaikovsky again after that terrible morning in early November. He was killed about an hour after he carried Barnes out of harm's way while saving *another* one of his precious Marines from an almost certain death. The date was 10 November, 1966 - my first Marine Corps Birthday in the Corps.

I'm sure I know where Gunnery Sergeant Tchaikovsky is today. Rest assured, he is taking care of those beloved Marines who have been called back to guard the pearly gates!

I REMEMBER

By Patrick Rogers

"I have just returned from visiting the Marines at the front, and there is not a finer fighting organization in the world!"
- General of the Army Douglas MacArthur; Korea, 1950

I was in my prep time for the two hundred yard rapid fire stage of the National Match Course "leg match" at the Virginia State Championships at Quantico. The scorer on an adjacent target had been occasionally looking at me since we squadded. Not mean looks, but inquisitive, as if he were trying to dig into the recesses of my mind. He was a my-age guy, wearing a Marine Corps sweatshirt, but obviously not on active duty. He looked vaguely familiar, but after twenty plus years as a cop most everyone looks familiar to me.

My curiosity overcame common sense. I should have been preparing to shoot, but suddenly I had an overwhelming desire to identify this guy. On a hunch I asked when he was in-country.

"65-66" he said, "You?"

"65-66," I replied. "Who were you with?"

"3rd Tank Battalion." Gee, I thought, what a coincidence. "So was I. I was an 1811."

Then his eyes got real wide. The earlier confusion was gone, and a grand smile spread across his face. "You're Mouse, I'm Whitehead! You were Alpha 34!"

I remember...

I remember a gangly kid from Georgia coming out to Hill 55 as a replacement on my tank. I don't even believe that

Gene Whitehead was a PFC yet. He was brand new, unblooded, untested. His sincerity was overpowering. He was trying so hard to do everything right that he wound up doing most everything wrong. Or maybe not. I had ten or eleven months in-country, and almost three years in the Marine Corps. I had seen the elephant. I had seen Marines killed and wounded, and it was not something I wanted to see again. Not if I could help it. I expected competence in a very imperfect environment. A tank is a very intimate place. You may sink, or you may swim, but rest assured you will all get wet together. I was so far intact, and wanted all in my sphere of influence to remain so. Circumstance might preclude survival, and I could accept that. But I could not accept a Marine dying because of a lack of training.

I remember...

I remember that we pushed Gene Whitehead hard. He probably believed that I considered him somehow unworthy. He once stated that I did not like him, but that was not the case. For all of his inexperience, he had that spark that differentiates the warrior from the rest. He had the makings of a good Marine. He just needed to survive long enough to be one.

I remember...

I remember that Hill 55 was not the best place to bring someone up to speed. The OJT was great, however. During the First Indochina War two French battalions were wiped out on, or near, this hill. The CO of 3/3, Lieutenant Colonel Muir, was killed there in September of 1965. When we occupied the hill in January of 1966 we had but two platoons of I/3/3, a light section of tanks, and an Ontos section. We were not on the hill for more than five minutes before one of our crewmen tripped a mine. In the book *Small Unit Action in Vietnam, Summer 1966* the author stated, "In the late spring and early summer of 1966, the most notorious area in I Corps was the flat rice paddy and hedgerow complex around Hill 55." I concur. The hill was probed, assaulted, and mortared constantly. Weather and terrain made movement difficult. The enemy apparently had an inexhaustible selection of mines, and he employed them effectively. More importantly, the VC R-20 (Doc Lap) Battalion had been actively engaging ARVN and US Marine units in the area. Well trained, well equipped, and extremely well led, this unit would continue to be a thorn in the side of Marines operating south of Da Nang.

I remember...

I remember that during the late morning of May 21st, 1966 a squad from C/1/9, operating on the west side of the Yan River, made contact with the R-20 Battalion near the village of An Trach (1). Hard hit, they received support from two tanks and additional Charlie Company grunts. A Sparrow Hawk, consisting of 3rd Platoon A/1/9 (rein), was attached to Charlie Company and deployed to and unsecured LZ that was believed to be north of the enemy position. They landed instead in the middle of the enemy battalion, and suffered horrible casualties in just a few minutes. The remainder of Alpha Company, attached amtracs, and our two tanks were ordered up to attack.

I remember...

I remember listening to the radio on the ride out, and hearing the frantic radio calls from the pinned down Marines, the requests for air and artillery support, and more ominously, the requests for multiple medevacs. Mr. Charles was not backing down. He was standing and fighting with all he possessed. It was apparent that this fight would be different.

I remember...

I remember that when we made contact it was sudden, and furious. The enemy was close. Engagement was rarely out to one hundred meters, and usually significantly closer. We were advancing north on the east side of the Yen River. The terrain was flat, with the paddies separated by thick hedgerows. The enemy had dug trenches along the river, and through some of the hedgerows as well. We assaulted these positions, supported by aviation, but it was the man with the rifle who ultimately had to remove the other man with a rifle from his position.

I remember that at one point I felt like I was in a kaleidoscope. The noise of incoming and outgoing rounds. UH-1 gunships flying at treetop height, hitting positions merely twenty-five meters in front of us. Friendly ordnance impacting as what can only be described as "Danger, *very* close." The constant radio noise, squawking over three channels simultaneously. The distinct whine of an OV-10 directing fast movers, and occasionally coming down to strafe positions when nothing else was available.

Gene expertly maneuvered O.G. Clank through the battlefield, punching holes in the hedgerows and making it a bit easier for the grunts to pass through. I remember moving through one hedgerow, and seeing the other side erupt in a wall of recoilless rifle, RPG and small arms fire. I had a canister round in the chamber of the main gun, and pressed the trigger. For a very few seconds, there was relative quiet.

I remember the Alpha Company commander issuing orders, moving his Marines, and overpowering a powerful foe. Many years later he received a Silver Star for his actions that day. The Marine Corps got away cheap on that one. He deserved more.

I remember...

I remember that after several hours of heavy fighting we were making terrific progress, overrunning enemy positions. Moving through one trench line, we momentarily stopped to let the grunts catch up. I looked out to either side of the TC's cupola and saw those wonderful, dirty, and tired warriors get on line and start shooting. I looked to the front and realized that no more than thirty meters away an enemy platoon was also on line and giving back everything they got. The image of two groups of hard men standing and firing almost shoulder to shoulder, neither giving nor seeking quarter, is one that I will take to my grave.

By now the enemy was endeavoring to leave, and we were not about to let him go. We pushed through another position, and stopped. 'Murphy,' who thrives on close combat, paid us a visit. A canister round broke open in the chamber, spilling out its deadly load of 1160 pellets and locking up the breech. The coaxial .30 caliber machinegun had finally overheated, quitting in fiery protest, and I had run the TC cupola mounted .50 caliber machinegun dry. Earlier I had shot an enemy soldier carrying a pistol and a map case with this weapon, at about ten meters - the effect was devastating. The mount, designed by Boeing, was difficult to load under normal peacetime conditions, and impossible to load now. O.G. Clank was effectively disarmed.

I remember...

I remember peering out of the TC's hatch and seeing a large number of enemy soldiers alongside the tank – we had outrun our support. The grunts had not yet caught up with us, and we were alone. We were in the unique position of having advanced past a retreating, disorganized enemy. I grabbed my M14, and as I climbed out of the tank one of the enemy raised his K-50 submachine gun and emptied his magazine at me at a range of ten feet. Above the noise of the rest of the battle, the sound of those bullets passing by my head were easily the most distinctive. I put the front sight on his chest and shot him. He went down, but there were many of his comrades close by. Some were retreating along a trench, and others were attacking O.G. Clank – the closest obstacle to their perceived survival. I will never again hear the term "target rich environment" without thinking about this incident. I started engaging as many as I could, one at a time. While changing magazines I caught sight of movement below me, and saw Gene standing in the driver's hatch shooting enemy soldiers off the tank and buying me time. I remember thinking, for a brief moment, that this kid was going to be alright.

We continued to shoot as many as we could, but it became rapidly apparent that there were more of them than we had bullets for. I called Gene on the intercom and ordered him to drive forward. About then I ran the M-14 dry, and called into the tank for another magazine. The pistol magazine I was handed did not even disturb the soldier I threw it at, but then I was handed a frag. I pulled the pin and threw it at a soldier in front of the tank. I called for Gene to stop, but my dancing on top of the turret had dislodged the yo yo cord, severing communications. The grenade detonated under the tank with no damage other than to my ego – which occurred when I had to explain to the CO why I had tried to blow up my own tank.

I remember driving down the trench line doing neutral steers on top of enemy soldiers, crushing them before they could hurt any more Marines. Off to the west I watched a grunt jump into a trench with two of the enemy who were firing a machinegun. His rifle apparently malfunctioned, because he picked up an e-tool and killed them both with it.

I remember a Huey flying low up the river shooting enemy soldiers who were swimming to the west bank in a vain attempt to escape the carnage in the hedgerows.

I remember...

I remember consolidating on the other side. Contact was established with what remained of the third platoon, and medevacs were brought in behind O.G. Clank to remove the wounded and dead. Communications were reestablished, malfunctions reduced, weapons reloaded. A grunt platoon commander came alongside the tank with a map in his hand and asked if I knew exactly where we were. I didn't have a clue at that point. He said, "To hell with it. Let's go north and kill some more of these sons of bitches!"

And I remember looking at Gene Whitehead and giving him a thumbs up.

As battles go this was not one of the big ones. It only lasted seven hours, although it seemed like seven eternities at the time. We destroyed two companies of the R-20 Battalion, killing between fifty and one hundred thirty of them. But we lost twelve Marines KIA, and thirty-one WIA. Things happened that day, things I have never seen or experienced before of since. Forever after I have seen life with a greater clarity, and have a much better understanding of certain emotions. And I completely understand what courage is – I saw it occur many times on that overcast day along the banks of the Song Yen.

I took the sling off my arm and stood up to hug Gene. Thirty-two years of emotions came out and we made lots of loud noises reminiscing about days gone by, much to the amusement of all the young shooters on the line. Gene then got down to the serious business of shooting. Already a Distinguished Pistol Shot, he needed four points to be among the very few who are "Double-D." He held hard and shot a 477-9X, enough to earn six points and his Distinguished Rifleman's Badge.

We went to dinner that night, and talked about what had transpired since that spring day thirty-two years ago. Married with three children, he had retired as a Master Sergeant with twenty-three years service to his country.

A member of the USMC rifle team told me that Gene had just received a Bronze Star for an action that occurred after my departure. He had picked up a frag that had been tossed into his tent and returned it to its original owners, saving several Marines. The Marine Corps got away cheap on that one too. He deserved at least one more, for helping keep his crew alive so many years ago.

This meeting of two broken-down warriors was too providential to be mere chance. It may not have been divine intervention but then again, maybe it was. It was extremely emotional for both of us, and brought back a flood of memories.

I remember…

I remember a time when we answered the clarions call, and strong men armed fought a war in a country that no longer exists. I remember a time when elected and appointed officials of a political party micro-managed its professional military and sacrificed the lives of the best and brightest on the altar of political expediency. I remember working with the finest men I have ever known.

...And I will never forget.

THE HANO JUMP

"Jumping out of a perfectly good aircraft is not a natural act. Just do it right and enjoy the view." - Mythical Gunnery Sergeant Tom Highway (played by Clint Eastwood) in the film "Heartbreak Ridge"

Anyone with the necessary desire can become airborne qualified. It doesn't take a great deal of intellect or athletic ability to fall out the open door of an aircraft in flight, and if you can keep your feet and knees together there is a good chance you will land safely on the ground. I am living proof of that. The skills necessary to become High Altitude, Low Opening (HALO) qualified are something else altogether.

I will never forget my first freefall. After two weeks on the ground learning to pack our rigs and practicing in the vertical wind tunnel the time finally arrived for an actual jump. As part of our preparation we sat through a slide show detailing procedures in the aircraft, and when the instructor reached a slide showing a C-130 in flight with its ramp down he paused. "When the ramp opens you will hear a loud banging noise," he said. Don't worry, it's normal. It's just the sound of forty assholes snapping shut simultaneously!"

It wasn't quite that bad, although there certainly was a bit of a pucker factor. My jump buddy was an Army Ranger, and we exited the aircraft at 12,500 feet followed closely by our instructor. I was a soup sandwich. My first couple of jumps I was what's known as a "yellow frisbee," which is what a student wearing a yellow jumpsuit looks like when he is in a flat spin. It's not a lot of fun.

On my third jump I managed to get stable but had a total malfunction of my main parachute – what they call in the business a "streamer." To this day I am amazed at how calm

I was. I attribute that calmness to the excellent training we had received on the ground, and I systematically applied the emergency procedures we had practiced so many times. My reserve eventually opened, and I watched the discarded main drift slowly to the ground. It was my first "HANO," or High Altitude NO Opening jump, which is what we jokingly called it when someone had a malfunction. I had managed to cheat death once again.

Unfortunately it doesn't always work out that way. After my graduation from HALO school I returned to my unit where I took part in parachute operations whenever possible. The bulk of our freefall evolutions were designed to develop skills and maintain proficiency, but tactical jumps were also part of many field operations. In the fall of 1988 one of our teams was making a twilight HALO insert into a patrol up in Fort Pickett Virginia when one of the jumpers failed to link up with his mates on the ground. It was originally thought he had begun to escape and evade, but when there was no trace of him after several days a search operation was launched. Eventually a helicopter spotted his canopy in the trees, and a search party on the ground found his body shortly thereafter.

Sergeant Robert Reyes had been seen fiddling with the legs straps on his rucksack just prior to the jump. Apparently one of them came loose in freefall and caused him to become unstable and go out of control. When Reyes deployed his parachute it became wrapped around him in what is known as a "horseshoe," and he was unable to successfully activate the reserve in time. It was a sad time in the company.

The day after Sergeant Reyes was found there was a company jump on the training schedule out at DZ Falcon, and I signed up for it along with my good friend James Goethe. I wanted to get one in as soon as possible after what had happened, and I think James felt the same way. We were uncharacteristically quiet as the aircraft climbed to jump altitude, and I couldn't wait to get out the door. When the parachute came off of my back I remember that it seemed to open in slow motion. I spiraled to the DZ and landed right on target – a perfect jump. I felt as if a huge weight had been lifted from my shoulders.

MORE THAN BROTHERS

By William C. Newton

"Genuine friendship is like your health – its value is seldom known until it is lost."

I was seventy-two years old. For over fifty years I'd had the same nightmares. I'd wake up in a cold sweat, often with tears running down my cheeks to my sweat-soaked pillow. I couldn't forget that last battle and the friend I'd lost to a Japanese shell.

In the late 1930s I had joined the Civilian Conservation Corps at the age of eighteen. The second of seven children, a six-foot, two-inch lanky boy from the Deep South, I wanted to help my family after the death of my father.

Four years later – a veteran and survivor of Roi Nanur, Saipan and Tinian – I found myself basking in the sun on the Hawaiian Island of Maui with my unit, the Second Battalion, Twenty-fourth Regiment of the Fourth Marine Division.

I was a machine gunner, first squad. My best friend was Richards, a broad-shouldered boy about an inch taller and a year older than me, who came from a town in the southern part of New York State. We did everything together.

We had been in Maui nearly three months, playing softball and going on trips to the town of Kahului, but most of our time was spent in the seemingly endless boredom of marching and training – preparing for our next objective.

Then all the boat rides, ball games, sunbathing and training came to an end. We were boarding transports to once again become part of the war, and we had no idea where our ships were taking us.

Swift, Silent and Surrounded

Our destination turned out to be a sulfur-smelling volcanic island called Iwo Jima. This island was near the end of Nanpo Shoto, a chain of islands in the South Pacific 750 miles from Tokyo. Twenty-three thousand Japanese soldiers and sailors occupied it.

On D-Day, we left the safety of our transports and boarded the landing craft around seventeen-hundred hours. We were to come in on the second wave; a section of the beach designated "Yellow" beach would be our landing zone. We were to take and hold this pork chop-shaped island as an emergency landing field for U.S. bombers and their fighter escorts returning from raids on Japan.

Leaving the landing craft, we struggled to get across the beach. Trying to walk in black volcanic sand was like trying to walk inside an hourglass – it shifted constantly beneath our feet. We made little progress because of the debris, the mines, and constant fire from the enemy. We also had the unpleasant task of wading through our fallen comrades.

We finally arrived at the crest of the beach and went across Motoyama Airfield Number One. We set up our guns and prepared to fight, staying there for what seemed an eternity. My buddy Richards, who had been in sickbay aboard the transport with a high fever, finally joined me on the third day. I felt a lot better with him by my side.

Our gun was set up halfway between two airfields near a place called Charlie Dog Ridge. We were under constant fire from snipers, small arms and machine guns. Plus a never-ending stream of shells came from the dreaded mortars, which were hidden in the jagged volcanic rock of this hell the Brass called an "objective." Hours passed as Richards watched my back and I watched his. Brothers in arms, we depended on each other totally.

As we repositioned our gun in what we believed to be a safer place, a Japanese shell suddenly exploded near our crater. Many were killed or wounded, including our ammo carriers and some of our riflemen. I was one of the injured. It seemed like hours, but it was only a few minutes until the angels of the battlefield, the Navy corpsmen, were helping me. As the stretcher bearers picked me up and carried me out, I kept reaching for my buddy. I did not want to leave him alone.

We had gone only a few yards when we were hit by another shell. One of the bearers was killed instantly, the other severely wounded, and I was hit for the second time. I lay there all night in the warm volcanic sand worrying about Richards and trying to ignore the pain from my wounds. Sometime during the night, I lost consciousness.

The next morning I was picked up and taken to the aid station on the beach. They told me I was the only one to survive the explosion. It was the last thing I remembered about those three awful days.

I woke up aboard a hospital ship headed for Guam. There, I was placed in a body cast and flown to the United States. Before and after my surgeries, I mourned Richards. I kept saying to myself, *'I should be the one who stayed behind.'*

I was discharged in December 1945 and went back home to Georgia to be with my family. I had married that August while on leave, and over the next fifty years helped raise three sons and a daughter. My life was as full as a man could ask for, yet there was a hollow place in my heart that could not be filled. Not a day went by that I did not think of my best buddy still on that island. And sometimes there were those awful dreams...

In 1995 I attended a "Veterans of Iwo Jima" reunion in Atlanta. At the reunion, I was asked to join several veterans'

Swift, Silent and Surrounded

groups. After talking with other vets, I finally wrote my name on a few different sign-up sheets. A copy of one of these pages ended up in the hands of a retired police detective in Endicott, New York, who immediately recognized my name.

The detective called me the very next day. I answered the phone, and the man asked, "Newton?" For the first time in fifty years, each of us heard a familiar voice – a voice we both thought we'd never hear again. The voices belonged to two Marines who had gone through the hell of war and who had each been told that his best buddy had been killed in action on that bloody island.

To this day we continue to phone, write and visit each other. The bad dreams are gone, the empty place filled. We are now, as then, closer than brothers.

This story originally appeared in "Chicken Soup for the Veteran's Soul"

308

THE COMMAND POST

"The more you sweat in peace, the less you bleed in war!"

Recon Marines are often characterized as a bunch of PT fanatics. That is not totally untrue. When a team is a hundred miles behind enemy lines there is no room for a weak sister, and everyone has to pull his weight.

A test called the Indoc was developed to screen out the "non-hackers." It commonly involved a PFT, swim test, obstacle course, calisthenics, and a "ruck march" carrying a sandbag. The Indoc is more than a rite of passage because it serves a practical purpose. The process screens Marines to ensure they are qualified for assignment and capable of successfully completing the formal schools to which they will be sent.

Our CO at 2nd Force Recon decided to take the process to another level. He implemented a "selection test" modeled after the ones used by the SAS and Delta Force. At a full two weeks, it was a far cry from the old one-day indoc! I was in one of the first groups to take the new test, and have to say it was quite a challenge.

At thirty-one I was the oldest Marine in the group by a fair margin. Marines, like athletes, are considered "old" once they get into their thirties. But what I lacked in youthful energy I made up for with experience. I had to, because those other guys were all stronger than I was. One way I did that was by caring for my feet. I was one of the few to periodically tend to his wheels, and it paid off. At a point when most of the others had a major problem with blisters, I had none at all, and that became especially important *after* the test had been completed.

The last week of the selection took place in the hills of Quantico, and I focused on a prize at the end as an incentive to keep going. I told the other guys we were all going to Quantico Town when it was over for a beer and a sandwich. Not just any beer and sandwich, but a San Miguel and a Chesty! During my visits to the Philippines I had acquired a taste for San Miguel beer, and the Command Post Pub serves a sandwich appropriately named the 'Chesty.' Everyone was down for it, and it became our rallying cry.

But once we were in the barracks and had an opportunity to shower and hit the rack, most lost their enthusiasm for a beer – although in some cases it was simply a matter of not being able to walk. I did manage to convince three of my buddies to go along though, and we grabbed a cab into "Q-Town."

A lot of times in life we have high expectations for things and end up disappointed when the reality doesn't live up to our hopes. But not this time. It was the best meal I've ever had!

THE WAR HERO

"A man will fight long and hard for a bit of colored ribbon."
- Napoleon Bonaparte

We've all known someone like 'George Brick' at one time or another. He and others like him are so insecure about themselves they grasp at superficial straws such as ribbons and badges in order to prove their manhood. Sergeant Brick was typical in that he was constantly trying to go somewhere, anywhere, that would add another trinket to his collection of "awards." He contemplated the drill field, recruiting duty, and the like not because he relished a challenge or sought a rewarding experience, but because he thought his chances of picking up a ribbon or two would improve. He even got himself transferred into Force Recon for the sole purpose of upgrading his wings from silver to gold, a status symbol to be sure, but not before the dreaded "indoctrination test" was discontinued for a while and all manner of riffraff were allowed to apply.

Brick's greatest coup came courtesy of the Gulf War. He was assigned to drive an officer around in a rear area for the duration of his stay in Saudi Arabia and by his own admission never heard a shot fired in anger - let along fire one himself. Even so, he somehow managed to cross a designated "line in the sand" while eating a pop tart and drinking an iced tea in the back of a Hummer long after the shooting had stopped, and in the process earned himself the coveted Combat Action Ribbon.

That Sergeant Brick so easily attained an award better men had earned walking point for thirteen months in the rice paddies of Vietnam would be shame enough in itself, but the magnitude of this particular travesty goes far beyond one man. A large percentage of those who wear the CAR will sheepishly tell you their unit had zero killed or wounded by the enemy, they only guarded (unarmed) prisoners, or they had never even gotten off their ship.

There was a time when the owner of a CAR was looked upon with respect and admiration because he was a bona fide combat veteran. These days the guy who *doesn't* have it is the conspicuous one. The glad-handed way this and other awards were handed out is nothing less than an insult to the warriors who earned them legitimately. The awards manual is very clear when it states that recipients must be actively engaged in ground combat to include returning fire. Provisos were included which took into account artillery fire and ships that were attacked, but of course these too were liberally interpreted. One ship striking a mine suddenly caused the crews and embarked troops of damn near every ship within a week's steaming time of the Persian Gulf to become instant combat veterans, sometimes while they slept.

I'm not trying to belittle or call into question the contributions and motivations of the vast majority of the armed forces, but I do question the judgment of the DOD and individual services for approaching this issue with a sweepstakes-like mentality. My guess is the Pentagon minted millions of medals in anticipation of a protracted struggle and when the expected ground war failed to materialize they decided to give them away as reparation for making so many people sit around in the desert (or on a ship) doing nothing for so long.

The Sergeant Bricks of this world, on the other hand, will always find a way to weasel and slide their way into anything they can get, any way they can get it. I like to think that way down deep, behind the facade of their ill gotten gains, they know who and what they really are.

As for the *real* combat veterans out there, there is no doubt that you know who and what *you* are. Semper Fi, and thanks!

Note: Since this was originally written we have seen the onset of Operation Iraqi Freedom. As anyone with CNN knows, most of the troops who fought there have not only earned their CARs and CIBs, but our everlasting respect and admiration as well.

BACK IN THE SADDLE

"The only thing we have to fear is fear itself – the nameless, unreasoning, unjustified terror which paralyzes needed efforts to convert retreat into advance." - President Franklin D. Roosevelt, March 4, 1933

In order for a reconnaissance unit to maintain a viable military freefall insertion capability it is vitally important for jumpers to make as many proficiency jumps as possible. It is no easy thing to freefall from an aircraft at night, fly your canopy to an unmarked drop zone, and land safely. It is even more difficult when doing it as part of a team trying to avoid detection.

Although combat jumps would almost certainly be conducted from fixed wing aircraft, we often used helicopters for training because it afforded us the opportunity to make multiple jumps. It was like riding an elevator. Upon reaching the ground we would grab a fresh chute, the helo would land, and we'd go up for another blast. During one such evolution at Camp Lejeune we were using a CH-53E Super Stallion, which was my favorite helicopter because it could carry a lot of jumpers and provided a stable platform. That day I got a bit more excitement than I had bargained for.

On the first jump of the day we exited the aircraft at 10,000 feet, and immediately our S-3 officer and I were caught up in the slipstream and bounced off one another. I didn't notice it at the time, but his foot had dislodged my main ripcord from its pocket and caused it to "float" behind my head. As you can imagine it a bit surreal when you go for the "pull" and there is nothing there to grab, but I followed procedures and pulled the cable instead. End of problem.

When the canopy came off my back I felt relieved, since a "floater" is not a normal occurrence. Unfortunately my relief was short-lived. My parachute malfunctioned by forming what is known as a "line-over." One of the suspension lines was routed over the top, and of the seven cells that comprise the canopy three were not inflated. I gauged my rate of descent against the other jumpers and decided to dump what I had and take my chances with the reserve, so I pulled the red cutaway handle and fell away from the partially inflated main canopy. It was much different from my first malfunction back in HALO school because that time I didn't have time to think about what was going on. I just acted.

As you can probably surmise from the fact I am writing this, my reserve functioned properly. The problem was by the time it deployed I had lost a lot of altitude and wasn't able to make it to the drop zone. As I descended between some tall trees the canopy snagged a branch, and I was slammed violently to the ground. I felt as if my back had been broken, and I just lay there for awhile as the chopper circled overhead in case I needed help. Eventually I managed to get up and collect my gear, and headed back to the zone to get a new chute.

We boarded the helicopter for the next jump, and after we had taken off the crew chief told me the pilot wanted to speak with me. He led me up to the flight deck and said "This is the guy, sir." The pilot looked at me and slowly shook his head. "You know I've always wanted to try skydiving, but after watching that... I'm over it!"

OPERATION FLUID DRIVE

"Lying offshore, ready to act, the presence of ships and Marines sometimes means much more than just having air power or ship's fire, when it comes to deterring a crisis. And the ships and Marines may not have to do anything but lie offshore. It is hard to lie offshore with a C-141 or C-130 full of airborne troops."
- General Colin Powell, U. S. Army, Chairman of the Joint Chiefs of Staff

Early in my career I volunteered to go on a six-month deployment to the Mediterranean – what is commonly called a "Med Float" – and our Battalion Landing Team was the amphibious combat element of the Mediterranean Amphibious Ready Group. The MARG's job was to maintain a presence in the region, and the BLT's job was to go ashore when somebody needed to be taught some manners. I'd like to say I signed up to do that sort of thing, but in actual fact I was in search of exotic liberty ports more than anything else.

Lebanon was embroiled in civil war at the time. Even back then Yasser Arafat was at the center of the storm, and we were dispatched to Beirut to protect Americans living there. Once we started steaming toward Beirut I forgot all about liberty. I was nineteen years old, and ready to go.

I remember one recruiting pamphlet that described the Marine Corps as "the cold hard fist of American sea power thrust ashore." I didn't really understand it sitting in my recruiter's office, but while sitting on an amphibious ship off the coast of Beirut with a loaded rifle in my hands its meaning became clear.

Unfortunately what started out as a charge to the rescue turned into a tedious routine. We made "holes in the ocean" off Beirut for seventy-two days while diplomats tried to resolve things, and knew our presence offshore gave them a hole card to play.

While the diplomats did their thing we did ours. A plan was drawn up to go ashore and use force if necessary. It called for two companies to assault the beach in amtracs while a third flew to the American University. We were seriously outgunned, but we were Marines and the other guys weren't. I had never been around such confident men in my life.

As we sat around waiting for the word to go the BLT honed itself to a fine edge, both literally and figuratively. Marines cleaned weapons that were already clean and sharpened K-Bars that were as keen as razors. At one point we loaded into our amtracs, they started their engines, and the stern gate went down. The Dogs of War were ready to be unleashed!

The order to go never came. I guess the bad guys realized what was about to happen to them, so they allowed landing craft to come ashore to peaceably evacuate our countrymen. It was the best possible outcome for all concerned, and proved using the threat of force can be just as effective as actually throwing the spear. Bottom line - mission accomplished!

NINE LIVES

"Far better it is to dare mighty things, to win glorious triumphs even though checkered by failure, than to rank with those poor spirits who neither enjoy nor suffer much because they live in the gray twilight that knows neither victory nor defeat." - President Theodore Roosevelt

Most of us have had close calls in our lives. Whether it's due to a car accident or food poisoning, we always have to be prepared for an unexpected brush with the grim reaper. And while it happens to us all, some people seem to push the envelope.

Staff Sergeant Rob Ward is one such fellow. One of the truly outstanding communicators I have known, he was so dedicated to his craft rumor had it he slept with his radio. He was also an accident looking for a place to happen. I have seen him wreck his motorcycle, "frap" in on a HAHO jump at China Lake, suffer an "O2 hit" while diving a Drager closed circuit rig, and who knows what else. He was also one of the lucky few to escape from a helicopter that crashed into the ocean and killed seven Marines. Rob somehow managed to squeeze through the gunner's hatch, and although he spent some time in the hospital he survived once again. Like a Timex watch he took a licking and just kept on ticking.

Ward may have been a prolific accident magnet, but the prize for leading the most charmed life has to go to a Lieutenant named 'Adams.' This guy actually drowned during a pre-Scuba course and lived to tell about it. He was in the process of taking a breath when his head became submerged, and he swallowed a lot of water. Sometime later an instructor on the other end of the pool noticed a body lying on the bottom and pulled the lieutenant to the surface. I helped pull him from the pool, and will never forget his blue lips and chalky complexion. I've seen dead people before, and I thought I was looking at another. But our corpsman somehow brought him back to life.

But that's not Lieutenant Adams' crowning achievement. I wasn't present for this one, but several reliable sources have verified how it happened. While a student at HALO school his main parachute malfunctioned, and in a moment of panic the lieutenant pulled his reserve ripcord instead of the cutaway pillow. His reserve tangled with the main parachute and he screamed toward the ground trailed by a double streamer. That should be the end of the story, but it isn't. As luck would have it there was a small clump of relatively tall trees in this particular drop zone, and that is precisely where he landed. The tree branches snagged the two canopies as Adams passed through and slowed him down to a speed something less than terminal velocity.

And he just walked away!

TO ANY SERVICE MEMBER

By Nick Hill

"Letters are expectations packaged in an envelope." – Shana Alexander

During the Persian Gulf War, I was stationed aboard the Navy amphibious ship *USS Nassau*. As a senior Marine intelligence analyst, my workdays were routinely twelve to sixteen hours long. Like all the veterans, we looked forward to receiving mail from home.

Unlike the Vietnam War, the Gulf War found support among most Americans. As a result, we soldiers received an enormous amount of "To any service member" mail from the States. I never took any of those letters since I wrote to my wife and two children on a daily basis, as well as occasionally writing notes to my daughter's classroom, and I didn't feel I had the time to write to anyone else.

After five or six months of hearing the mail orderly announcing the availability of "To any service member" mail, I decided to take a few of the letters. I planned, as time permitted, to drop them a line telling them "Thanks" for their support.

I picked up three letters, placed them in my cargo pocket, and proceeded back to work. Over the next week or so I started responding to the letters. When it came time to answer the third letter I noticed it had no return address, but had a Colorado postmark, which made me think longingly of home. I had missed spending Thanksgiving, Christmas, and New Year's with my family, and I was really lonesome for them.

I opened the card and started to read the enclosed letter. About the third or fourth sentence down it read, "My Daddy is a Marine over there, if you see him tell him hi and I love and miss him." This statement really touched me and made me miss my family even more. I looked down to the signature - and sat in stunned silence as tears filled my eyes.

My own daughter Chris had signed the letter.

This story originally appeared in "Chicken Soup for the Veteran's Soul."

BLACKBEARD THE PIRATE

"There are only two types of people who understand Marines – the Marines themselves, and the enemy. Everyone else has a second hand opinion."

"It's easy to be hard, and it's hard to be smart" is an old Recon saying. It means 'don't be so motivated that you allow yourself to do unnecessary things that are unpleasant or even detrimental to your well being,' and I can think of no better example than Corporal Thompson of First Reconnaissance Battalion.

One of the things which sets a Marine apart from the average Joe Blow is the ability to tolerate unpleasant situations while in the pursuit of an objective. This characteristic has enabled wounded Marines to take hills and establish beachheads for over two centuries, and it is part of the Marine persona even during peacetime. When a good Marine sets his sights on a goal or is assigned a task he rarely lets anything stand in his way, even if it causes him to suffer. Corporal Thompson was just such a Marine, and his story should be a lesson to all.

It has always been difficult for the Marine Corps to get enough quotas to the formal schools run by other services, and Army Airborne school is no exception. Since quotas are in such short supply it is considered an honor to be selected to attend, and it is unthinkable for a Marine to fail to graduate for any reason short of death.

In the weeks preceding Thompson's departure for jump school he had been experiencing pain and a gradual loss of vision in one eye, but failed to report it for fear of losing the opportunity to become jump qualified - deciding instead to wait until he returned. He went ahead and completed the school as planned, but by that time was all but blind in one eye. An examination revealed cancer as the problem, and it became necessary for the eye to be removed - but that didn't slow Thompson down. He wore a black patch while waiting to be fitted with a glass eye and just continued to train.

One morning shortly after returning from a long range patrol the company formed up on the parade deck along with the rest of the battalion for the Colonel's customary Friday formation. After calling the battalion to attention the Sergeant Major eyeballed each company in turn until his gaze finally came to rest on Corporal Thompson. The Sergeant Major had just returned to the area and was unaware of Thompson's situation, so his obvious displeasure with what he saw is quite understandable.

Thompson was of course unshaven, and the residue of camouflage paint clung to his five day growth of beard. Over his field (i.e. filthy and torn) cammies he wore a Ka-Bar knife strapped to his side, and like some others he preferred to tie a green triangle bandage around his head rather than wear a cover. This, in combination with his eye patch, served to present quite a visual effect.

After a pause the Sergeant Major looked Thompson squarely in his good eye and asked, "And *who* in the hell do you think *you* are, Black-fucking-beard the pirate?"

GUYS THAT KEEP US IN

"I love the Corps for those intangible possessions that cannot be issued: pride, honor, integrity, and being able to carry on the traditions for generations of warriors past." - Corporal Jeff Sornij, USMC; in Navy Times, November 1994

The following is an e-mail from a Battalion Commander to his Regimental Commanding Officer:

"Sir, I was going for a run late Sunday afternoon and noticed the lights on in our motor transport maintenance bay. This caught my eye because I had directed the Motor Transport Section to enjoy the MLK 72 based on their work and on the positive feedback received to date from the LRI inspectors, so I investigated. As I entered the maintenance bay I heard country western music, and then saw a Marine in overalls and tennis shoes covered in grease under the hood of a Hummer - it was Sergeant Niles.

I asked Sergeant Niles what he was doing and he replied, 'Sir, just doing a little work.' I then asked why he was working on a Sunday afternoon, and that we had time next week. He replied, 'Sir, we really need to get these old Hummers fixed and I wanted to get a head start so my Marines don't have to work so hard next week and can concentrate on the LRI.' I asked how many were fixed and how long had he been working. Sgt Niles said, 'I have been working over the last two days and got six up sir, but I need another part to fix the others.' I then questioned him regarding the parts because I thought all the parts came in. He stated that the part/bolt he had would work, but was technically the wrong size, so he wanted to order the right

324

one in order to properly fix the vehicles for 1/7. I thanked him and again stated that it was not absolutely necessary to work over the 72. He then looked at me very seriously with grease all over his face and said, 'Sir, I also want to get ahead in our work so I can go on the Iwo Jima trip... I really want to see where those Marines fought and died... it means a lot to me.

I said, 'Sergeant Niles, I will make sure you are on the Iwo trip roster,' and turned away very quickly before he saw the tears welling up in my eyes. As I write this, I am bursting with pride that we have such fine Marines. These are the guys that keep me motivated and keep me in!!!

ONE TOUGH MARINE

"The mind is the limit. As long as the mind can envision the fact that you can do something, you can do it, as long as you really believe one hundred percent." - Arnold Schwarzenegger

One of the true warriors I have had the privilege of meeting through the Force Recon Association is a retired First Sergeant by the name of Don "Woody" Hamblen. He is something of a legend in the reconnaissance community, and for good reason. Woody lost one of his legs on a parachute jump back in 1962 when he drifted into some high-tension wires, but fought tooth and nail to stay on active duty in spite of his handicap. In a situation where most people would feel sorry for themselves, take the disability pay and retire to their porch swing, he instead decided to move forward with his life and in the process became an inspiration for us all.

When the accident occurred Hamblen was a Staff Sergeant with 1st Force Recon Company at Camp Pendleton. In order to remain on active duty the injured Marine pursued an aggressive letter writing campaign and eventually managed to convince the brass he could still serve. He asked for no special treatment, and received none. Hamblen was still required to complete the Marine Corps PFT along with everyone else, and successfully negotiated every event including the three mile run. That is particularly impressive when you consider that the prosthetic leg he did it on was far more primitive than what is available today.

Three years after the accident, in 1965, Woody saw action in Vietnam. He spent a total of thirty months in-country, much of it with special operations units. Just think of all the 4Fs who escaped military service because they had flat feet, and here's this guy running around in the jungle for two and a half years with only one leg. Amazing!

Hamblen's exploits were documented in detail in the book "One Tough Marine," and I used his story both to motivate myself and to set an example for my troops. Most of the time the lesson learned was a general one, but on at least one occasion I credit the First Sergeant's story with helping a Marine overcome a seemingly insurmountable obstacle. I had an otherwise squared-away Marine who just couldn't manage to pass the company Indoc, despite taking it several times. I think he had gotten to the point where he didn't believe he could do it, but if I had learned one thing in the Corps it's the word "can't" should not be part of a Marine's vocabulary.

I threw a copy of Hamblen's book at him and said "read this over the weekend. If you still don't think you can do it on Monday let me know and I'll take you off the list." Monday came and went, and not another word was spoken about the indoc. That Marine must have taken the lesson of Don Hamblen's story to heart, because he finally passed.

Anytime you find yourself in a difficult situation and in need of some inspiration I suggest picking up a copy of Don Hamblen's book. After all, when the going gets tough, tough Marines get going!

AN EMBEDDED REPORTER
Fondly Recalls the Marines in Iraq

Richard Tomkins

"Freedom is like the air we breathe – we don't miss it until we are deprived of it!"

What's the face of the Iraq war? Is it the scenes of physical destruction people see on their televisions and in their newspapers? Is it a glimpse of sullen - but more often relieved - Iraqi prisoners or celebrating civilians? Or is it the wave of camouflaged U.S. troops routing an enemy and, in typical American fashion, then embracing the children of a foe vanquished?

It's all that and more. For journalists embedded with U.S. forces the dominant feature of Operation Iraqi Freedom is, and always will be, the faces of the individual Marines, soldiers, airmen or sailors with whom they lived, sweated and feared during the long slog to Baghdad.

There is, for example, the unidentified Marine with his mouth set in a grimace from the bullet that passed through his knee. He tried to wave off comrades who eventually carried him to cover during the heaviest fighting for al-Azimiyah Palace in east Baghdad. While being carried he continued to fire his weapon at the enemy until his ammunition ran out.

There is Marine Private Aaron Davis, a jovial and slightly pudgy kid from California, who moved nearby with unbelievable speed and abandon, braving explosions and flying fragments from rocket-propelled grenades to help carry wounded to an evacuation.

There is Captain Shawn Basco, a forward air controller, who handed out candy from Meals Ready to Eat packs to village children and food to their parents with the same personal sense of mission that earlier had saved scores American lives and snuffed out many an Iraqi one while calling in air strikes.

"You hear about the World War II generation being 'the Greatest Generation,'" Lieutenant Colonel Fred Padilla, commander of the 1st Battalion, 5th Marines, told this correspondent. "In a sense that's true – we're certainly living off the equity they earned. But this generation - call it Generation X or whatever - is also every bit as extraordinary. They measure up."

For thirty-six days this correspondent was in a unique position to gauge that sentiment. As part of Pentagon policy for media coverage of the war, I was embedded with Bravo Company, 1st Battalion, 5th Marines, or simply Bravo 1/5. Bravo 1/5 was one of the first two units to cross into Iraq from Kuwait at the start of the land war (we would have been first, but Alpha Company broke the line of march and moved ahead of us).

Bravo 1/5 captured a gas and oil separation plant in the al Ramallah oil fields in southern Iraq, routed Iraqi defenders while capturing a key bridge over the Saddam Hussein Canal in central Iraq, liberated village after village and a children's prison, fought its way into Baghdad through a gauntlet of RPG fire, and seized and held Saddam's seventeen-acre complex on the Tigris River despite a five-hour onslaught from Baath Party gunmen and foreign extremists. It was one of the heaviest battles of the Iraq conflict, with the besieged Marines nearly running out of ammunition. Thirty-five Marines were wounded that morning, and one killed. Luckily for Bravo, only three of the wounded came from its ranks.

In battle, the men of Bravo 1/5 fought with tenacious courage. In liberating a people long cowed by the repression of dictatorship, they acted with great compassion, and in many cases a great tenderness. 'Operation Iraqi Freedom,' a name they initially greeted with scorn and expletives, gained poignant currency as the Marines viewed the plight of the Iraqi people - lives in unbelievable squalor - and their explosions of joy at being set free from the grip of fear.

Earlier mutterings that the war to topple Saddam Hussein should be called Operation Sandstorm because of weather, or Operation Stand Still for the delays to allow logistics vehicles to catch up with advancing front line units, were quickly forgotten.

"I feel pretty good today," First Sergeant Bill Leuthe said after liberating a town near Baghdad and a prison for children, where charges were reportedly beaten every morning simply for being there. "I think we all do."

Leuthe, Davis, Shevlin, Washburn, Malley, Lockett, Jones, Moll, Lyon, Bishop, Avilos, Nolan, Lockett, Meldoza, Craft, George -- the list of names of the men who did themselves proud, the Marines proud and their nation proud is too long to recite. There were more than one hundred and eighty in the company; more than two hundred when you add in attachments, such as armored vehicle crews and additional Navy corpsmen.

They were a cross-section of America. There were whites, blacks, Hispanics, Asians, American Indians and every hue and mixture in between. Private Dustin Pangelinann was from Saipan in the U.S. Commonwealth of the Marianas. Fifteen members of Bravo Company were not U.S. citizens and represented the newest wave of immigrants to our country. Some were from Mexico, and one was from Haiti. There were also several from Russia and the Ukraine.

Some came from poor backgrounds, others were solidly middle class. One Marine, who didn't need to work because of a family fortune, enlisted in his late twenties in the aftermath of the terrorist attacks of September 11, 2001.

And yes, some even had had youthful brushes with the law. But they all shared two things. They were Marines and "Devil Dogs." Not hyphenated Marines, just Marines - the "Few and the Proud," carrying on the tradition of courage their regimental forebears showed at Belleau Wood and the Argonne, at Guadalcanal and Okinawa, at the Chosen Reservoir and Inchon, and at Hue.

"None of you had to be here," company commander Captain Jason Smith told his men before crossing the border berm into Iraq from Kuwait. "You all chose to be here by becoming Marines, by doing something good for the world. Take a look around you. We are all different... what other military force or country in the world can say that? The fact that we are all different and live with each other and focus together under adverse circumstances tells me and the world a lot."

This group of men, this collection of Marines, he said, comes from a nation that "is going to war to defend an idea" of freedom, the rule of law and human dignity. "We're going to war to make the world a better place because we don't want to happen again what happened on September 11."

It's difficult to convey the rich texture of the men who make up Bravo 1/5 and the special camaraderie among them. Words just aren't adequate enough. But they are truly a band of brothers. Even the company oddball, the Marine who somehow never seemed to fit in or pull his own weight, was looked out for and protected with concern like that of a big brother looking out for an awkward sibling.

Bravo 1/5, in a very real sense, proves two truisms this correspondent has discovered in thirty years of reporting, much of it in war zones: Sharing a foxhole is the ultimate bonding experience, and the word "cliché" needs a new definition. According to the American Heritage College dictionary, "cliché is a trite or overused expression or idea or stereotype." All too often it is used with a negative cast. Yet clichéd characters and generalizations are based on truths.

Take the characters in any war move you've ever seen. There is the jokester, the screw-up, the smart mouth, the lothario, the kindhearted sergeant with a tough-as-nails exterior, the good-natured medic and the caring-but-firm commander. It's no wonder these characters exist on paper and celluloid. They exist in real life, just as the scenes of GIs passing out candy to civilians, sharing their last smoke or holding up a magazine pin-up to troops in a passing convoy. Clichéd in the context of Bravo 1/5 should be a label of honor, because it mirrors America and is replicated throughout our society and military services.

The commander of Bravo Company is Captain Jason Smith, from Baton Rouge. He fits the image - tall, square-jawed, a good-natured, decent and erudite man who requires things be done correctly. A graduate of Louisiana State University with a B.A. in history, his main goal in Operation Iraqi Freedom - other than accomplishing unit missions - was bringing everyone home. Watching him one night, when troops were out setting an ambush, was like watching a parent of a teenager waiting for his or her child to return home from a New Year's Eve party to which they had driven. The silent pacing was enough to drive one crazy. Any casual mention about how the company had been lucky in the casualty department would result in a quick, sharp look of reproach – don't jinx good fortune by talking about it.

The executive officer is First Lieutenant David Gustafson, a quiet, shy Swede from Maynard, Minnesota, with a wicked sense of humor. The only graduate of the Naval Academy among the company's officers, his educational background is often a butt of jokes. So too his efforts to conceal the cigarette smoking he'd taken up since crossing into Iraq.

And then there is Gunnery Sergeant Ron "my first name is Gunny" Jenks, the company logistician. Before battle, the Gulf War veteran would sternly but lovingly caution his men on mistakes to avoid and advise on lessons learned the hard way. His "Okay gents, let's get a move on," inevitably followed his barked orders. But for all the sternness, there was the old clichéd heart of gold. Gunny Jenks always had words of encouragement, always knew who was married and who was expecting a child and made it a point to inquire about them. He loaded up on cigarettes, parceling them out to his "knuckleheads" when they ran out in the Iraqi desert.

Bravo 1/5 has now left Baghdad. It is heading south toward Kuwait and an eventual return home to California. But there will be no rest for the weary. After an expected parade in Oceanside and a few weeks of reunion with family, the band of brothers will ship out to Okinawa to complete a previously scheduled deployment. Operation Iraqi Freedom will become just a memory, and another ribbon of honor for men serving their country.

This reporter took his leave of Bravo 1/5 on April 15. It was one of the hardest farewells I've ever had to make. In the thirty-six days I spent with them, I had been welcomed and made part of the family. The idea of leaving my band of brothers was wrenching, yet my family at home was also calling. In the end, I left quickly, with few goodbyes. The sight of a blubbering reporter was something best avoided. Speaking with other formerly embedded reporters in Kuwait turned up similar emotional pulls.

So how to say thank you? How to say how much I love and respect them? Words can't do it. So like other reporters, I give them the smartest, snappiest salute I, as a civilian, can muster. God speed, Bravo 1/5, and Semper Fi.

REVERSE DRAFT DODGER

"Marines I see as two breeds, Rottweilers or Dobermans, because Marines come in two varieties, big and mean, or skinny and mean. They're aggressive on the attack and tenacious on defense. They've got really short hair and they always go for the throat." - Rear Admiral "Jay" R. Stark, USN

One of the most legendary Reconnaissance Marines I have known was not even from the United States. He is a French Canadian named Herve St. Pierre, and I remember him as being tougher than a one dollar steak. But there are a *lot* of tough Marines. What made him really unique is he came *to* the United States *from* Canada during the Vietnam War. Imagine that. One theory put forth by some joker is the vacuum created by all of those draft dodgers leaving our country sucked him across the border - but in reality he just wanted to go fight for something he believed in. Ironically, he was never sent to Vietnam.

I first met St. Pierre in the '70s when he was with 2nd Force Recon Company at Camp Lejeune. Even then he had a reputation for being "harder than petrified woodpecker lips," and was reputed to have run regularly from French Creek to Onslow beach while barefoot. If that is true (it's a long way) it says a lot about him. Back then my friend James Goethe was a young troop under St. Pierre, and he loves to tell people what his team leader would say when James would screw up. First he would spit, and then say in his French accent, "Goethe... the name, I cannot keep it in my mouth!"

We next crossed paths some years later at the Jungle Warfare Training Center located at Fort Sherman, Panama. St. Pierre was then a Gunnery Sergeant assigned to the

Inspector and Instructor Staff for a recon reserve unit, and had brought his charges down for their annual training cycle. He hadn't changed a bit. There was one reserve Lieutenant who couldn't find his own ass in the dark with both hands, and the Gunny made no secret of his disdain for him. One morning I heard St. Pierre tell the inept butter-bar "Lieutenant, I am not going to let you go on patrol today. You are too *stupid*!"

One evening the reservists were conducting a night hydrographic survey, which involves making depth soundings at regular intervals in order to determine the suitability of a beach for an amphibious landing. Everything was going smoothly until the voice of one of the weekend warriors began to resonate from the darkness in a terrified voice, saying that a shark had brushed up against him. St. Pierre was unmoved, and immediately hollered back, "Shut up, you fool. They have to eat too!"

A couple of years later my platoon was training at the Mountain Warfare Training Center in Bridgeport in preparation for a deployment to Norway. The First Sergeant of one of the grunt companies was none other than St. Pierre. He obviously missed Recon, but being a consummate professional he was enjoying the leadership challenges that came with being a First Sergeant. We didn't see a lot of him during that deployment, but he did take part in our Biathlon, which is an event that combines cross country skiing and marksmanship. He smoked everyone like a cheap cigar despite being twice the age of most of the participants.

A friend who knew St. Pierre told me he ended up marrying a WM, and whenever she called him at work he would ask "Did you PT today?" If she said no he would say, "Call me back after you PT!" and hang up the phone. Ooh-Rah!

A LEAGUE OF OUR OWN

"Once a Marine, always a Marine!"

Once a Marine, always a Marine. That's much more than just a slogan. As any Marine will tell you, there is no such thing as an "ex-Marine." Those of us no longer serving prefer to be called *former* Marines, because we remain always faithful to the Corps. A study a few years back found that airmen leaving the military make the transition to civilian life almost seamlessly, soldiers are able to do so in a matter of weeks, and sailors lost the last vestiges of their military service within a year. The same study found that the vast majority of Marines NEVER completely divest themselves of the traits and characteristics of the Corps. Ever notice how Marine Corps bumper stickers outnumber those of the other services by a huge margin, even though we are the smallest service? It's a small thing, but it says a lot. Once a Marine, always a Marine.

My first exposure to the Marine Corps League came when I was a young sergeant on Long Island. I was driving along Sunrise Highway out in Suffolk County with another Marine when I spotted a sign containing an Eagle Globe and Anchor. We decided to investigate, and found we had stumbled upon the local MCL Detachment. The members bought us a couple of beers, and we got to listen to tales of Tarawa, Iwo Jima and Khe Sahn for the rest of the night.

Many years later I retired and moved to Florida, where I became affiliated with the Morris Dixon Jr. Detachment in Clearwater. They are a real slice of the "Old Corps," living history in fact, and I wish there was enough space to tell tales about them all. Each has a unique story, and they are all

337

heroes to me. Even after all these years these guys still gather to celebrate the Marine Corps Birthday with the same camaraderie as when they were still in. The detachment also provides JROTC scholarships, works on behalf of Toys for Tots, and so much more. Once a Marine, always a Marine.

Among the members of the "greatest generation" that I met via the League is a gentleman named John Residence. John is a veteran of Iwo Jima, and his unabashed pride in being a Marine is overwhelming. He is in his seventies now and no longer drives a car, and because of that I had the privilege of transporting him up to Pensacola for the commissioning of *USS Iwo Jima*. There were many Iwo vets there, and even after spending a quarter of a century in the Corps it was a humbling experience for me. Once a Marine, always a Marine.

Another great example of Marine Corps camaraderie is my friend and fellow League member Bill Moore. I first met Bill when he approached me in an Irish pub one evening to introduce himself. He had noticed I was wearing a Marine Corps t-shirt, and wanted to say "Semper Fi," despite being out of the Corps for over forty years. It's funny, but if Bill hadn't been a Marine we never would have been friends - in fact we would probably be mortal enemies. His political views are the polar opposite of mine, and more importantly our favorite baseball teams are archrivals. Even so we do agree that Ted Williams, who happened to be a Marine himself, is the greatest hitter who ever lived! The ties that bond Marines together run deeper than politics, baseball teams, and even blood.

Once a Marine, *always* a Marine!

For more information about the League write them at Marine Corps League, PO Box 3070, Merrifield VA 22116, call (703) 207-9588, or visit www.mcleague.org on the worldwide web.

WHY AMERICA LOVES
THE CORPS

By William J. Peters

"Marines know how to use their bayonets. Army bayonets may as well be paper-weights." - Navy Times, 1994

I retired after twenty-one years in the Corps in 1989 and never really understood why America loved the Marines. Maybe some of the following examples will explain why.

I was an Inspector-Instructor for Company G, 2nd Battalion, 25th Marines in Dover New Jersey for three years. It was my first "independent duty" assignment and my first time on an Army base. My job was to provide training for the reserves and "gung-ho" stuff to that research oriented base. While serving in this billet I saw the range of emotion surrounding the Corps, a range that transcended age and time.

As an I&I, I received many burial requests from members of all the services whose own parent service had neither the time nor manpower to deal with them. I and my cohorts found both.

In 1979 I presented a Bronze Star to a former Marine who had earned it on Iwo Jima. The Corps was thirty-four years late, but we had a mass formation and watched as this ramrod straight Marine walked in perfect step to receive his award while his son and buddy from Iwo watched through teary eyes. After the ceremony every reservist present shook his hand.

While at I&I, I received letters from boys in the third grade asking how to be Marines and a letter from a World

War II Marine, dying of cancer, asking how he could ensure being buried as a Marine because it would give his wife and him "peace of mind."

On each Marine Corps birthday I would get a cake, and my staff and I would go to the VA hospital at Basking Ridge and personally give a piece to each patient. One time, one of the Marines was way the hell on the other side of the hospital grounds, causing my young sergeant to think it "really wasn't worth it" to wheel a cake cart through the falling snow dressed in blues just to give this guy a piece of cake.

When we got there the nurse told us he was from World War I, and had one lung destroyed by mustard gas. He couldn't talk, but had been looking forward to our visit for days. I gave him his piece, the last on the tray, and thanked him for fighting so well that the Germans gave us the name *Teufel Hunden* – sons of the bitches of hell – or Devil Dogs.

I shook his hand and rose to leave, but he wouldn't let go. I looked into his eyes and he didn't have to say anything. His exploits were not in vain. We of today hadn't let him of the "Old Corps" down. He was important. He wasn't forgotten. I finally bent over, kissed him on the forehead, and told him "Semper Fi." We walked back to the car. The sergeant thought it was worth it.

In November of 1979 I led the Long Island procession for a Corporal Crowley, killed in Pakistan, from the funeral home to his church. Masses of Marines turned out and acted as escorts, marchers, and pew guides in the church. All were reservists taking a day off from work, without pay, because they "had" to do it. Along the way hundreds came out to wave flags or salute, because their hometown Marine was taking his last ride home.

Perhaps the following most clearly shows America's love for the Corps. My unit paraded down Fifth Avenue in New

York for the giant Armed Forces day parade while I walked along the curb looking at the company's dress and cover. As we were marching behind an Army unit, also dressed like us in utilities, a young boy no older than five saw the Eagle, Globe and Anchor and exclaimed, "Look Mom, here come the Marines!"

Later on, as we stood on a side street taking a break and waiting for the buses to come to take us back to New Jersey, an older lady came out from a boutique, walked toward the curb, and stood there watching the Marines. I walked over and kiddingly asked, "Are you over eighteen? Do you want to join?" She smiled, shook her head, and replied, "No, my husband was a Marine before he died. I just wanted to see how my Marines were doing today."

Why America loves the Corps – I think the answer lies with the boy and the woman. The boy knew we were different. The emblem meant something to him even at his age. Maybe it's getting the job done, the universal respect we hold, the fear of us by our enemies, whatever. We're special, and there's an intangible people pick up on. The woman wanted to see *her* Marines. She wasn't even in the Corps, but her husband was, and that makes her part of an extended, yet select, family. Even after his death she wanted to see – had an interest in, a right to see – *her* Marines.

I came back early from a Christmas vacation in New York one cold December day to see Lieutenant Colonel William "Rich" Higgins – killed by terrorists in Beirut – buried at Quantico, Virginia. It was something that had to be done.

I attended my Vietnam reunion of Company D, 1st battalion, 7th Marines – the famed Delta Death Dealers – at "The Wall" and watched guys march in platoon formation for the first time in twenty-five years in near perfect dress and alignment to read the names of our dead. Later I helped a

Marine from 1/9 dressed in utilities who was coming to the Wall for the first time in twenty-six years to see his Marines. He was the only one left of a twenty-man recon team and questioned how he could get a Silver Star when all of his people were on the Wall.

I talked to a State Department type who had been trapped in the U.S. Embassy in Kuwait during Iraq's invasion. He had tears in his eyes as he spoke of the hardships imposed by the Iraqis and the guts and strength of the Marine Security Guards. He marveled at their arrogance in the face of overwhelming Iraqi troops, how they stayed awake all night, were disciplined, worked out every day with wind sprints and weights, taught him how to use weapons, and always, always told them, "You are with Marines. You are safe. Nothing will happen to you." All of this from men not even in their twenties, men who will risk their lives and die for a cause.

Finally, when at Harpers Ferry Virginia two months ago, I saw a backpacker walk past me. On his pack was sewn, "U.S. Marines." I called out "Hey, Marine!" and there was an immediate "Yes, sir?" The man turned around and instead of a young Marine, this guy was older than I.

I learned he had fought in some Marine anti-air unit during World War II at Guadalcanal, Tarawa, Okinawa and other places where few men survived. He had been in for four of the toughest years in our Corps' history, and was discharged almost fifty years ago to the month of our meeting. I shook his hand, and thanked him for his courage and for giving meaning to the name "Marine."

I told him "Semper Fi." He was hiking the Appalachian Trail and had thought enough about his Marine service fifty years ago that he wanted people to know about it now. He was seventy years old.

I guess I'm still not sure why America loves us, but maybe a good guess is pride. We're not perfect, but Marines try very hard to be fair and are jealous of their brotherhood. You new Marines are nothing until you meet our standards, standards that have held us in good stead in war and peace and have made us respected around the globe.

Once you prove yourself to us you have a responsibility to honor our emblem and to maintain our traditions so that you are not the first to lose a battle or the first to dishonor those who have gone before and given all they had to make the name "Marine" stand for something.

That desire to excel, to honor and not tarnish our reputation, to win and never lose, to be ready to rescue an Air Force Pilot or deliver food to starving kids, gives pride. Why does America love us? Maybe because in a confusing world of political correctness, the Marines stand for something. For commitment, for honor, for the pride of doing it right the first time.

William J. Peters is a retired Marine Corps Major.

DUTY CALLS

"Gone to Florida to fight the Indians. Will be back when the war is over." - Colonel Commandant Archibald Henderson, USMC in a note pinned to his office door, 1836

One of the most difficult aspects of being a Marine is the frequent and often lengthy separations from your family. It is not uncommon for a child to be born while the father is deployed, and it isn't easy missing all of those recitals, first steps and graduations. Like most who have served I missed many important events in the lives of my children as they were growing up, but when I read this it helped put the comparatively minor sacrifices I had to make into proper perspective:

When Major Hal Sellers learned his infant son was living on borrowed time awaiting a heart transplant, the Marine and his wife had to choose between duty to family and to nation. Should he stay and aid his critically ill son, or help lead his battalion as it readied for a looming war in the Middle East? Sellers "'did a lot of soul-searching,'" said his wife, Betsy. Since there was nothing he could do to help four-month-old Dillon, Major Sellers chose to help his unit.

"It was a hard decision to make,'" Betsy said. "He had to come to the hospital and say goodbye to Dillon, and not know what would happen." A little more than a week after Sellers left, Dillon had only days to live unless he received a new heart. "I am doing what I have to do, and my husband is doing what he has to do,'" Betsy Sellers said. "We're doing what we need to do for our family and, hopefully, for other families.'"

Dillon was ten days old when he was diagnosed with Hypoplastic Left Heart Syndrome, which occurs when a heart is unable to pump or circulate blood. Although the condition can sometimes be corrected with surgery, doctors said his heart was too damaged. Dillon was placed at the top of the heart transplant list at Loma Linda University Medical Center, although it was not immediately clear where he had been placed on the list by the United Network for Organ Sharing. There is a twenty-five percent mortality rate for those awaiting transplants. "Every day could be an end-of-life issue for him,'" the transplant coordinator said. "We're probably talking days rather than weeks.'"

As the family struggled with Dillon's diagnosis, the Marine Corps offered Major Sellers a desk job at the Marine Corps Air Ground Combat Center in Twentynine Palms. But the thirteen-year veteran was XO of the 3rd Light Armored Reconnaissance Battalion, and had trained for months to deploy to the Middle East. His wife said ultimately he was concerned about bringing in a new member so late in the training.

"I think this situation sheds light in a very tangible way on the sacrificial nature of service to country. While no one would want to be in the Major's position, we understand the difficulties," said Captain Rob Crum, a base spokesman.

The Major's mother, Betty Sellers, said the family supported her son's decision. "We didn't say, 'Hal, do this or do that.' We tried to convey the message that Dillon was getting the best possible care he could have, and maybe Hal had to do in life what he could do best,'" she said in a telephone interview from her home in Des Moines, Iowa.

Lying in a crib at the medical center, Dillon was breathing with the help of a ventilator as tubes snaked from his chest, arms and legs. A patch from Sellers' unit, known as the Wolf

Pack, was among the pictures and stuffed animals that decorated Dillon's crib.

When Major Sellers called home from an undisclosed location for an update on Dillon, his wife delivered a message to their son: "Daddy loves you."

THE FINISH LINE

"Marines die, that's what we're here for. But the Marine Corps lives forever... and that means YOU live forever."
- The mythical GySgt Hartman (portrayed by R. Lee Ermey) in the film Full Metal Jacket

Retirement is a difficult thing for many of us to accept after spending our lives in the Corps, but like death it is a fact of life. After all, even Chesty Puller had to retire. Even so it is a bittersweet time in your life. On the one hand you are on the verge of beginning a new life with the freedom to go wherever you want, whenever you want, and do whatever you please (within limits of course). On the other you will be surrounded by undisciplined civilian pukes instead of steely eyed warriors. Ugh - all of those people out there just milling around aimlessly with no one in charge. If you don't believe that try shouting "fall in" down at your local mall. Nothing happens!

As the fateful day approached for me I was the recipient of a lot of good natured teasing. I was called an old man, soon to be "retarded," a washed up has-been, and so on. It was great! I sure was going to miss these guys.

During that time our 4th platoon was preparing to deploy to the Persian Gulf, and were aboard *USS Bonhomme Richard* in the final days of their grueling MEU/SOC workup. One evening while they were at sea there was a knock on my door. It was my OIC, Captain Warren Dickey, and he said there had been an accident. He then asked if I had any adult beverages, so I broke out a couple of the Australian beers I had been hoarding for the day of my retirement. What we really needed was a bottle of scotch.

347

The platoon had been making an assault on a target ship while it was underway. Their mission was to board the vessel from the air while Navy Seals came alongside in inflatable boats. As they approached the flight deck and prepared to fast rope onto the ship the CH-46 helicopter they were riding in somehow got snagged on a safety net. The pilot wasn't sure what happened and added power, and suddenly the helo flipped over and crashed into the ocean. It began to sink quickly. Eleven of the eighteen who were aboard managed to escape, and were plucked from the sea by the Seals.

Among the seven missing Marines were five from our company. Three of those, Vince Sabastaenski, Jay "Doc" Asis, and Jeff Starling, I knew well. Just before they left Ski told me his platoon was flying back a day early just to be at my retirement, and every time I saw Doc he asked "How many more days, Top?" with a big smile. And silly as it was, I felt partially responsible for Starling because I had been instrumental in getting him into the company. I didn't know Staff Sergeant Galloway and Corporal Baca as well as the others, but by all accounts they were outstanding Marines.

By a total coincidence, or perhaps divine providence, our company was scheduled for our annual group photo on the *very day* I retired. That photo hangs above my desk as I write this, and as always my eyes are drawn to the five inverted rifles, bush covers and pairs of boots in the foreground which represent the absence of our comrades.

A memorial ceremony was scheduled to be held in the base theater the following Monday, and I delayed my departure for three days so that I could attend. The theater was packed with friends and family members of the fallen men, and once the ceremony concluded I got into my car and began the long drive to my new home in Florida. It was a hell of a way to end a career.

Vince Sabastaenski left a wife, Julie and son, Nicholas; Dave Galloway left a wife, Holly and three sons, William, Stetson and Frederick; Mark Baca left a wife, Jean Marie, son, Derek, and daughter, Kylie; Jay Asis left a wife, Kathryn; Jeff Starling was the only unmarried member of the platoon to perish, but I later go to know his Mom and Dad, Charlotte and Grandle – who was himself once a Marine – in Florida.

I will never forget them.

The Force Recon Association has established the "15th MEU Memorial Fund" to provide support and financial assistance to the families of these fallen comrades. All funds collected will be distributed to surviving family members. Donations can be sent to 15th MEU Memorial Fund, c/o Force Recon Association, PMB 1775, 3784-B Mission Avenue, Oceanside CA 92054-1460, or visit forcerecon.com for more information.

ABOUT THE AUTHOR

Andy Bufalo retired from the Marine Corps as a Master Sergeant in January of 2000 after more than twenty-five years service. A communicator by trade, he spent most of his career in Reconnaissance and Force Reconnaissance units but also spent time with Amtracs, Combat Engineers, a reserve infantry battalion, and commanded MSG Detachments in the Congo and Australia.

He shares the view of Major Gene Duncan, who once wrote "I'd rather be a Marine private than a civilian executive." Since he is neither, he has taken to writing about the Corps he loves. He currently resides in Tampa, Florida.

Semper Fi!

CPSIA information can be obtained at www.ICGtesting.com
Printed in the USA
269472BV00005B/11/P